ACCOUNTS FOR SOLICITORS

ACCOUNTS FOR SOLICITORS

Jacqueline Kempton BA (Hons), Solicitor

Lesley King LLB, Dip Crim (Cantab), Solicitor

Published by

College of Law Publishing,
Braboeuf Manor, Portsmouth Road, St Catherines, Guildford GU3 1HA

British Library Cataloguing-in-Publication Data

A catalogue record for this book is available from the British Library.

ISBN: 978 1 912363 42 1

Typeset by Style Photosetting Ltd, Mayfield, East Sussex

Tables and index by Moira Greenhalgh, Carnforth, Lancashire

Preface

This book is written primarily for the Legal Practice Course but it is hoped that it will be useful for others.

It is divided into two parts. The first part provides an introduction to business accounting. The second part deals with the accounts of solicitors and, in particular, the need to account for client's money.

For the sake of brevity, the masculine pronoun has been used to include the feminine.

The authors would like to thank their colleagues at The University of Law at Store Street for their help in the preparation of this book, and College of Law Publishing for their support during the production process.

The law is stated as at 1 April 2018.

JACQUELINE KEMPTON
LESLEY KING

Contents

Table of Statutes, Rules and Accounting Standards

Table of Abbreviations

COFA	Compliance Officer for Finance and Administration
COLP	Compliance Officer for Legal Practice
FRS	Financial Reporting Standards
GAAP	generally accepted accounting principles
HMRC	HM Revenue and Customs
IAS	International Accounting Standards
IASB	International Accounting Standards Board
IFRS	International Financial Reporting Standards
pa	per annum
PAYE	Pay As You Earn
REL	registered European lawyer
TPMA	third party managed account
VAT	value added tax
VATA 1994	Value Added Tax Act 1994

Introduction

WHY DO I NEED TO KNOW ABOUT ACCOUNTS?

The short answer is because a knowledge of accounting principles is a required element of all Legal Practice Courses. However, that does give rise to a further question – 'Why?' The answer to this question is that knowledge and understanding of accounting principles will help you enormously in your professional and personal life, in the following ways.

To deal with the affairs of clients

A great deal of the work done by solicitors requires an understanding of accounts:

- In commercial work, you may be involved in shares or asset takeovers and will need to be able to 'read' the accounts of the company involved to understand the problems of the transaction.
- In private client work, you may be involved in the valuation of shares for taxation purposes.
- In family work, you may have to look critically at the accounts of a business run by a spouse when you are trying to agree the amount of a financial settlement.

To liaise with accountants

Particularly in commercial work, you may have to work closely with accountants on certain aspects of transactions. You will find it helpful to understand some of the concepts and jargon accountants use. Accountants have studied law and have some understanding of the solicitor's job. Therefore, as a profession, we will be at a disadvantage if we have no understanding of their job.

To deal with your own financial affairs

It is likely that you will have money to invest, if not now then in the not too distant future. An understanding of the principles of investment is vital to your financial well-being.

To run your own business

If you become a partner you will have to manage the financial affairs of your firm. To do so adequately you must understand profitability and solvency, and the crucial importance of cash flow.

To comply with the SRA Accounts Rules 2011

The SRA Accounts Rules 2011 require anyone regulated by the SRA who handles money belonging to clients to keep particular accounts and to record dealings with such money in a particular way. While you are unlikely to have to make the entries yourself, you will be responsible if errors are made by others. You may have to decide whether a payment which is to be made by your firm for a particular client can be made from the client bank account or must be made from the office bank account. Similarly, when money is received from a client, you may have to decide whether it should be paid into the client or office bank account.

HOW TO USE THIS BOOK

This book is not designed for passive reading. It is a work book. You will find that there are exercises for you to do throughout the text. These exercises are an integral part of the course. They are designed to develop your understanding and confidence, not merely to test you on the material you have just read. Solutions to the exercises appear at the end of the relevant chapter. It is essential that you study these solutions as you go through the text.

PART I

BUSINESS ACCOUNTS

INTRODUCTION TO BUSINESS ACCOUNTS

LEARNING OUTCOMES

After reading this chapter you will be able to:

- explain the importance for a business of keeping financial records
- describe the role of accountants
- explain the basic information to be found in business accounts
- distinguish between different business types.

1.1 INTRODUCTION

In this chapter you will be introduced to the topic of business accounts. You will begin by looking at the purpose and importance of record keeping, before going on to examine some key accounting concepts.

1.2 KEEPING RECORDS

Most people keep some sort of record of what happens to their money. You probably keep pay slips, bank and building society statements, loan agreements and credit card bills. These documents provide a useful personal record. These records enable you to calculate your financial position and are essential when dealing with HM Revenue and Customs (HMRC) as they provide the information necessary to calculate your tax liability.

Anyone who runs a business needs similar information to keep track of the financial position of the business. However, because so many different events occur in the life of a business, it is impractical to rely on individual documents to provide the full picture. It is preferable to take the relevant information from the individual documents and enter it on separate records. These records summarise the individual documents and are usually referred to as accounts.

While a business is small, the proprietor will probably do everything himself, including keeping the accounts. However, once a business expands, it is common to employ a bookkeeper to undertake the vital but time-consuming task of keeping the accounts on a day-to-day basis. This leaves the proprietor free to concentrate on securing the success of the business by planning strategy, and improving the quality of the product and the level of customer satisfaction.

1.3 THE NATURE OF ACCOUNTS

Accounts then are nothing more, and nothing less, than summaries of financial information. The term 'accounts' is frequently used in two senses. It is used to describe the day-to-day records which a business keeps of its financial transactions – you will also hear these records referred to as 'the books'. The term is also used to describe the summary statements which a business produces at the end of its accounting year.

The focus in the first part of this book will be on understanding and interpreting accounts in the sense of the year-end summary accounts. However, in order to be able to read a set of year-end accounts you must first understand the day-to-day record keeping which underlies them.

1.4 USERS OF BUSINESS ACCOUNTS

The financial affairs of a business will be of interest to a variety of individuals, both inside and outside the business itself. A number of people will therefore need to use the accounts for a variety of different purposes.

1.4.1 Internal users

The person most directly interested in the accounts of a business will be its owner or proprietor. The proprietor needs the accounts to provide accurate, up-to-date information which the proprietor can interpret correctly to draw conclusions about the past performance of the business. This enables the proprietor to make decisions as to future development and plan a business strategy. The proprietor therefore uses the accounts retrospectively, to see what has already occurred, and prospectively, to see where the business might be headed.

In anything but the smallest of businesses, there will also be employees and executives, managers and directors, who will similarly need to use the accounts to manage and direct the affairs of the business. Employees may also demand information about the financial health of the business, usually as a prelude to wage negotiations

1.4.2 External users

Those who deal with the business, such as its bankers, those who lend money or advance credit to it, will often need to look at the accounts. The main purpose is to monitor the performance of the business in order to safeguard their position against financial loss.

Those who work alongside the business and are involved in its financial affairs – for example analysts, lawyers and accountants – will look at the accounts to assess the state of the business in order to advise on past events and assist in the planning of future decisions.

Those who invest in the business will want to review the accounts to see what is happening to their investment and what returns or gains they can expect.

1.4.3 Government

The government body that will need to see the accounts regularly will be HMRC. The accounts are the starting point for establishing liability for tax. Other government agencies, such as the Competition and Markets Authority or the Registrar of Companies, will need to see the accounts from time to time.

1.5 THE ROLE OF ACCOUNTANTS

A business may have its own in-house accountant or, more commonly, it will buy in accountancy services in much the same way as it buys in legal services.

A business will involve accountants in one or more of a number of different aspects of managing the finances of a business.

1.5.1 Recording information

We have already seen that it is very important to have records so that the proprietor of a business can make informed decisions. The accountant will follow rules that govern the way in which information is recorded. It is important that there are rules, since it means that anyone who has learnt the rules can understand accounts kept by another person on the basis of those rules.

1.5.2 Reporting

The accountant will analyse the information contained in the day-to-day accounts, summarise it and present it to management. Management can then use that information as the basis for decisions on strategy. However, it is not just management who need financial reports. As we have seen, there is also a demand for information from outside the business – HMRC demands tax returns and, in the case of companies, the Government, potential investors and shareholders require published accounts.

1.5.3 Auditing

Not all accountants are qualified to audit accounts. Only those who are registered auditors are authorised to sign a statutory audit report.

Most companies are required to have their accounts examined by a qualified auditor, who must provide an opinion as to whether the accounts give a 'true and fair' view of the affairs of the company and its profit (or loss) for the relevant period. The auditors will have access to all the books and documents of the company. They are under an obligation to the members of the company and are also subject to disciplinary action by their professional body for misconduct.

In addition to the statutory audit required by the Companies Acts, auditors may be invited by management to carry out an audit as a means of obtaining an independent appraisal of the efficiency of the organisation.

1.5.4 Dealing with HMRC

Accountants frequently prepare tax returns for submission to HMRC on behalf of individuals and businesses. They can advise on the availability of deductions, exemptions and reliefs, and on the correct treatment of income and capital gains.

1.6 ACCOUNTS AND TAX

Accounts are very important as a record for taxation purposes. The Government imposes a variety of different taxes, all of which require detailed records. The accounts of the business are the starting point for assessing tax liability in a number of situations.

If the business is unincorporated, the proprietor (or proprietors, if it is a partnership) will include the profit or profit share of the business (ie the financial benefit which he derives from the business) in his income tax return. If the business is a company, the company itself will be liable for corporation tax based on the information given in the accounts.

If the business employs staff, it will have to operate the Pay As You Earn (PAYE) scheme. This requires the employer to deduct income tax from the employees and to account for it to HMRC. Records will have to be kept of salaries so that HMRC can check that the correct amount of tax has been deducted and so that certificates of deduction of income tax can be issued to employees. The business will also have to deduct National Insurance contributions from the employees. Again, detailed records will have to be kept for HMRC.

Lastly, if the business is registered for value added tax (VAT), it will need to keep records of VAT charged to customers and of VAT charged to the business by suppliers. It will have to account to the Government for the correct amount of VAT every quarter.

1.7 REGULATION OF ACCOUNTS

There is a great deal of regulation of accounts. Some of it is self-imposed by the accountancy profession and some of it is imposed externally, for example the Government insists that companies produce final accounts at the end of the accounting year in a particular form.

A person could prepare a set of accounts for his own use on any idiosyncratic basis he wished, but such accounts would be useless to an outsider trying to understand the affairs of the business. Clearly, if accounts are prepared on a uniform basis (ie if the same conventions have been followed and the same practices adopted), they will be usable by anyone.

Frequently, people want to compare the accounts of one business with the accounts of another (eg when investing or considering the purchase of a business). It is impossible to make a valid comparison unless the accounts have been prepared on a uniform basis.

The accounting profession has therefore tried to achieve a measure of uniformity.

The UK Financial Reporting Council (the main standard setter in the UK) lays down definitive standards of financial accounting and reporting (known as Financial Reporting Standards (FRSs)). These standards describe methods of accounting for application to all financial accounts (although we will consider them in the context of company accounts in **Chapter 7**). The aim is to give a true and fair view of the financial position of an enterprise and its profit or loss. Although these standards have no statutory force, non-compliance by an accountant could lead to disciplinary action by the appropriate governing body in a similar way to disciplinary proceedings against a solicitor.

In recent years, accounts regulation has begun to reflect the increasing globalisation of commerce and finance. The International Accounting Standards Board sets standard applicable at an international level.

1.8 INFORMATION PROVIDED BY ACCOUNTS

Accounts provide information about the financial affairs of the business. A business needs to know:

(a)   the income it has generated in a particular period; and

(b)   the expenses it has incurred in the same period.

Deducting expenses from income enables the business to calculate the profit it has made.

A business also needs to know:

(a)   the assets it has at a given moment; and

(b)   the liabilities it has at a given moment.

Deducting the total liabilities from the total assets will establish the net worth or value of the business.

On a daily basis, therefore, a business must keep records of income, expenses, assets and liabilities. The classification of items into these four categories is a fundamental aspect of bookkeeping and accounts.

Income is what the business is trying to produce. It is the result either of the labour of the business's employees, or of the investment of its capital. Examples of income are professional charges for services supplied, the price charged for stock sold, interest received and insurance commission received.

Expenses are items paid, the benefit of which is obtained and exhausted in a relatively short time (often within a single accounting period) and where the expenditure is necessary to maintain the earning capacity of the business. Examples of expenses are the price paid for stock bought for resale, gas, electricity, wages, interest paid, hire charges, petrol and repairs.

Assets must be carefully distinguished from expenses. Like expenses, assets are the result of expenditure. The difference is that an asset gives rise to a benefit which can be spread over a longer period and which will increase the earning capacity of the business. Examples of assets are premises, machinery, fixtures and fittings, vehicles, cash and debtors.

Liabilities are amounts owing from the business. Examples of liabilities are bank loans and creditors.

Accounts then show and distinguish between the income, expenses, assets and liabilities of the business. The classification is crucial to gaining an understanding of accounts. You will therefore need to keep this classification in mind as you work through the book.

1.9 TYPES OF BUSINESSES

Businesses may take a variety of forms. In this first part of the book we shall be looking at the accounts of two different types of business: a trading business, which generates income through the buying and selling of stock; and a professional business, such as a firm of solicitors, which sells services to its clients.

We shall also consider three different business mediums:

(a)   businesses which are run by a single individual as a sole trader or practitioner;

(b)   partnerships where two or more people join forces to run the business together; and

(c)   companies which are owned by shareholders and run by directors.

SUMMARY

(1) Accounts are summaries of financial information.

(2) Accounts are read by a number of different users for a variety of purposes.

(3) Financial items can classified as income, expenses, assets and liabilities.

DOUBLE ENTRY BOOKKEEPING

LEARNING OUTCOMES

After reading this chapter you will be able to:

- explain the purpose of bookkeeping
- explain the rules which underlie double entry bookkeeping
- make basic entries using the double entry system
- draw up a trial balance.

2.1 INTRODUCTION

In order to be able to interpret a set of business accounts you must first understand the records on which those accounts are based. In this chapter you will be introduced to the system businesses use to collate financial information – double entry bookkeeping.

2.2 THE PURPOSE OF DOUBLE ENTRY BOOKKEEPING

In order for the accounts to provide accurate information, the business must have a system in place to record its financial dealings. The process of recording financial transactions in the accounting records of a business is called bookkeeping. This terminology harks back to the days when these records were hand-written, or 'entered', into large bound books; and indeed these day-to-day records are often referred to as 'the books' of the business. Today, of course, most businesses keep their financial records using computerised systems.

All businesses use the same bookkeeping system to record their day-to-day transactions. This system is called the double entry bookkeeping system. The double entry system was developed in the 15th century by Venetian traders. The fact that it continues to be used today is a tribute to their ingenuity and its efficiency.

There is nothing to stop anyone inventing his own personal accounting system. However, there is a great deal to be said for uniformity. We have seen that the accounts need to be understood by outsiders. This is achieved by using the double entry system, which has been developed over hundreds of years and is understood by people all over the world.

The double entry bookkeeping is a system of recording financial dealings built upon a series of rules. As we look at the double entry system some of the rules may appear arbitrary to you, perhaps even counter-intuitive. The fact is that the Venetian traders could have decided to set up the whole system differently, but they chose not to. However, once you have accepted that initial decision, everything which follows builds methodically, and you will soon appreciate that the system has its own internal logic.

2.3 PRINCIPLES OF DOUBLE ENTRY

Double entry bookkeeping is based on one very simple idea: every business transaction has two aspects to it, so, to give an accurate picture of the state of the business, both aspects need to be recorded. Consider the following examples which illustrate the two aspects of a number of transactions:

(a)   The business pays cash to buy premises:

Aspect 1 – The business has less cash

Aspect 2 – The business has acquired premises

(b)   The business sells goods to a customer for cash:

Aspect 1 – The business has earned income

Aspect 2 – The business has more cash

(c)   The business provides services to a client on credit:

Aspect 1 – The business has earned income

Aspect 2 – The business has a debt owing to it

(d)   The client pays the business the money owed:

Aspect 1 – The business has lost the debt that was owing to it

Aspect 2 – The business has more cash

(e)   The business pays wages:

Aspect 1 – The business has less cash

Aspect 2 – The business has incurred an expense

No matter what type of transaction you consider, there will always be two aspects to it.

Both aspects of a transaction are recorded in the books of the business. Each aspect must be recorded in a different account. The double entry bookkeeping system requires the business to have a number of separate accounts, so, for example, there is one account for cash, one account for each type of asset, one for each type of expense, one for each person to whom the business owes money, one for each debtor that owes money to the business.

In order to record the two aspects, accounts are divided into two sides. The two aspects of any transaction are recorded on different sides of the two accounts.

2.3.1   Rules for recording transactions

The rules for recording transactions may conveniently be summarised as in the following table:

Left column	Right column
Expense incurred	Income earned
Asset acquired/increased	Asset disposed of/reduced
Liability reduced/extinguished	Liability incurred/increased
Cash gained	Cash paid

We have seen that every transaction has two aspects. When an individual transaction is recorded, one aspect appears in the left-hand column of the grid and will therefore be recorded on the left-hand side of one account. The other aspect appears in the right-hand column of the grid and will therefore be recorded on the right-hand side of another account. For every transaction these two aspects must first be identified and then each of them recorded in two separate accounts.

There is no magic about whether entries are made on the left or the right. The system would have worked just as well if the different aspects were recorded on the opposite sides. The rules summarised in the grid simply need to be learned and followed.

Example

A business carries out the following transactions:

(a) *The business buys a machine for £20,000 cash.*

Expense incurred	Income earned
Asset acquired/increased	Asset disposed of/reduced
Liability reduced/extinguished	Liability incurred/increased
Cash gained	Cash paid

The business gains an asset in the form of a machine (recorded on the left of the machine account) and pays cash (recorded on the right of the cash account).

(b) *The business buys stock for £1,000 cash.*

Expense incurred	Income earned
Asset acquired/increased	Asset disposed of/reduced
Liability reduced/extinguished	Liability incurred/increased
Cash gained	Cash paid

The purchase of stock is an expense of the business. The business incurs an expense (recorded on the left of the purchases account); there is a payment of cash (recorded on the right of the cash account).

(c) *The business sells stock for £3,000.*

Expense incurred	Income earned
Asset acquired/increased	Asset disposed of/reduced
Liability reduced/extinguished	Liability incurred/increased
Cash gained	Cash paid

By selling stock the business earns income (recorded on the right of the sales account); there is a gain of cash (recorded on the left of the cash account).

You may have noticed already an important point about the double entry system. At this stage of recording the transactions, there is no need to worry about how well the business is doing. Transactions are simply recorded as they occur. The system is a mechanical method of recording transactions as they happen and involves no value judgements about the state of the business. In the above example, when recording the initial purchase or sale of stock, there is no need to worry about whether the goods bought were 'worth' £1,000, or whether the sale price of £3,000 was a high or low price. A record is simply made of what happens.

2.3.2   The business is separate from the proprietor

Another important principle of double entry bookkeeping is that the business is regarded as completely separate from its proprietor. So, when a proprietor sets up a business and puts in some cash, the transaction must be recorded from the point of view of the business. The two aspects of the transaction are that the business is gaining cash and is incurring a liability, in that it now owes money to the proprietor. This liability to repay its proprietor is normally referred to as the 'capital' of the business.

Exercise 2A

Yasmin starts a business buying and selling goods.

Identify the two aspects involved in the following transactions and say whether they would be recorded on the right or the left of the accounts:

(1) To start the business, Yasmin puts in £20,000 cash.

(2) Business buys premises for £90,000 cash.

(3) Business buys trading stock for £2,000 on credit from Fred, a supplier.

(4) Business sells some of the trading stock for £4,000 cash.

(5) Business pays Fred, the supplier, £2,000.

2.3.3 Debit and credit

So far, when talking about the two sides of the accounts, we have referred to the left-hand side and the right-hand side. However, the double entry system uses the labels 'Debit' and 'Credit'.

'Debit' is used as a label for the left-hand side and 'Credit' as a label for the right-hand side. They are shortened to 'DR' and 'CR' respectively.

Example

(a) Joe sets up a business and pays in £120,000 to start it.

The business gains cash (recorded on the left of the cash account with a DR entry) and incurs a liability to its proprietor (recorded on the right of the capital account with a CR entry).

(b) The business buys premises for £100,000.

The business pays cash (recorded on the right of the cash account with a CR entry) and gains an asset in the form of the premises (recorded on the left of the premises account with a DR entry).

2.4   THE FORM OF ACCOUNTS

Accounts may be presented in a variety of different forms. The most common is the tabular form, as shown below:

Name of Account				
Date	Details	DR	CR	Balance

When the transaction is recorded, the date of the transaction is entered in the 'Date' column. The 'Details' column contains a cross-reference to the name of the account where the other part of the double entry is made, often with a brief description of the nature of the transaction as well. The amount involved is entered in the left-hand debit column (DR) or the right-hand credit column (CR), as appropriate. The 'Balance' column shows the running balance on the account. If the DR entries exceed the CR entries, the balance is described as a DR balance, and vice versa.

Example

A business pays three electricity bills: £1,000, £2,000 and £3,000. Each payment will be recorded on the electricity account and the cash account. The electricity account will show debit entries as the business is incurring an expense, and will look as follows:

Electricity				
Date	Details	DR	CR	Balance
1	Cash	1,000		1,000DR
2	Cash	2,000		3,000DR
3	Cash	3,000		6,000DR

The corresponding entries appear in the cash account as credit entries because the business is paying cash, and will look as follows:

Cash				
Date	Details	DR	CR	Balance
1	Electricity		1,000	1,000CR
2	Electricity		2,000	3,000CR
3	Electricity		3,000	6,000CR

2.5 MAKING ENTRIES

Every financial transaction must be recorded in the accounts of the business as it happens. To help you to understand how the double entry system works in practice, we shall now look at a series of simple transactions which may typically occur in the early stages of the life of a business.

Example

Miriam sets up a business selling handmade designer knitwear. She buys the knitwear from a small group of producers in Scotland, and she then sells it to the public from a rented shop in Camden.

The following financial transactions occur:

June

1   Miriam starts a business and puts in £10,000 cash
2   Business buys a computer for £2,000
4   Business pays rent of £1,000
7   Business buys knitwear for £2,000
8   Business sells knitwear for £750

To record these events the business will need the following accounts:

–   a capital account
–   a cash account
–   an asset account for the computer
–   two expense accounts: one for rent, and one for the purchase of the knitwear stock
–   an income account for the sale of the knitwear stock

The following entries are required in the accounts of the business:

1 June   Miriam puts in £10,000 cash
The two aspects of this transaction are that the business:
–   gains cash
–   incurs a liability to Miriam

There will be a DR entry on the cash account and a CR entry on the capital account:

Cash				
Date	Details	DR	CR	Balance
1 June	Capital	10,000		10,000DR

Capital				
Date	Details	DR	CR	Balance
1 June	Cash		10,000	10,000CR

2 June   Business buys a computer for £2,000

The two aspects to this transaction are that the business:

– loses cash

– gains an asset

There will be a CR entry on the cash account and a DR entry on the computer account:

Cash				
Date	Details	DR	CR	Balance
1 June	Capital	10,000		10,000DR
2 June	Computer		2,000	8,000DR

Computer				
Date	Details	DR	CR	Balance
2 June	Cash	2,000		2,000DR

4 June   Business pays rent of £1,000

The two aspects of this transaction are that the business:

– pays cash

– incurs an expense

There will be a CR entry on the cash account and a DR entry on the expense account for rent:

Cash				
Date	Details	DR	CR	Balance
1 June	Capital	10,000		10,000DR
2 June	Computer		2,000	8,000DR
4 June	Rent		1,000	7,000DR

Rent				
Date	Details	DR	CR	Balance
4 June	Cash	1,000		1,000DR

7 June   Business buys knitwear for £2,000

The two aspects of this transaction are that the business:

– pays cash

– incurs the expense of purchasing stock

There will be a CR entry on the cash account and a DR entry on the expense account for purchases:

Cash				
Date	Details	DR	CR	Balance
1 June	Capital	10,000		10,000DR
2 June	Computer		2,000	8,000DR
4 June	Rent		1,000	7,000DR
7 June	**Purchases**		**2,000**	**5,000DR**

Purchases				
Date	Details	DR	CR	Balance
7 June	**Cash**	**2,000**		**2,000DR**

8 June   Business sells knitwear for £750

The two aspects of this transaction are that the business:
- gains cash
- earns income by selling stock

There will be a DR entry on the cash account and a CR entry on the income account for sales:

Cash				
Date	Details	DR	CR	Balance
1 June	Capital	10,000		10,000DR
2 June	Computer		2,000	8,000DR
4 June	Rent		1,000	7,000DR
7 June	Purchases		2,000	5,000DR
8 June	**Sales**	**750**		**5,750DR**

Sales				
Date	Details	DR	CR	Balance
8 June	**Cash**		**750**	**750CR**

The above example is of a trading business. Trading businesses make their profit by buying and selling goods (stock). They may do so for cash or on credit. The purchase of stock is considered an expense of the business and is recorded in the purchases account. The business earns income by selling stock and this is recorded in the sales account.

Solicitors and other professionals do not sell trading stock to produce income; they sell their services. When a bill is issued, a solicitor wants to record the two aspects of the transaction. The first aspect is the sale of the solicitor's services and the second aspect is the gain of the debt now owed by the client to the firm. Charges for professional services are recorded as a CR entry on an income account, often called 'profit costs'. The client's debt is recorded as a DR entry on an account in the name of the client. When the client eventually pays, the solicitor will record a receipt of cash and the loss of the debt owed by the client to the business. It is important to notice that no entry is made on the profit costs account when the client pays the cash due. The profit costs account merely records the bill issued. It does not show whether or not clients have paid their bills.

Exercise 2B

Using the blank accounts below, make the double entries to record the following transactions:

1 July   Sally starts to practise as a solicitor. She puts in £5,000 cash.

2 July   Business pays £1,000 rent for office premises.

8 July   Business sends out a bill for £300 profit costs to Sidney, a client.

10 July Business pays £1,000 cash in staff wages.

Cash				
Date	Details	DR	CR	Balance

Date	Details	DR	CR	Balance

Date	Details	DR	CR	Balance

Date	Details	DR	CR	Balance

Date	Details	DR	CR	Balance

Date	Details	DR	CR	Balance

2.6 CASH AND LEDGER ACCOUNTS

You will have noticed that a large number of transactions have one aspect which will be recorded in the cash account. Most businesses operate by banking all receipts and making virtually all payments by cheque. The so-called 'cash' account is in reality a record of receipts into and payments out of the bank account. However, a business will usually need a small amount of cash in the office to cover small, day-to-day expenses. This is referred to as 'petty cash'. A petty cash account is required to record the periodic receipts of cash from the bank and the various payments made from petty cash.

We mentioned earlier that, traditionally, accounts were kept together in a bound book referred to as the 'ledger'. The cash account was the busiest account and was kept in a separate book. This distinction is of no practical importance, as accounts are now usually computerised.

However, it makes a difference in terminology, since all the accounts are referred to as 'ledger accounts' apart from the cash account and, where there is one, the petty cash account.

2.7 DRAWINGS

Anyone running a business will almost certainly need to withdraw some cash from time to time to live on. A withdrawal by the proprietor reduces the cash in the business and also reduces the amount the business owes to the proprietor. Rather than record these withdrawals on the capital account each time, it is usual for a business to keep a separate account entitled 'Drawings' on which to record withdrawals made by the proprietor during the accounting period.

The drawings account is a temporary account. At the end of the accounting period, the balance on the drawings account is transferred to the capital account so that the picture on the capital account is brought up to date, showing the total amount now owed to the proprietor.

2.8 TRIAL BALANCE

Periodically, a bookkeeper checks the accuracy of the bookkeeping. Depending on the nature of the business and the frequency with which financial transactions occur within it, this may be done at the end of every day or every month. However, every business will always carry out a check of its bookkeeping at the end of its accounting period (usually one year).

We have seen that every transaction has two aspects, and the double entry system requires that, for every DR entry made on an account, a CR entry for an identical amount must be made on another account. If every transaction has been properly recorded, the total of DR entries will equal the total of CR entries. If an entry has been made on only one side of the accounts, or if an entry has been written incorrectly on one side of the accounts, there will be a discrepancy between the two totals.

It should therefore be possible to check the accuracy of bookkeeping by comparing the two totals. However, over an entire accounting period, a bookkeeper will make an enormous number of entries. Adding them all up would be a tedious task. As a short-cut, it is possible to add together all the DR balances from the various accounts and then all the CR balances; if no errors have been made, the two totals will agree. You will see why this works if you think about what the balance on an individual account represents. It is the difference between the DR and CR entries on each account. If the correct DR and CR entries have been made on each account, the differences between the DR and CR sides of each and every account should agree. The process of adding together all DR and CR balances and comparing the total is referred to as preparing a 'Trial Balance'.

Example

Look at the solution to 2B below. We are going to use the figures to prepare a Trial Balance.

Trial Balance

	DR	CR
	£	£
Capital		5,000
Cash	3,000	
Wages	1,000	
Rent	1,000	
Profit Costs		300
Debtors (Sidney)	300	
	5,300	5,300

The Trial Balance is used as a check on the accuracy of the bookkeeping. If one half of an entry has been omitted or written as a wrong amount, the error is revealed because the total debits will not equal the total credits. However, the Trial Balance will not reveal all bookkeeping errors. If, for example, the bookkeeper has failed to make any entries relating to a particular transaction, the Trial Balance will not reveal the error because the debit and credit totals will add up to the same amount, but it will be the wrong amount.

Exercise 2C

Prepare a Trial Balance from the following list of balances:

Profit Costs	£10,000CR
Rent	£5,750DR
Electricity	£150DR
Wages	£2,500DR
Cash	£2,000DR
Creditors	£300CR
Debtors	£750DR
Fixtures and Fittings	£1,400DR
Capital	£1,750CR
Bank Loan	£500CR

Preparing a Trial Balance enables the bookkeeper to check the accuracy of the records. However, a Trial Balance will always be prepared at the end of the accounting period as a first step in preparing the year-end summary accounts, or 'Final Accounts', of the business. We examine Final Accounts in **Chapter 3** below.

SUMMARY

---

(1) Businesses use the double entry bookkeeping system when recording day-to-day transactions.

(2) The double entry bookkeeping system recognises that every business transaction has two aspects.

(3) Each aspect is recorded on an account.

(4) There will be one DR entry and one CR entry for each transaction.

(5) There are conventions which govern whether a DR entry or a CR entry is made.

(6) A Trial Balance is a list of the debit and credit balances on the accounts of the business.

(7) A Trial Balance is used:

    (a) to check the accuracy of the bookkeeping;

    (b) as a preliminary to drawing up Final Accounts.

SOLUTIONS

Exercise 2A

(1) Business gains cash	(1) Business incurs liability to proprietor
(2) Business gains asset (premises)	(2) Business pays cash
(3) Business incurs expense (cost of stock)	(3) Business incurs liability to Fred
(4) Business gains cash	(4) Business earns income
(5) Business extinguishes liability to Fred	(5) Business pays cash

---

Exercise 2B

Cash

Date	Details	DR	CR	Balance
1 July	Capital	5,000		5,000DR
2 July	Rent		1,000	4,000DR
10 July	Wages		1,000	3,000DR

Capital

Date	Details	DR	CR	Balance
1 July	Cash		5,000	5,000CR

Rent

Date	Details	DR	CR	Balance
2 July	Cash	1,000		1,000DR

Profit Costs

Date	Details	DR	CR	Balance
8 July	Sidney		300	300CR

Sidney

Date	Details	DR	CR	Balance
8 July	Profit Costs	300		300DR

Wages

Date	Details	DR	CR	Balance
10 July	Cash	1,000		1,000DR

Exercise 2C

Trial Balance

	DR £	CR £
Profit Costs		10,000
Rent	5,750	
Electricity	150	
Wages	2,500	
Cash	2,000	
Creditors		300
Debtors	750	
Fixtures and Fittings	1,400	
Capital		1,750
Bank Loan		500
	12,550	12,550

CHAPTER 3

FINAL ACCOUNTS

LEARNING OUTCOMES

After reading this chapter you will be able to:

- explain the purpose of Final Accounts
- draw up a basic profit and loss account
- draw up a basic balance sheet
- interpret the information provided by a simple set of Final Accounts.

3.1 INTRODUCTION

So far we have looked at the bookkeeping entries made by a business to record its financial transactions as they occur day to day. We have also seen that periodically the bookkeeper will prepare a Trial Balance. In this chapter we shall see how the basic financial information recorded using the double entry system may be presented as Final Accounts. Understanding this method of presentation will enable you to begin to use the accounts to make assessments as to the performance of the business.

3.2 THE PURPOSE OF FINAL ACCOUNTS

The records kept using the double entry system give the business information on every single transaction carried out, for example payment of a gas bill, purchase of a fixed asset, delivery of a bill to a client, receipt of cash from a client in payment of costs. However, neither the records produced using the double entry system nor the Trial Balance are particularly helpful in enabling us to assess the financial state of the business.

Consider the following Trial Balance:

Trial Balance as at . . .		
	DR	CR
Sales		15,000
Purchases	12,000	
Cash	5,000	
Rent	3,000	
Capital		10,000
Bank Loan		5,000
Wages	5,000	
Machinery	5,000	
	30,000	30,000

At first sight it is difficult to work out how well the business is doing. All the information that we need is there, but it is not presented in a way that makes interpretation easy.

For any proprietor, of course, it is vital to know how well the business is doing. The proprietor will want to know:

(a)   Has the business made a profit?

(b)   How much is the business worth?

The profitability of the business may be calculated by preparing a Profit and Loss Account. The worth or value of the business may be seen by preparing a Balance Sheet. The purpose behind preparing a Profit and Loss Account and a Balance Sheet is essentially to bring together the detail of the day-to-day records as summarised in the Trial Balance and present it in such a way that this key information about the performance of the business may readily be seen.

Typically a business prepares a Profit and Loss Account (also known as an Income Statement) and a Balance Sheet (also known as a Statement of Financial Position) once a year at the end of the accounting period. Collectively these end-of-year accounts are referred to as 'Final Accounts'. (Other year-end statements are produced, such as cash flow statements, which are extremely important to investors and lenders, but we shall consider these in the context of company accounts in **Chapter 7**.)

We shall now consider the Profit and Loss Account and the Balance Sheet in turn. Remember that the starting point for both is the Trial Balance. The figures from the Trial Balance are transferred across to the Final Accounts.

3.3   THE PROFIT AND LOSS ACCOUNT

The first element of the year-end Final Accounts is the Profit and Loss Account. The purpose of the Profit and Loss Account is to present information from the Trial Balance, so that it can readily be seen whether the company has made a profit during the accounting period.

3.3.1   The period covered

The accounting period will normally (but not necessarily) be one year. The Profit and Loss Account is headed with the period to which it relates.

> **Examples**
>
> Profit and Loss Account for ABC & Co for year ended 30 September [201–]
> Profit and Loss Account for ABC & Co for 1 October [201–] to 30 September [201–]

3.3.2   Income and expenses

In essence the Profit and Loss Account shows us a very simple calculation:

Income – Expenses = Profit

Using this calculation, you will see that if the income of the business exceeds its expenses, the business has made a profit. Conversely, if the expenses exceed the income then the resulting figure will be a negative one, showing that the business has made a loss.

An important point to note here is that only those items appearing on the Trial Balance which can be classified as income and expenses will appear on the Profit and Loss Account. It is therefore vital to identify these items accurately, and to distinguish them from the assets and liabilities of the business. Those items which can be classified as assets and liabilities will appear on the Balance Sheet. We considered this classification at **1.8**.

Having prepared the Trial Balance, looking at the items to distinguish between income and expenses on the one hand and assets and liabilities on the other is the next step in preparing the Final Accounts.

Exercise 3A

Study the following Trial Balance. Identify those accounts which will appear on the Profit and Loss Account as income, and those which will appear as expenses.

Trial Balance as at . . .

	DR	CR
Capital		61,000
Bank Loan		50,000
Premises	200,000	
Machinery	6,000	
Rent Paid	1,500	
Wages	3,500	
Electricity	700	
Interest Paid	450	
Interest Received		300
Professional Charges		114,000
Cash	4,850	
Debtors	12,000	
Creditors		3,700
	229,000	229,000

3.3.3 Preparation

Once the items appearing in the Trial Balance as income and expenses have been identified, the balances on those accounts are transferred to the Profit and Loss Account. Essentially all the income figures are grouped together, followed by the expenses. Then the total expenses are deducted from the total income to calculate the profit.

The Profit and Loss Account is usually set out vertically. So the calculation of profit appears as:

Income

–

Expenses

=

Profit

Example

Here is an extract from the Trial Balance prepared for Ann, a solicitor in sole practice. It shows the income and expense accounts for the year 1 March 2017 to 28 February 2018.

Ann, a firm
Extract from Trial Balance 28 February 2018

	DR	CR
Profit Costs		120,000
Interest Received		20,000
General Expenses	10,000	
Wages	30,000	

Ann's Profit and Loss Account will show income less expenses and will look like this:

Profit and Loss Account for Ann for year ended 28 February 2018

	£	£
Income		
Profit Costs	120,000	
Interest Received	20,000	
		140,000
Expenses		
Wages	10,000	
General Expenses	30,000	
		(£40,000)
NET PROFIT		100,000

Although you will see that the figures on the Profit and Loss Account are shown in columns, these no longer represent debits and credits. The columns are simply used to make the Profit and Loss Accounts appear as clear as possible. The convention is to show workings in column(s) to the left and carry the main figures across to the right-hand column. You should also note the convention of indicating that a figure is to be deducted, or shown as a minus, by placing that figure in brackets.

The net profit shown on the Profit and Loss Account (£100,000 in the above example) is owed to the proprietor (Ann). However, this does not mean that the proprietor will simply take the profit out of the business at the end of the year. A business needs to retain at least some of its profits to fund investment and growth.

Exercise 3B

Prepare a Profit and Loss Account for Smith for the year ended 31 December 2017 based on the Trial Balance set out below:

Trial Balance as at 31 December 2017

	DR	CR
Profit Costs		20,000
Wages	14,000	
Rent	3,000	
Electricity	500	
Fixtures and Fittings	6,500	
Computers	7,000	
Debtors	2,000	
Creditors		2,000
Cash	2,000	
Drawings	2,000	
Capital		15,000
	37,000	37,000

Understanding the Profit and Loss Account enables the proprietor, or anyone else reading the accounts, to begin to assess the performance of the business. A key measure of the success of a business is whether it is making a profit; consequently if the business has low profits, the proprietor will usually want to take steps to improve them. From the simple calculation which we now know to be shown in the Profit and Loss Account (Income – Expenses = Profit) it is clear that there are only two ways of improving profits: increasing income and/or decreasing expenses. A business can increase its income by selling more stock (perhaps by better marketing or introducing new products), or by increasing prices (this will require careful consideration of the market and business competitors to see if it is viable). Decreasing expenses could be achieved by finding a cheaper supplier, but might involve taking commercial decisions such as cutting the number of staff. Sometimes it may be possible for a business to change the nature of its products sold to those with a higher 'mark up'; this will have the effect of increasing profits.

3.3.4 Trading Accounts

A business which buys and sells goods has a Profit and Loss Account, but it also has a preliminary account called a Trading Account. A business which provides professional services, for example a firm of solicitors, does not need a Trading Account.

The Trading Account shows income from sales less the cost of those sales (ie, the cost of buying the trading stock). The difference between the two is the gross profit. The gross profit is then carried forward to start the Profit and Loss Account; any other income is added and the expenses of running the business are deducted to produce the net profit.

To prepare the Trading Account the balance on the sales account for the year will be transferred from the Trial Balance to the Trading Account as income. The balance on the purchases account for the year will be transferred to the Trading Account as an expense. The difference between the sales income and the cost of buying trading stock will represent the gross profit.

Example

A business has the following balances on its sales and purchases accounts for the year 1 January to 31 December 2017. The balances are transferred to the Trading Account.

Extract from Trial Balance as at 31 December 2017

	DR	CR
Sales		400,000
Purchases	280,000	

Its Trading Account will show sales less the cost of the goods sold:

Trading Account for year ended 31 December 2017

	£
Sales	400,000
Less Cost of goods sold	
Purchases	(280,000)
Gross profit	120,000

The Profit and Loss Account then follows with the addition of any other income and the deduction of the remaining expenses to produce the net profit.

The reason for having a separate Trading Account is to highlight the difference between what the business pays for its trading stock and what it sells it for. This is achieved by separating these items from other income and expenses. This is then usually presented in the Final Accounts with the Trading Account at the top of the page and the Profit and Loss Account following below. Highlighting the gross profit in this way is helpful to the proprietor. If a business has a low net profit figure overall, the proprietor will try to identify the cause and take steps to try to improve the profitability of the business. A low net profit figure could be caused by high running expenses, or by stock being bought at too high a price. Separating the two types of expenses by moving the expense of purchasing stock into the Trading Account makes it easier to spot where the problems have occurred.

3.4 BALANCE SHEET

The second element of the year-end Final Accounts is the Balance Sheet. The purpose of the Balance Sheet is to present the figures from the Trial Balance in order to show the worth or value of the business.

3.4.1   The date of preparation

The Balance Sheet is a list of the assets and liabilities of the business. It lists the assets and liabilities on the last day of the accounting period, and is accurate only for that one day. It must be headed with that date.

> **Example**
>
> Balance Sheet for ABC & Co as at 31 December [201–].

3.4.2   Assets and liabilities

We saw at **3.3.2** that only those items from the Trial Balance which can be classified as income and expenses for the year appear on the Profit and Loss Account to calculate net profit. The remaining items represent assets and liabilities, and these are the items which will appear on the Balance Sheet.

Just like the Profit and Loss Account, in essence the Balance Sheet shows a simple calculation, although, as we shall see later, the way in which the calculation is presented is a little more complicated. The calculation shown on the Balance Sheet is:

Assets – Liabilities = Net worth of the business

So, the presentation of the Balance Sheet shows that if all the assets of the business are added together and all the liabilities then deducted, the figure that remains is the net worth, or value, of the business. However, the Balance Sheet does not simply show assets in one section and liabilities in the other. It shows what the business is worth *to the proprietor*. Therefore, one section of the Balance Sheet shows the value of assets less liabilities owed to third parties; the other shows the amount owed to the proprietor as capital. The two amounts should be the same.

The Balance Sheet calculation (Assets – Liabilities = Net Worth) is shown vertically. In the example set out below, we show the first part of the calculation (Assets – Liabilities) followed by the value to the proprietor, labelling the sections 'Employment of Capital' and 'Capital Employed' respectively. Different titles are often used for the two sections of the vertical Balance Sheet. The assets section is often entitled simply 'Assets' and the liabilities section is often labelled 'Financed By' or 'Represented By'.

Example

Balance Sheet as at 30 September 201–

	£	£	£
EMPLOYMENT OF CAPITAL			
Fixed Assets			
Premises		50,000	
Machinery		50,000	
			100,000
Current Assets			
Debtors	10,000		
Cash	102,000		
	112,000		
Less Current Liabilities			
Creditors	(2,000)		
Net Current Assets			110,000
			210,000
Less Long-term Liabilities			
Five-year Bank Loan			(100,000)
Net Assets			**110,000**
CAPITAL EMPLOYED			
Capital			
Opening balance		80,000	
Net profit		60,000	
Drawings		(30,000)	
			110,000

You will see that a layer of complexity has been added here because, having identified the assets and liabilities from the Trial Balance, they must be sub-divided:

(a) Assets are divided into fixed assets and current assets:

Fixed assets are those which are bought not for resale but to improve the efficiency of the business, for example premises, machinery.

Current assets are short-term assets, for example cash and debtors. These are sometimes referred to as 'circulating assets' because they change their character as one asset turns into another: for example, when a debtor pays, the business no longer has the debtor as an asset; it has the cash paid instead.

(b) Liabilities are divided into current liabilities and long-term liabilities:

Current liabilities are those which are repayable in 12 months or less from the date of the Balance Sheet.

Long-term liabilities are those repayable more than 12 months from the date of the Balance Sheet.

By convention, assets are listed in decreasing order of permanence (or, to put it another way, in increasing order of liquidity). So, fixed assets are shown before current assets. Listing in decreasing order of permanence means that premises will always be shown first in the list of fixed assets. Within the current assets, debtors will always be shown above cash because cash is more liquid.

The Balance Sheet shows current liabilities being deducted from current assets to give a figure called 'net current assets'. This is an important figure for a business. It shows the extent of the assets which the business can most readily turn into cash in order to meet its most pressing liabilities. In other words, it represents the liquid funds available to the business. A business may have substantial assets and be very profitable, but if it has insufficient liquid assets, it will be unable to meet its debts as they fall due and will be unable to continue trading. The Balance Sheet therefore highlights this. A low (or negative) figure for net current assets is usually an indication that the business is in financial difficulty.

Long-term liabilities are deducted from the total of fixed and net current assets to give a figure for the net assets of the business. Net assets will always equal the amount owing to the proprietor as capital at the end of the year.

The 'Capital Employed' section reflects the value of the business to the proprietor. This starts with the balance on the capital account. The net profit from the Profit and Loss Account is 'owed' to the proprietor and must be added. Any withdrawals made by the proprietor during the accounting year will be shown on the drawings account, and therefore the balance on the drawings account is deducted.

As we have seen already, when the proprietor starts a business, he will normally contribute some money to the business. From the perspective of the business, the capital contributed is a liability owed to the proprietor. The proprietor of a business hopes that at the end of the accounting period the business will have made a net profit. Any profit the business makes will be 'owed' to the proprietor. Therefore, once the net profit has been calculated on the Profit and Loss Account, it will be credited to the capital account to increase the amount shown as owing to the proprietor.

Exercise 3C

Prepare a Balance Sheet for Smith as at 31 December 2017 based on the Trial Balance set out in Exercise 3B. Remember that in Exercise 3B you calculated the net profit. You will add this to the balance on the capital account.

Understanding the Balance Sheet enables the proprietor or anyone else reading the accounts to begin to assess the current state of the business. A business whose liabilities exceed its assets is in financial difficulty. If the business cannot meet its liabilities, there is a risk that unpaid creditors may take some kind of insolvency proceedings. The nature of the assets and liabilities is also important. A business may have high-value fixed assets but little cash. Whilst the net value of such a business may be high, the business lacks the cash with which to pay immediate liabilities. If a business has to start to sell fixed assets in order to pay current liabilities, it is usually an indication that the business is in financial difficulties.

3.4.3   Client bank account

A firm of solicitors will have an additional asset – a bank account containing money held for clients. This asset will always be equalled by the amount the firm 'owes' its clients. The two items are normally shown as self-cancelling items on the Balance Sheet after the net figure for current assets.

Example

	£	£
Net Current Assets		110,000
Client bank account	100,000	
Due to clients	(100,000)	

3.5   THE IMPORTANCE OF FINAL ACCOUNTS

The proprietor of a business will need to know how much profit the business made in the most recent accounting period, how much cash is in the bank, and what liabilities and other assets the business has at the end of the accounting period. All this information can readily be seen from the way in which the information is presented in the Final Accounts.

The Final Accounts also enable the proprietor, and others, to assess the past performance of the business and make informed decisions for the future. If the business is fundamentally profitable, but currently short of cash because of over-enthusiastic expansion, the proprietor may decide to borrow money in order to increase the cash in the business. If the machinery is outdated, it may be sensible to scrap the existing machinery and to buy something more modern. If the business is thriving, the proprietor may consider taking on more staff and expanding the business.

Whatever the type of business medium you are considering, however large or small the business may be, at the heart of its Final Accounts will be a Profit and Loss Account and a Balance Sheet. You will often see some added complexity, and you will certainly see different terminology. However, whenever you are looking at any set of Final Accounts, remember that they will in essence be showing you this basic information – the Profit and Loss Account, revealing the profit that the business has made, and the Balance Sheet, showing the worth of the business.

SUMMARY

(1) The Final Accounts of a business comprise a Profit and Loss Account and a Balance Sheet.

(2) A Profit and Loss Account shows income less expenses to give net profit.

(3) Businesses which buy and sell goods have a Trading Account as well as a Profit and Loss Account. The Trading Account shows income from sales, less the cost of goods sold to give gross profit. The Profit and Loss Account shows gross profit less expenses to give net profit.

(4) The Balance Sheet shows assets and liabilities. It is set out as follows:

    (a) first fixed assets are added together;

    (b) then the net current assets figure is calculated – this is total current assets less total liabilities;

    (c) the total fixed assets and net current assets are added together;

    (d) any long-term liabilities are deducted;

    (e) the result is labelled 'Net Assets';

    (f) it should equal the new capital figure found by adding net profit to the figure for capital on the Trial Balance and deducting drawings.

SOLUTIONS

Exercise 3A

Expenses	Income
Rent Paid	Professional Charges
Wages	Interest Received
Electricity	
Interest Paid	

The remaining items represent assets or liabilities which will appear on the Balance Sheet.

Exercise 3B

Profit and Loss Account for Smith for year ended 31 December 2017

	£	£
Income		
Profit Costs		20,000
Expenses		
Wages	14,000	
Rent	3,000	
Electricity	500	
		(17,500)
NET PROFIT		2,500

Exercise 3C

Balance Sheet for Smith as at 31 December 2017

EMPLOYMENT OF CAPITAL

Fixed Assets

Fixtures and Fittings	6,500	
Computers	7,000	
		13,500
Current Assets		
Debtors	2,000	
Cash	2,000	
	4,000	
Less Current Liabilities		
Creditors	(2,000)	
Net Current Assets		2,000
Net Assets		15,500
CAPITAL EMPLOYED		
Capital		
Opening Balance	15,000	
Net profit	2,500	
Drawings	2,000	
		15,500

ADJUSTMENTS

LEARNING OUTCOMES

After reading this chapter you will be able to:

- explain the concept of accruals
- describe the purpose of year-end adjustments
- make the key adjustments required to produce accurate Final Accounts.

4.1 INTRODUCTION

Up to now we have recorded financial transactions as they occur. So, the recording of the payment of, say, an electricity bill is made when the bill is actually paid, and the appropriate entries are made on the electricity and cash accounts respectively. If an electricity bill has been received but not yet paid, there will be no entries in the accounts. This can mean that the books present a somewhat distorted picture with, for example, expenses being recorded in the accounting period when they happen to be paid, rather than being recorded in the accounting period to which they relate. In this chapter we shall look at how the figures recorded using the double entry system may be adjusted so that the Final Accounts present a more accurate picture of the performance of the business.

4.2 THE CONCEPT OF ACCRUALS

The Final Accounts of most businesses are prepared and adjusted on what is called the 'accruals basis'. The accruals basis requires that income and expenditure are recorded in the period to which they relate rather than that in which payment or receipt happens to occur. Relying simply on when cash is paid would result in the Final Accounts being distorted by the almost accidental timing of payments in relation to the beginning and end of the accounting year. Using the accruals basis instead means that the Final Accounts provide a more accurate picture of how the business has performed during the accounting year.

Final Accounts, then, must include all expenses which relate to the accounting period, irrespective of whether the expense has yet been paid or whether bills have yet been received. So far as income is concerned, the accruals basis requires the Final Accounts to include all income 'earned' during the period, irrespective of whether cash has yet been received or whether bills have yet been delivered.

Conversely, if an expense has been paid in the current accounting period which actually relates to an earlier or later period, it will not be included in the current Final Accounts. Similarly, income received in the current accounting period which actually relates to an earlier or later period will not be included in the current Final Accounts. Instead, such items will be included in the Final Accounts for the earlier or later period.

You can think of the process of determining which items relate to which period as 'matching'. The task is to 'match' the expense to the period in which the benefit of the expense was obtained, and to 'match' the income to the period in which the work producing the income was done.

Exercise 4A

You are preparing Final Accounts for Smith & Co for the accounting year ending 31 December 2017. Decide which of the following items relate to the accounting year ending 31 December 2017:

(a) electricity bill paid 10 January 2017 for period July–December 2016;

(b) electricity bill paid 10 July 2017 for period January–June 2017;

(c) electricity bill unpaid for period July–December 2017;

(d) stationery bill paid 30 November 2017. Three-quarters of the stationery purchased remains in the stationery cupboard on 1 January 2018;

(e) rent for new premises paid in advance on 28 December 2017 for period January–March 2018;

(f) work done for clients during 2017 but not yet billed by 31 December 2017, estimated at £15,000.

We have seen that the Final Accounts are prepared using the figures from the Trial Balance. These Trial Balance figures are themselves derived from the records made using the double entry system, and so it is sometimes necessary to make adjustments to the Trial Balance figures before inserting them into the Final Accounts in order to ensure that the Final Accounts follow the accruals concept.

We are now going to look at a number of different types of adjustments. However, there are a couple of general points to bear in mind. First, adjustments are always made *after* the preparation of the Trial Balance at the end of the accounting period. Secondly, each adjustment will always be reflected on both the Profit and Loss Account and the Balance Sheet.

4.3 OUTSTANDING EXPENSES

As and when expenses are paid during an accounting period, entries are usually made on the cash account and on the relevant expense account. Assume that a Trial Balance for a business includes a balance on the electricity account of £1,000. This figure reflects those electricity bills paid during the accounting period. We shall assume that the business receives a further bill for £200 for electricity used during the current year, but the bill has not be paid by the time the Trial Balance is prepared at the end of the accounting period.

As the electricity bill has not been paid, no double entries have been made and the bill is therefore not included in the Trial Balance figure. The electricity has been used in this accounting year and it therefore properly relates to this year. The Trial Balance figure for electricity is consequently too low. In order for there to be an accurate reflection of the expense incurred in relation to electricity for this year, we need to adjust the Trial Balance figure. The adjustment is made by increasing the Trial Balance figure of £1,000 by the amount of the outstanding bill of £200. The increased expense of £1,200 is then shown on Profit and Loss as the true expense for the current accounting period.

The adjustment will also be reflected on the Balance Sheet. The amount of the unpaid bill, £200, is shown on the Balance Sheet as a current liability. This shows that the business will start the next accounting year with the bill still owing. The unpaid expense can simply be shown as an additional item in the current liabilities section of the Balance Sheet. However, in practice a business is likely to have a number of unpaid expenses at the year end, it is usual to add these together and show one composite figure for unpaid expenses, labeled 'Accruals'.

Example		
(Extract) Profit and Loss Account Year ended . . .		
	£	£
Income		
Expenses		
Electricity	1,200	
Wages		
Stationery		
(Extract) Balance Sheet as at . . .		
	£	£
Current Liabilities		
Creditors		
Accruals	200	

4.4 PAYMENTS IN ADVANCE

Payments in advance are essentially the opposite of outstanding expenses. It will sometimes be the case that a business pays an expense this year but will not get the benefit until next year, for example rent paid in advance. The payment will have been made and recorded in the current accounting year, but the expense properly relates to the following year.

Assume that the Trial Balance for a business includes a balance on the stationery account of £600, which includes £50 for stationery bought this year but which the business will use next year. The Trial Balance figure for the expense of stationery is too high. We need to adjust the Trial Balance figure of £600 by reducing it by the amount of the payment in advance, £50. The reduced expense of £550 is then shown on Profit and Loss as the true expense for stationery for the current accounting period.

The amount of the payment in advance is shown on the Balance Sheet as a current asset (usually after cash). The 'asset' for the business is the benefit of the payment already having been made. It shows that the business will begin the next accounting year being able to use something in the future without any further payment. As with outstanding expenses, it is usual to add all payments in advance for the year together and show one composite figure in the current assets section of the Balance Sheet labeled 'Prepayments'.

Example		
(Extract) Profit and Loss Account Year ended . . .		
	£	£
Income		
Expenses		
Electricity		
Wages		
Stationery	550	

(Extract) Balance Sheet as at . . .		
	£	£
Current Assets		
Work in Progress		
Debtors		
Cash		
Prepayments	50	

4.5 WORK IN PROGRESS

A firm of solicitors, like any other business providing services, earns income by sending a bill to a client for the work done on his behalf. This is recorded when the bill is delivered to the client, and the relevant entries are then made in the client's account and the profit costs account. It will often be the case that a solicitor will reach the end of the accounting year having done work for a client which has not yet been billed. As a bill has not been delivered, no entries will have been made on the profit costs account to show the income earned, and yet the work has been done in the current year and it properly relates to the current year. A firm of solicitors will therefore want to adjust its profit costs account at the end of the year to reflect the value of this work in progress at that date.

The estimated value of work done but not yet billed increases the profit costs properly attributable to the current period and must be added to the balance on the profit costs account appearing on the Trial Balance. The increased figure for profit costs must be shown in the income section of the Profit and Loss Account. It is usual, however, to show the costs actually billed and the value of work in progress at the end of the year as two separate items, which are then added together on Profit and Loss Account.

The estimated figure for work in progress at the end of the year is also shown on the Balance Sheet. The figure will appear as an additional item in the current assets section. Work in progress is normally shown as the first of the current assets. This shows that the business will start the next accounting period with the benefit of that work in hand.

A firm of solicitors will begin each year with some work in progress from the previous year. It is normal to show the value of work in progress at the start of the year as a deduction on Profit and Loss Account from the value of bills issued during the year.

Example

(Extract) Profit and Loss Account Year ended . . .		
	£	£
Income		
Professional Charges	478,000	
Less Opening Work in Progress	(30,000)	
Plus Closing Work in Progress	40,000	
		488,000
Expenses		

(Extract) Balance Sheet as at . . .		
	£	£
Current Assets		
Work in Progress	40,000	
Debtors		
Cash		
Prepayments		

A point to note here is that the modern approach generally adopted by professional firms is to calculate work in progress by treating the right to payment as accruing gradually as the work is done. The result is that much work in progress is shown as part of the debtors figure on the Balance Sheet instead of as a separate item. However, in order to illustrate the principles clearly, we shall show work in progress separately in our examples and exercises.

4.6 CLOSING STOCK

When we calculated gross profit on the Trading Account (see **3.3.4**), we deducted the cost of goods sold from sales and we used the purchases figure to represent the cost of goods sold. However, the purchases figure does not, by itself, represent the correct value for cost of goods sold. It is highly unlikely that a business will buy, say, £10,000 worth of stock during the year and then reach the end of the year with each and every item of stock having been sold and its warehouse empty. In reality the business will have some stock which remains unsold. It is therefore necessary for a trading business to make an adjustment for the value of any stock purchased during the year and left unsold at the end of the year. The adjustment is made by showing the value of closing stock appearing in the Trading Account as a deduction from purchases in order to calculate the cost of goods sold.

The figure for closing stock will also appear as an additional item in the current assets section of the Balance Sheet. This shows that the business will be starting the next accounting year with the benefit of that stock having already been purchased. Closing stock is usually shown as the first item in the current assets section.

Unless it is the first year of trading, the business will have started the year with some stock in the warehouse left over from the previous year and still waiting to be sold. The value of this opening stock must also be taken into account when calculating the cost of goods sold.

Example		
Trading Account for . . .		
	£	£
Sales		12,000
Less Cost of Goods Sold		
Purchases	5,000	
plus Opening Stock	1,000	
less Closing Stock	(2,000)	
		(4,000)
GROSS PROFIT		8,000

You will see from the above example that the cost of goods sold is calculated as follows:

Cost of Goods Sold = Purchases + Opening Stock – Closing Stock

By convention, stock is valued in the Final Accounts at the *lower* of its acquisition cost or its realisable value. There is of course no guarantee that the stock left over at the end of the year can be sold even for the price that the business paid for it in the first place. The goods may be perishable or have become unfashionable, or they may have been damaged or lost. The business should inspect its stock at the end of the year to check its condition and place a realistic value on it. The value given for closing stock is therefore an estimate. This means that when you are analysing accounts, you should always look critically at the figure given for closing stock. The value given may not be a realistic assessment of its value. Overvaluing stock is an easy way to distort the accounts by making the profit figure look better. This is illustrated in the following example.

Example

In its first year of trading, a business has sales of £20,000 and purchases of £10,000. The closing stock is valued at £1,000. The Trading Account will be as follows:

Trading Account for . . .

	£	£
Sales		20,000
Less Cost of Goods Sold		
Purchases	10,000	
less Closing Stock	(1,000)	(9,000)
GROSS PROFIT		11,000

We shall now set out the Trading Account again, but this time on the basis that the closing stock is valued at £7,000. Look at the effect this has on the gross profit.

Trading Account for . . .
Year 1

	£	£
Sales		20,000
Less Cost of Goods Sold		
Purchases	10,000	
less Closing Stock	(7,000)	(3,000)
GROSS PROFIT		17,000

You will see that increasing the value for closing stock has the effect of increasing gross profit. Obviously, therefore, it is very important that the closing stock figure should be accurate. If it is not, the gross profit figure will also be inaccurate.

4.7 BAD AND DOUBTFUL DEBTS

4.7.1 Bad debts

Debtors are a current asset of a business, and they therefore increase the net value of the business appearing on the Balance Sheet. However, in reality not every debtor will pay the amount owed to the business. A debtor may become insolvent and be unable to pay; or a debtor may simply refuse to pay, and the business takes the commercial decision that it is not worth the time and expense of suing for the debt. If these so-called bad debts were to continue to be included in the Balance Sheet figure for debtors, that figure would be inaccurate and as a consequence the net value of the business would be inflated. Periodically, therefore, a business will review its debtors during the year to ascertain whether any should be declared bad and written off.

The effect of writing off a debt as bad is that the debtor is no longer shown as owing the firm money. The debtors figure from the Trial Balance is adjusted by deducting the amount of the bad debt. This adjusted figure for debtors appears on the Balance Sheet, and therefore the total of assets will be reduced.

Bad debts are regarded as an expense of the business. The value of a bad debt which has been written off will appear in the Profit and Loss Account as an additional item of expense labeled 'Bad debts'.

As well as writing off debts during the accounting period, it is common to review debtors at the end of an accounting period, to consider whether any further debts need to be written off as bad. It is the final figure for bad debts which will be shown on Profit and Loss as an expense reducing the net profit. Any further bad debts written off at that point will be deducted from the debtors figure and added to the bad debts figure before these are transferred across to the Final Accounts.

Exercise 4B

At the end of an accounting period you have already written off £1,500 debts as bad. Your remaining debtors amount to £20,000. You decide to write off a further £1,000 of debts as bad.

(a) What figure will you show on the bad debts account?

(b) What figure will you show on Profit and Loss for bad debts?

(c) What figure will you show on the Balance Sheet for debtors?

4.7.2 Doubtful debts

At the end of an accounting period after the known bad debts have been written off, the books will still show that the business is owed a certain amount by its debtors. The business may be owed this amount on paper, but the business will know from past experience that whilst it may not be able to identify any more specific debts as bad, in practice it never manages to collect all its debts.

The business knows that the debtors figure in the Trial Balance is likely to be too high and that it would therefore be inaccurate to calculate net profit on the basis that all debtors will pay, and inaccurate to include the full debtors figure on the Balance Sheet. An adjustment must be made to take account of the uncertainty regarding the debtors by making provision for doubtful debts.

To make this adjustment a business will calculate the value of debtors it thinks may never pay. Doubtful debts are considered an expense of the business. There will therefore be an additional item of expense in the Profit and Loss Account labeled as 'Provision for Doubtful Debts' (although sometimes this is added to the bad debts to give a composite figure for 'Bad and Doubtful Debts').

The adjustment must also be reflected on the Balance Sheet to demonstrate that some of the debtors figure is considered doubtful. It is usual to show the amount of the 'Provision for Doubtful Debts' on the Balance Sheet as a deduction from debtors.

Example

At the date of the Trial Balance a business has written off £15,000 of debts as bad and has £82,000 of debtors remaining. The business then decides to write off an additional debt of £2,000. Having reviewed its debtors, it concludes that £8,000 of them are doubtful; it therefore makes a provision for doubtful debts of £8,000.

The Final Accounts will appear as follows:

(Extract) Profit and Loss Account Year ended . . .

	£	£
Income		
Expenses		
Bad Debts		17,000
Provision for Doubtful Debts		8,000

(Extract) Balance Sheet as at . . .

	£	£
Current Assets		
Debtors	80,000	
Less Provision	(8,000)	
		72,000
Cash		
Prepayments		

Exercise 4C

Mabel is a solicitor in practice on her own. The bookkeeper prepares a Trial Balance and then has to make the following adjustments. There are outstanding electricity expenses of £200 to take into account, and stationery left over at the end of the year amounts to £300. A provision is to be made for doubtful debts of £175.

For questions (1)–(3) below, tick which *one* of the options you think is correct.

(1) **In relation to the £200 outstanding electricity bill:**

    (a) The £200 will increase the amount shown on Profit and Loss for electricity. It will not appear on the Balance Sheet.

    (b) The £200 will reduce the amount shown on Profit and Loss for electricity and will appear on the Balance Sheet as a current asset.

    (c) The £200 will increase the amount shown on Profit and Loss for electricity and will appear on the Balance Sheet as a current asset.

    (d) The £200 will increase the amount shown on Profit and Loss for electricity and will appear on the Balance Sheet as a current liability.

(2) **In relation to the pre-paid stationery stock of £300:**

    (a) The £300 will increase the amount shown on Profit and Loss for stationery. It will not appear on the Balance Sheet.

    (b) The £300 will reduce the amount shown on Profit and Loss for stationery and will appear on the Balance Sheet as a current asset.

    (c) The £300 will increase the amount shown on Profit and Loss for stationery and will appear on the Balance Sheet as a current asset.

    (d) The £300 will increase the amount shown on Profit and Loss for stationery and will appear on the Balance Sheet as a current liability.

(3) **Making provision for doubtful debts will:**

    (a) Increase debtors.

    (b) Reduce debtors.

    (c) Reduce bad debts.

    (d) Have no effect on debtors.

4.8   DEPRECIATION

We have seen that when a business acquires fixed assets, such as cars, computers or machinery, this will be recorded in the books of the business. The price paid for an asset will be included in the Final Accounts at the year end in the fixed assets section of the Balance Sheet. The business will have acquired the asset to benefit the business in the long term, and is therefore likely to own the asset for several years. In reality many fixed assets lose some of their value each year. You may have experienced this yourself. If, for example, you have ever owned a car, you will know that when you come to sell it, the sale price is likely to be much less than the price you paid for the car. This annual loss in value is called 'depreciation'.

Depreciation is a hidden expense of the business and must be shown on the Profit and Loss Account as an item reducing net profit.

> **Example**
>
> A business buys a machine in Year 1 for £15,000. By the end of Year 5 it is worn out and has to be scrapped. Over the five years, it has depreciated by £15,000. To look at it another way, it has cost the business £3,000 a year to keep the machine for the five years. The Profit and Loss Accounts for those years must show the annual expense of keeping the machine.

The Balance Sheet will not show just the original purchase price of the asset. Instead, it will show the original purchase price with a deduction for the amount of depreciation incurred to date. This depreciation is referred to as 'accumulated depreciation'.

> **Example**
>
> A business bought a van at the beginning of Year 1 for £20,000. Each year, the business depreciates the van by £3,000. At the end of Year 3, the business will have depreciated the van three times (once at the end of Years 1, 2 and 3). Accumulated depreciation will therefore amount to £9,000. The Balance Sheet as at the end of Year 3 would include the following item for vans:
>
> | | £ | £ |
> |---|---|---|
> | Fixed Assets | | |
> | Van | 20,000 | |
> | less Depreciation | (9,000) | |
> | | | 11,000 |

The £11,000 in the above example is referred to as the 'book value' of the van – its value in the business's books or accounts. Each year, the amount of accumulated depreciation shown on the Balance Sheet will increase by £3,000.

The Profit and Loss Account each year will record the loss in value over the one-year period. Thus, each year, the depreciation expense shown on Profit and Loss will be £3,000.

4.8.1 Calculation

Accountants have different methods of calculating the amount of depreciation, for example the 'straight line' method and the 'reducing balance' method. In this book, we look only at the 'straight line' method.

A business using the straight line method will decide on the likely length of the life of an asset. The loss in value is spread evenly over the projected life of the asset. Thus, if the projected life is 10 years, the business will use up 10% of the asset's original value each year. If the projected life is four years, the asset will be reduced by 25% of its original value each year.

The reason that this method is called 'straight line' is that the asset suffers the same amount of depreciation each year. If the asset is kept for the whole of its projected life, the value of the asset will eventually be reduced to zero.

The straight line method of calculating depreciation is to some extent artificial in that it presupposes an even loss of value year by year, whereas in reality an asset is likely to suffer a greater drop in the value of the asset in the first years of its life. Calculating depreciation by the straight line method also depends on an estimate being made of the useful life of an asset. The business will therefore keep the depreciation of its assets under review. If, for example, an asset looks likely to last for longer than expected, its rate of depreciation should be slowed down.

4.8.2 Date of purchase and sale

It is common practice:

(a) to depreciate all assets held at the end of an accounting period for an entire accounting period, irrespective of the point in the period at which the purchase was made;

(b) not to depreciate assets sold part way through an accounting period.

This helps to simplify the calculations.

Exercise 4D

Ruddle has been in practice as a solicitor for some years. The Trial Balance for the year ended 31 December 2017 includes the following:

	£
Interest Received	22,567
Furniture and Library at cost	15,000
Motor Cars at cost	40,000
Provision for Depreciation at start of 2017:	
Furniture and Library	4,500
Motor Cars	16,000

Depreciation is to be charged at the following rates (straight line basis):

Furniture and Library 15% pa

Motor Cars 20% pa

For questions (1)–(3) below, tick which *one* of the options you think is correct.

(1) **Depreciation on furniture and library will be:**

    (a) £2,250 on Profit and Loss.

    (b) £1,500 on Profit and Loss.

    (c) £4,500 on Profit and Loss.

    (d) £450 on Profit and Loss.

(2) **Depreciation on the furniture and library will be:**

    (a) £4,500 on the Balance Sheet.

    (b) £6,750 on the Balance Sheet.

    (c) £2,250 on the Balance Sheet.

    (d) £1,500 on the Balance Sheet.

(3) **Depreciation on motor cars will be:**

    (a) £16,000 on Profit and Loss.

    (b) £8,000 on Profit and Loss.

    (c) £8,000 on the Balance Sheet.

    (d) £16,000 on the Balance Sheet.

4.9 REVALUATION

Assets which are not depreciated, such as premises, will continue to be recorded at their acquisition value. Over time, the real value may increase. As it does so, the value recorded in the accounts will become increasingly inaccurate.

The proprietor of a business may decide to revalue the asset. The figure given for the asset in the Balance Sheet will be increased to its true value.

A business may revalue an asset at any time, but typically a proprietor will want to do so if he is considering bringing someone else into the business to run it jointly with him as a partner. The revaluation is made just before admitting the partner, so that the accounts show the increase in value as belonging to the original proprietor.

4.10 DISPOSAL OF A FIXED ASSET

4.10.1 Disposal at 'book' value

When a fixed asset is sold, this will be recorded in the books to show that the business has lost the fixed asset and gained cash.

Provided the asset is sold for exactly the value at which it is recorded in the accounts of the business, no gain or loss over book value arises as a result of the transaction. The only effect of the sale will be on the Balance Sheet, where there will be fewer fixed assets and more cash. The business has simply transformed one asset (premises) into a different sort of asset (cash). Therefore, total assets on the Balance Sheet remain the same.

4.10.2 Disposal not at 'book' value

It is fairly unusual for an asset to be sold for exactly the amount recorded in the accounts. If the asset is sold for more than its book value, the excess will be a profit on the sale. The profit will be recorded on the Profit and Loss Account and will increase net profit. If the asset is sold for less than its book value, there will be a loss on the sale. The loss will be recorded on the Profit and Loss Account and will reduce the net profit.

Only the excess or shortfall over book value is recorded on Profit and Loss. It is important to differentiate profits and losses of this type from trading profits and losses. Failure to do so will make the Final Accounts misleading. Accounts should show profit resulting from trading activities and other items such as gains and losses on sale of assets separately.

Exercise 4E

Premises recorded in the accounts at £170,000 are sold for £200,000.

(a) What is the gain over book value?

(b) What will be recorded on Profit and Loss?

(c) What effect will the sale have on the Balance Sheet, assuming the Balance Sheet is prepared immediately after the sale?

CONSOLIDATION EXERCISE

Exercise 4F

Consider the following Trial Balance.

TRIAL BALANCE AS AT 31 DECEMBER 2017

	DR	CR
Sales		250,000
Purchases	150,000	
Opening Stock	6,000	
General Expenses	60,000	
Debtors	15,000	
Capital		70,000
Drawings	10,000	
Creditors		4,000
Office Furniture	55,000	
New Cars	23,000	
Cash	1,000	
Rent Paid	3,000	
Bad Debts	1,000	
	324,000	324,000

Prepare a Profit and Loss Account and Balance Sheet, taking into account the following year-end adjustments:

(a) unpaid general expenses of £2,000;

(b) rent has been paid in advance but £1,000 of it relates to the following year;

(c) the firm wishes to create a provision for doubtful debts of £2,000;

(d) closing stock at the end of the year is estimated at £7,000;

(e) the firm decides to depreciate the new cars by 10% pa.

SUMMARY

---

(1) *Accruals and prepayments*

    (a) Adjustments are made to income and expense accounts at the end of each accounting period to make sure that the figures on those accounts accurately reflect the expenditure and income of the accounting period.

    (b) An outstanding expense will increase the expense figure on the Profit and Loss Account and it will produce an additional current liability on the Balance Sheet.

    (c) A prepayment will reduce the expense figure on the Profit and Loss Account and it will produce an additional current asset on the Balance Sheet.

(2) *Closing Work in Progress and Closing Stock*

    (a) Closing Work in Progress will be added to the Profit Costs figure and so will increase the income of the current year; it will be shown on the Balance Sheet as a current asset.

    (b) Closing Stock will be deducted from the Cost of Goods Sold figure and so will increase the income of the current year; it will be shown on the Balance Sheet as a current asset.

(3) *Provision for doubtful debts*

    (a) The business will estimate the debts which are doubtful.

    (b) The estimate (called a provision) is included on Profit and Loss as an extra expense and deducted from Debtors on the Balance Sheet.

(4) *Depreciation*

    (a) Many fixed assets lose value over time. One method of recording this loss of value is the 'straight line' method. The annual fall in value is recorded on the Profit and Loss Account.

    (b) Each year the asset will lose a percentage of the original value – this will be the same figure each year.

    (c) Each year the Balance Sheet will show the original value of the asset less all the depreciation incurred to date (the 'book value' of the asset). Each year the book value of the asset will fall.

(5) *Disposing of fixed assets*

    (a) If the asset is sold for more than book value, the gain will be shown on Profit and Loss (it should be clearly differentiated from ordinary profits from trading activities).

    (b) If the asset is sold for less than book value, the loss will be shown on the Profit and Loss Account (it should be clearly differentiated from ordinary business expenses).

SOLUTIONS

Exercise 4A

(a) This expense relates to an earlier accounting period and will not be included in the Profit and Loss Account for the current year even though it is paid in the current period. The amount of the expense will have been included in the previous year's Profit and Loss Account.

(b) This expense relates to the current accounting year and will be included in the Profit and Loss Account for the current year.

(c) This expense relates to the current accounting year and will be included in the current Profit and Loss Account even though not yet paid.

(d) The stationery bill should be apportioned. One-quarter of the stationery purchased has been used in the current accounting period; three-quarters will not be used until the following period. Therefore, one-quarter of the bill should be shown as an expense on the current Profit and Loss Account, and three-quarters should be carried forward as an expense to the Profit and Loss Account for the following period.

(e) The rent has been paid in the current accounting period, but the benefit will not be obtained until the following period. Therefore, the whole of the expense should be carried forward to the Profit and Loss Account for the following period.

(f) The work has been done in the current accounting period and therefore the benefit of it should be attributed to the current accounting period. It will be included on the current Profit and Loss Account as additional income.

Exercise 4B

(a) £2,500. Bad debts were £1,500; you have now written off a further £1,000.

(b) £2,500.

(c) £19,000. The debtors on the last day of the accounting period, having already written off bad debts of £1,500, were £20,000. You then wrote off a further £1,000, which will reduce debtors to £19,000.

Exercise 4C

(1) (d) Outstanding expenses increase expenses shown on Profit and Loss and are shown on the Balance Sheet as a current liability.

(2) (b) Prepaid amounts reduce expenses shown on Profit and Loss and are shown on the Balance Sheet as current assets.

(3) (b) Making provision for doubtful debts reduces debtors and appears as an expense on the Profit and Loss Account.

Exercise 4D

(1) (a) Depreciation on furniture charged to Profit and Loss is 15% of the acquisition value shown on the Trial Balance:
15% × £15,000 = £2,250

(2) (b) Accumulated depreciation shown on the Balance Sheet is the total of accumulated depreciation from previous years plus current depreciation:
£4,500 + £2,250 = £6,750

(3) (b) Depreciation on cars charged to Profit and Loss is 20% of the acquisition value shown on the Trial Balance:
20% x £40,000 = £8,000

Exercise 4E

(a) Book value was £170,000. The sale was for £200,000. Therefore, the gain over book value is £30,000.

(b) Only the gain over book value, £30,000, is recorded on Profit and Loss. Thus, the net profit of the business will be increased by £30,000.

(c) Premises will no longer be shown in the fixed assets section of the Balance Sheet. Fixed assets will therefore be reduced by £170,000.

Cash will be increased by £200,000. Overall, therefore, the assets of the business will have been increased by £30,000. The Capital Employed section will also be increased by £30,000, since the net profit of the business goes up by £30,000 and net profit is shown in the Capital Employed section of the Balance Sheet representing an amount owed to the proprietor by the business.

Exercise 4F

TRADING AND PROFIT AND LOSS ACCOUNT YEAR ENDED 31 DECEMBER 2017

Income

Sales			250,000
Less: Cost of Goods Sold			
Purchases		150,000	
Opening Stock		6,000	
Closing Stock		(7,000)	
			(149,000)
GROSS PROFIT			101,000
Less: Expenses			
General (£60,000 + £2,000)		62,000	
Rent Paid (£3,000 – £1,000)		2,000	
Bad Debts		1,000	
Provision for Doubtful Debts		2,000	
Depreciation on cars		2,300	
			(69,300)
Net Profit			31,700

BALANCE SHEET AS AT 31 DECEMBER 2017
EMPLOYMENT OF CAPITAL

Fixed Assets

Office Furniture		55,000	
Vehicles	23,000		
Depreciation	(2,300)		
		20,700	
			75,700
Current Assets			
Closing stock		7,000	
Debtors	15,000		
Less Provision For Doubtful Debts	(2,000)		
		13,000	
Cash at Bank		1,000	
Prepayments		1,000	
		22,000	
Current Liabilities			
Creditors	4,000		
Accruals	2,000		
		(6,000)	
NET CURRENT ASSETS			16,000
NET ASSETS			**91,700**
CAPITAL EMPLOYED			
Capital	70,000		
Drawings	(10,000)		
Profit	31,700		
			91,700

PARTNERSHIP ACCOUNTS

LEARNING OUTCOMES

After reading this chapter you will be able to:

- explain how the nature of a partnership affects the form of its Final Accounts
- draw up an appropriation account
- distinguish between capital and current accounts
- describe how partnership changes are reflected in the accounts.

5.1 INTRODUCTION

So far we have concentrated on the accounts of a sole trader or sole practitioner. We are now going to turn to those businesses owned by two or more people in partnership.

5.2 THE NATURE OF PARTNERSHIPS

In a partnership, capital is contributed by a number of different proprietors (the partners) and the firm's profit is 'owed' to those partners. The business will have to keep separate records for each partner, showing:

(a)   the amount of capital contributed;

(b)   the amount of profit 'owed' at the end of each year by the business to the partner;

(c)   the amount withdrawn from the business during the year by the partner.

The accounts of a partnership will have to show this information. This joint ownership means that there will therefore be some differences between the accounts of a business run by one person and the accounts of a partnership. The keeping of records and the presentation of the Final Accounts for the partnership will still follow the same format we have been considering so far, but there will be some additional elements in the accounts which reflect the joint nature of the business.

When a partnership is set up, the partners will usually reach an agreement on how they intend to run the business. Even if the partners themselves fail to turn their minds to this, the Partnership Act 1890 will imply terms into their business arrangement. The accounts will reflect the financial terms of the partnership agreement.

Both trading and professional businesses can be run through the medium of a partnership. In this chapter, for convenience, we shall use a solicitor's firm for our illustrations.

5.3 CAPITAL ACCOUNTS

By definition a partnership has more than one proprietor. At the outset each will contribute money to start the business. The partners may decide to contribute in equal or unequal amounts.

Each partner will have a capital account in his or her own name. This account will show the amount contributed by the partner.

> **Example**
>
> Mary and Syed set up a partnership and contribute £30,000 and £20,000 respectively as capital. The capital employed section of the Balance Sheet will show separately the balance on each capital account
>
> Extract Balance Sheet as at …
>
> | Capital Employed | | |
> |---|---:|---:|
> | Mary | 30,000 | |
> | Syed | <u>20,000</u> | |
> | | | 50,000 |

The capital account will also show the partner's share of an increase (or decrease) in value of an asset recorded in the accounts by way of revaluation. The ratio in which partners are to share increases and decreases in the value of capital assets may be set out in the partnership agreement. If the partnership agreement is silent on this point, the partners will share capital increases and decreases in the ratio in which they agreed to share profits and losses.

5.4 PROFIT SHARING

You will now be familiar with the idea of the profit produced by a business being 'owed' to the proprietor. In a partnership, the profit will be owed to the proprietors or partners and shared between them.

A well-drafted partnership agreement should set out the profit-sharing ratio upon which the parties have decided. So, for example, if partners A and B have agreed to a profit-sharing ratio of 2:1, this means that the net profit will be divided so that A receives two-thirds and B receives one-third. If the partnership agreement is silent, the partners will share profits and losses equally.

The partnership agreement may provide for a simple profit-sharing ratio. Alternatively, the agreement may contain a more complex method of dividing the profits, whereby the partners receive 'interest on capital' and/or 'salaries'. The terminology here can be confusing because we are not using these terms in the same way as we have been using them so far, ie as an additional source of income (interest) and the wages paid to employees (salaries). In partnership accounts, 'salaries' and 'interest on capital' are simply labels given to different shares of net profit.

A salary is a set sum taken from the profit. So the partnership agreement may provide for Partner A to receive a salary of £10,000. This means that A will receive the first £10,000 of profit. This type of agreement is common where one partner is doing more of the day-to-day work in the business – the salary reflects the extra workload.

If the partnership agreement provides for the partners to receive interest on capital, this simply means that the partners will receive a share of profit calculated by reference to how much capital each partner contributed to the business. So if partners A and B contributed capital of £5,000 and £2,000 respectively, and the partnership agreement provides for them to receive 10% interest on capital, this means that A will receive £500 and B will receive £200 from the net profit. This type of agreement is common where the partners have contributed capital unequally; the interest on capital reflects the extra investment made by those partners who have contributed more.

When the net profit of the partnership has been calculated, the partners must then take that net profit figure and share it between the various partners in accordance with the terms of the partnership agreement. The amount due for 'interest' and 'salaries' is allocated first, and then any balance is divided amongst the partners in the agreed profit-sharing ratio.

Unless the partnership agreement provides otherwise, 'salaries' and 'interest' must be appropriated to partners by the partnership irrespective of whether the net profit is sufficient to cover the amount due. The result may be to produce a loss for the year, which must then be appropriated among all partners in the agreed profit-sharing ratio. A well-drafted partnership agreement should, therefore, provide that salaries and interest are due only if profits are sufficient to cover them.

5.5 THE APPROPRIATION ACCOUNT

The Profit and Loss Account of a partnership is prepared in exactly the same way as the Profit and Loss Account of a sole trader or practitioner. However, the Profit and Loss Account is extended to an appropriation account on which the allocation of net profit among the partners is shown.

Example

Wendy and Peter set up in partnership. Wendy contributes capital of £5,000 and Peter contributes £2,000. The net profit for the year has been calculated at £21,700. The partnership agreement provides for interest on capital of 10% pa, a salary for Peter of £1,000 pa and remaining profits to be divided 3:1.

Extract Profit and Loss Account for year ended ...

	£	£	£
Net Profit			21,700
Appropriations	**Wendy**	**Peter**	
Interest on Capital	500	200	700
Salary	–	1,000	1,000
Profits	15,000	5,000	20,000
	15,500	6,200	21,700

You will note that the column on the right keeps a running total of how the profits have been allocated.

5.6 CURRENT ACCOUNT

The net profit is owed to the proprietor(s) of the business. Where there is only one proprietor, we have seen that the profit is usually credited directly to the capital account. In the case of a partnership, it is usual to have a separate current account for each partner to which the appropriation of net profit (including salary and interest) is added and from which drawings are deducted. The reason for separating capital and current accounts is that, as we have seen, partners are often entitled to interest on capital contributed. It is therefore desirable to keep the original capital contribution of each partner readily identifiable and unaffected by subsequent appropriations of profits and drawings.

Exercise 5A

Pam and Theresa are in partnership as solicitors. The partnership agreement provides for interest on capital of 10% pa. Theresa is to receive a salary of £9,000 pa. Remaining profits are to be shared equally.

The Trial Balance of Pam and Theresa as at 31 December is as follows:

Trial Balance

		DR £	CR £
Capital:	Pam		120,000
	Theresa		80,000
Current:	Pam		2,000
	Theresa		1,000
Drawings:	Pam	3,000	
	Theresa	2,000	
Bank Loan			34,000
Premises		200,000	
Profit Costs			260,000
General Expenses		150,000	
Travel Expenses		4,000	
Debtors		153,000	
Creditors			25,000
Cash		10,000	
Client Bank Account		400,000	
Due to Clients			400,000
		922,000	922,000

Prepare a Profit and Loss and Appropriation Account from the above figures.

5.7 THE BALANCE SHEET

The capital and current account balances of each partner are shown separately on the Balance Sheet in the capital employed section.

Example

(Extract) Balance Sheet at at ...

Capital Employed		
Capital		
Partner A	50,000	
Partner B	40,000	
Current		
Partner A	20,000	
Partner B	10,000	
		120,000

5.8 DETAILS OF MOVEMENTS ON PARTNERS' CURRENT ACCOUNTS

You will notice that, in the previous example, we showed only the final balances for the current accounts on the Balance Sheet. This is because the Balance Sheet would be very cluttered if full details of salaries, interest, profit shares and drawings were included, especially where there are several partners. It would be difficult to pick out the important figures. However, it is helpful to show information as to how the balances were arrived at. It is therefore usual to provide an appendix to the Balance Sheet which sets out the detailed picture of movements on partners' current accounts.

A common form of presentation is set out in the practical example below.

Example

Movements on partners' current accounts

	A	B
	£	£
Balance at start of accounting period	2,000	2,000
Appropriations	40,000	34,000
Drawings	(22,000)	(18,000)
Closing balance	20,000	18,000

Exercise 5B

Prepare a Balance Sheet and details of movements on partners' current accounts from the figures given in Exercise 5A and your calculation of the net profit from that exercise.

5.9 PARTNERSHIP CHANGES

The number of partners may change part of the way through an accounting period either because a new partner is admitted, or because an old partner leaves. Unless the partners agree otherwise, the net profit for the year of the change will be apportioned on a time basis to the period before and the period after the change.

Two appropriation accounts will be prepared, one allocating the pre-change profit in accordance with the pre-change partnership agreement and one allocating the post-change profit in accordance with the post-change partnership agreement.

5.10 TAXATION OF PARTNERSHIPS

Each individual partner makes a tax return claiming personal allowances. The senior partner of the firm makes a return of partnership income. HMRC then makes a joint assessment to tax in the partnership name. This assessment is based on each partner's share of profit less reliefs and charges, and supplies the senior partner with information on the method of calculation so that the tax burden may be apportioned among the partners. The tax liability of the individual partners is not shown in the partnership accounts.

SUMMARY

(1) The Profit and Loss Account of a partnership is continued to an Appropriation Account which shows the allocation of profit (interest on capital, salary and profit share) amongst the partners.

(2) Each partner has a separate capital and current account.

(3) The current account records the partner's share of net profit and drawings.

(4) The capital and current account balances for each partner are shown on the Balance Sheet.

SOLUTIONS

Exercise 5A

Profit and Loss Account for year ended 31 December ...

Income

Profit Costs			260,000

Expenses

General Expenses		150,000	
Travel Expenses		4,000	
			(154,000)
NET PROFIT			106,000

Appropriations

	Pam	Theresa	
	£	£	£
Interest	12,000	8,000	20,000
Salary		9,000	9,000
Profits	38,500	38,500	77,000
	50,500	55,500	106,000

Exercise 5B

Movements in Partners' Current Accounts

	Pam	Theresa
	£	£
Opening Balance	2,000	1,000
Appropriations	50,500	55,500
Drawings	(3,000)	(2,000)
	49,500	54,500

Balance Sheet as at 31 December ...

Employment of Capital

Fixed Assets

Premises			200,000

Current Assets

Debtors		153,000	
Cash		10,000	
		163,000	

Current Liabilities

Creditors		(25,000)	
Net Current Assets			138,000
Client Bank Account		400,000	
Due to Clients		(400,000)	

Less Long-term Liabilities

Bank Loan			(34,000)
Net Assets			**304,000**

Capital Employed

Capital: Pam		120,000	
Theresa		80,000	
Current: Pam		49,500	
Theresa		54,500	304,000

INTRODUCTION TO COMPANY ACCOUNTS

LEARNING OUTCOMES

After reading this chapter you will be able to:

- explain how the nature of a company affects the form of its Final Accounts
- describe how company profits are allocated
- explain the concept of reserves
- outline the purpose of deferred taxation.

6.1 INTRODUCTION

So far we have considered the Final Accounts of sole traders and partnerships. In this chapter we turn to the accounts of companies.

6.2 THE NATURE OF COMPANIES

The accounts of a company are prepared on exactly the same accounting basis as those of a sole trader or a partnership. Financial transactions will be recorded using the double entry system, and the information will be summarised and presented in the Final Accounts at the end of the year. There are, however, some differences in the presentation of the Final Accounts because of the different legal nature of a company. Understanding company accounts therefore requires an understanding of how a company operates.

A company is a distinct legal entity which is separate from its owners. A company can enter into contracts in its own name and has its own tax liabilities. A company is owned by its members (also called 'shareholders') who put money into the business by buying a 'share' in the company. A company is run on a day-to-day basis by its directors.

The directors manage the company, but they do not own the company unless they also happen to be shareholders. In small companies it is common for an individual director to be a shareholder too. In the case of large companies the directors and shareholders will usually be different.

People who want to run a business will often choose to do it through the medium of a limited company for a number of reasons. An important consideration is that there is less financial risk to the owners. Shareholders have no financial liability to the company beyond paying for their shares. If the company runs into financial difficulties, it may be wound up as insolvent but the shareholders will not be asked to cover the company's debts. The separation between those running the business and the owners also means that there is the opportunity to raise capital from 'outsiders' – the shareholders can provide the funding, leaving the directors to run the business.

Company accounts are closely regulated by a combination of legislation and accounting practices. We consider regulation in **Chapter 7**, but for now you just need to be aware that part of this regulation does influence the form and content of accounts.

The different nature of companies and the regulative requirements means that you will see some differences in layout and terminology between company accounts and the accounts of a sole trader/practitioner or partnership that we have been looking at in previous chapters. However, you should remember that the accounts are still showing the same basic information that we have seen in the Profit and Loss Account and the Balance Sheet.

6.3 SHAREHOLDERS

A person who wants to invest money will often buy shares in a company as a way of profiting from a successfully-managed business without having to fund the whole of the cost of the business. Each year the directors of the company will review the profits of the company and will decide how much of the profit, if any, can be returned to the shareholders. The payment to the shareholders is called a dividend.

For example, a company with 40,000 shares may make a £100,000 profit in a particular year. The directors may decide that they need to retain £80,000 within the company to cover expected liabilities and future expansion, but that they can pay £20,000 to the shareholders. Each shareholder will receive a dividend of 50p per share held.

Dividends are normally paid at the end of the company's trading period, although some companies will make smaller payments during the year. Dividends paid at the end of the year are referred to as 'final' dividends; those paid during the year are referred to as 'interim' dividends.

There is an element of uncertainty for the shareholders, since they depend on the decision of the directors as to the amount they will receive by way of dividend. Directors may decide, if profits are low or if substantial expansion is required, to pay no dividends in a particular year. The level of dividends paid by many companies is often quite low, and many people who invest in shares do so to obtain the increase in the value of the shares themselves as the business prospers.

> **Example**
>
> Mark sets up a company. He contributes £10,000 and his father contributes £40,000. In return Mark is issued with one-fifth of the shares in the company and his father is issued with four-fifths. The company's assets are currently £50,000, ie the cash contributed by Mark and his father. So if Mark's father tried to sell his shares he would probably get £40,000. Suppose that the company trades successfully for the next 10 years and the assets increase to £1 million. If a third party offers to buy the shares, Mark's father would receive four-fifths of £1 million (£800,000). The third party would then own the shares and would receive any future dividends and the benefit of any further increases in asset values.

6.4 ISSUING SHARES

A shareholder puts money into a company and in return the company issues shares to the shareholder. When a company issues shares, this is recorded in the same way as when a sole trader/practitioner or partner introduces capital. However, rather than use a separate capital account for each shareholder, the company will record the transaction in a composite share capital account.

Using one share capital account makes recording the entries much easier. There could be a large number of different shareholders, for example, so that having a separate capital account for each one would be unmanageable. Having one account also avoids the company having to keep updating the names of different capital accounts every time a shareholder sells his shares.

You will now be familiar with the capital account for a sole trader/practitioner or for individual partners appearing in the 'capital employed' section of the Balance Sheet. This is also the case for the capital introduced by the shareholders when being issued with their shares. However, in a company Balance Sheet this section is usually headed differently. There is no absolute consistency in the terminology used, but 'Financed By', 'Equity' and 'Capital and Reserves' are commonly seen as headings.

Example

Extract from Balance Sheet for X Ltd as at 31 December 201–

Net Assets	**200,000**
Capital and Reserves	
Share capital	**200,000**
	200,000

6.4.1 Issuing shares at par

A company may issue shares either at par or at premium. (It is not possible for shares to be issued at a discount: see Companies Act (CA) 2006, s 580.) Each share has a nominal or par (ie face) value, eg £1. The issue of shares at par means that the shares are 'sold' to the shareholder for their nominal value.

6.4.2 Issuing shares at a premium

The issue of shares at a premium means that the shares are 'sold' to the shareholders for more than their nominal value. So, a share with a nominal value of £1 may be issued to a shareholder for £1.50; the premium is 50p. When the issue of shares is recorded in the books, the premium element is recorded separately in a share premium account and is shown separately from the share capital on the Balance Sheet.

6.4.3 Types of shares

A company may issue shares of different types. For example, it may issue ordinary shares, which carry the usual rights of a shareholder to receive dividends and vote when company decisions are referred to the shareholders, and preference shares, which carry preferential rights such as entitling the preference shareholder to dividends in priority to ordinary shareholders. If there is only a small profit, the preference shareholders may receive a dividend and the ordinary shareholders nothing. A company may also issue shares of the same type carrying different rights, for example voting and non-voting ordinary shares.

The company law distinctions between these different shares are beyond the scope of this book. The important point to appreciate is that, whatever type of share is issued, the basic entries are precisely the same. However, the different kinds of shares will be shown separately in the Balance Sheet.

> **Example**
>
> **(Extract) Balance Sheet for Y Ltd as at 31 December Year 1**
>
> | | |
> |---|---:|
> | Net Assets | **500,000** |
> | **Capital and Reserves** | |
> | Preference Shares | 100,000 |
> | Ordinary Shares | 300,000 |
> | Share Premium Account | 100,000 |
> | | **500,000** |

6.5 MAINTENANCE OF CAPITAL AND A COMPANY BUYING ITS OWN SHARES

6.5.1 Maintenance of capital

A general principle of company law is that capital, once raised, must be maintained. After members have paid for their shares, the money produced constitutes the company's capital. Creditors will expect this fund to remain in the company to be available to meet the company's debts and, because the liability of the members of the company is limited, this capital sum should not be diminished (although, of course, assets can be lost through unsuccessful trading).

To provide this protection for creditors of companies, it is not normally permissible for the company to return the shareholders' initial investment during the lifetime of the company. The impact of this on the members of the company is that, having bought their shares, they cannot normally hand back their share certificate to the company in exchange for the consideration they originally provided. However, if the business is successful the owners will often be able to sell their shares to third parties. They will receive a price based on the value of the company's assets at the date of the sale, plus something for the 'goodwill' of the business generated by their successful past trading.

6.5.2 Company buying its own shares

One of the consequences of the need for a company to maintain its share capital is that a company must not generally purchase its own shares (CA 2006, s 658).

However, there are often circumstances where it is helpful for a company to be able to buy its own shares. This is particularly the case for small and medium-sized private companies because there is not usually a ready market for the shares of such companies. A small company might want to buy out a dissident shareholder who may be harming the company's business, buy the shares of a deceased shareholder where the personal representatives or beneficiaries under the will do not wish to keep them, or buy the shares of a proprietor of a company who is retiring to make way for new management.

The CA 2006, s 690 permits a company, provided various conditions are complied with, to purchase its own shares. Once purchased, the shares are cancelled and the issued share capital reduced by the nominal amount of the shares.

6.6 DEBENTURES

If a company borrows money, it will commonly do so by issuing debentures. A debenture is a document evidencing a loan made to the company. Thus, if a company issues debentures of £50,000, this basically means that the company is borrowing £50,000.

A debenture differs from a share in that a debenture holder is not an owner of the company (ie he is not a shareholder) and the payment of interest on a debenture is not dependent on the making of profits by the company. From the point of view of the company, this has advantages and disadvantages.

Exercise 6A

You are a director of Company X. You wish to raise additional capital of £50,000 and are trying to decide whether to issue more shares, or whether to borrow.

What are the advantages and disadvantages of each course of action from the company's perspective?

6.7 A COMPANY PROFIT AND LOSS ACCOUNT

Whether a company is in the business of dealing in goods or services, much of the Profit and Loss Account will look very similar to the accounts of a sole trader practitioner business. It will show the same type of trading income and other types of income, as well as similar expenses. The same accounting principles and concepts, such as accruals, depreciation, etc, will govern the way in which the figures are arrived at.

The Profit and Loss Account of a company shows the company's income and deducts expenses to show the company's profit. There are, however, some minor differences in the types of expense which may appear on a company's Profit and Loss Account. These differences flow from the fact that a company is a separate legal person, with its own legal identity separate from those of its shareholders and directors. A salary paid to a director is, from the company's point of view, an expense incurred in earning profit and will therefore appear on the Profit and Loss Account as an expense. This is so even if the director is a shareholder and therefore an 'owner' of the business. It is an expense in the same way as wages paid to ordinary employees. In contrast, a 'salary' paid to a partner under the terms of the partnership agreement is merely a method of allocating the profit and will appear on the appropriation section of the account.

6.7.1 The appropriation of profit

The Profit and Loss Account of a partnership shows the calculation of net profit and then continues into an appropriation account to show how that profit is to be allocated or appropriated. The net profit of a company is also allocated for particular purposes. For a company there are three main purposes: taxation; dividends; and retention of profits.

6.7.1.1 Taxation

Tax is not a feature of the accounts of sole traders/practitioners or partnerships simply because these types of business do not have a tax liability. Instead tax is paid by the sole trader/practitioner or the individual partners on the benefits they derive from the business. In contrast, a company has its own tax liability, and this will appear in the accounts.

The first item to be considered after the net profit has been ascertained is the company's liability to corporation tax on that profit. A company is no different from an individual in that it has a legal liability to pay tax and must be sure that provision is made to meet its tax bill. Until tax has been provided for, the directors cannot make a decision on the declaration of a dividend.

For most companies corporation tax is not normally payable until nine months after the end of the accounting period. So when the Final Accounts are prepared at the end of that accounting period, the company will not actually have paid any tax on its profits from that year. On its Profit and Loss Account the company will show that a certain amount of profit is needed to pay the company's tax bill by setting out the company's profits before and after tax.

> **Example**
>
> In its first year of trading, a company has income of £200,000 and expenses of £100,000. It estimates that corporation tax of £20,000 will be payable
>
> (Extract) Profit and loss Account for the year ending ...
>
> | | |
> |---|---:|
> | Net Profit before tax | **100,000** |
> | Tax | **(20,000)** |
> | Post Tax Profit | **80,000** |

The company has a liability to pay the tax when it falls due. The amount of tax due to HMRC will therefore appear on the Balance Sheet as a current liability.

> **Example**
>
> (Extract) Balance Sheet as at ...
>
> | | |
> |---|---:|
> | **Current Assets** | |
> | Cash | 30,000 |
> | **Current Liabilities** | |
> | Creditors | (xxx) |
> | Provision for Tax | (20,000) |
> | **Net Current Assets** | **xxx** |

When the tax is eventually paid the provision will disappear from the current liabilities section and cash will be reduced in the current assets section.

Large companies are treated rather differently for tax purposes. A 'large' company for this purpose is one whose profits in the accounting period in question exceed a set amount (currently £1.5 million). A large company has to pay its corporation tax in four instalments.

In practice, the company will makes the first payment six months and 14 days after the start of the company's accounting period, and subsequent payments will be made quarterly. The first instalments will obviously have to be based on an estimate of the company's profits. At the date of the Balance Sheet at the end of the accounting period a large company will already have paid two instalments of tax and the rest will still be outstanding.

6.7.1.2 Dividends

A dividend represents a distribution of part of the net profit to the owners of the company (ie the shareholders). A company is most unlikely to distribute the whole of its profit after tax. There are two reasons for this:

(a)   it will need to retain funds to meet future costs of running or expanding the business;

(b)   much of the profit is not actually available in the form of cash – profit may be represented by any assets (eg stock, debtors or fixed assets).

The directors will decide how much cash can, in their opinion, safely be distributed to the shareholders by way of a dividend. The balance of the profit after tax is retained within the company. Company law requirements mean that the company cannot actually pay the dividend until the shareholders approve its size in the annual general meeting, which will take place after the end of the accounting period.

Strictly speaking, dividends which have been recommended but not approved are not yet payable. A recommended dividend will not be shown in the accounts, but it will be mentioned in the accompanying Notes to the accounts.

Once a dividend has been paid, it could, as it is an allocation of profit, be shown in an appropriation account in the same way as a partnership's allocation of profit appears in an appropriation account. However, in practice, the payment of a dividend is usually included in the Notes to the accounts or in a separate statement (see **Chapter 7**).

6.7.1.3 Retained profit

Once provision has been made for taxation and dividends, the balance of the net profit is retained in the business.

The retained profit is profit which could be distributed to the shareholders should the directors decide to distribute it. The retained profit is therefore 'owed' to the shareholders and will be shown on the Balance Sheet. In just the same way as the net profit for a sole trader is transferred across to the 'capital employed' section of the Balance Sheet to show the total amount owed to the proprietor, so in a company the retained profit is carried across to the Balance Sheet. The retained profits are often referred to as a 'Profit and Loss Reserve', and are normally shown on the Balance Sheet immediately after the share capital to show the total amount 'owed' to the shareholders.

6.8 A COMPANY BALANCE SHEET

6.8.1 Capital and reserves

The main difference in a company Balance Sheet is contained in the 'Capital Employed' or, as it is often headed in company accounts, 'Capital and Reserves' section.

Example	
(Extract) Balance Sheet as at . . .	
NET ASSETS	**220,000**
CAPITAL AND RESERVES	
Share Capital	100,000
Debenture Redemption Reserve	20,000
Profit and Loss Reserve	100,000
SHAREHOLDERS FUNDS	**220,000**

We have already looked at the 'capital' element of this as the shareholders' original capital contribution to the company in return for the issue of shares. Now we shall turn to the reserves element.

6.8.2 Reserves

The term 'reserve' can be confusing, because at first sight it suggests an extra pot of cash at the company's disposal. However, this is not the case. The reserves appear in the equivalent to the 'Capital Employed' section of the Balance Sheet. This section of a Balance Sheet shows the amount which a business 'owes' to its owners. So, reserves are 'owed' to the shareholders but not distributed to them. Reserves essentially arise through profits being retained within the company.

A company Balance Sheet may show different types of reserves. The principal division is between revenue reserves and capital reserves. A revenue reserve is one which (in theory at least) could be distributed to the shareholders at any time, for example through the payment of a dividend. A capital reserve is one which is not available for distribution in this way.

6.8.2.1 Revenue reserves

Most reserves are revenue reserves. A revenue reserve may be created by retaining profits for a specific purpose, or merely by retaining profit generally. In either case, the assets represented by the reserve profit can be used for the payment of dividends in future years, always assuming that the necessary cash is available.

The Profit and Loss Reserve is the main example of a revenue reserve. We have seen that after tax has been provided for and a decision taken on the payment of a dividend, the remaining profits will be retained in the company. This figure will appear on the Balance Sheet as the Profit and Loss Reserve. As the company generates profits year on year, they will be added to this figure so that over time the retained profit figure increases.

Exercise 6B

Study the following extract from the Profit and Loss Account and Balance Sheet.

Profit and Loss Account for year ending . . .

	£
Profit before tax	**70,000**
Tax	**(22,000)**
Profit after tax	**48,000**

Balance Sheet as at . . .

Share Capital	100,000
Reserves	100,000

Tick which one you think is correct.

Assume no dividend has been paid. On last year's Balance Sheet, reserves would have been:

(a) £100,000;

(b) £148,000;

(c) £52,000;

(d) £48,000.

It is often difficult for people not directly involved in the management of the company (eg shareholders, employees) to understand why large amounts of profit are being retained in the company instead of being returned to the shareholders as dividends or being used to pay salaries for employees. It is quite common, therefore, for directors to indicate why profits are being retained by attaching labels to portions of retained profit, such as 'debenture redemption reserve', indicating that some of the profits have been retained in anticipation of the company having to repay a debenture in the future. A debenture redemption reserve is a revenue reserve. It is important to realise that the labels are for convenience only; the reserves remain undistributed profits *owed* to shareholders.

Example

Consider the following Balance Sheet. The company has a debenture and has created a Debenture Reserve to show that profits are being retained in the company so that the debenture can be paid back when required.

Balance Sheet as at ...

	£	£
	£	£
ASSETS		
Fixed Assets		40,000
Current Assets		
Cash	25,000	
less Current Liabilities		
Creditors	(5,000)	
Net Current Assets		20,000
		60,000

Long-term Liabilities

Debenture		(10,000)
		50,000

CAPITAL AND RESERVES

Share Capital	20,000	
Debenture Reserve	10,000	
Profit and Loss	20,000	
		50,000

Now we shall look at the Balance Sheet as it will appear after the debenture has been paid back:

Balance Sheet as at ...

	£	£
Fixed Assets		40,000
Current Assets		
Cash	15,000	
less Current Liabilities		
Creditors	(5,000)	
Net Current Assets		10,000
		50,000
CAPITAL AND RESERVES		
Share Capital	20,000	
Debenture Reserve	10,000	
Profit and Loss	20,000	
		50,000

Cash has been reduced by £10,000. The debenture of £10,000 has disappeared. Notice that the debenture redemption reserve has remained on the Balance Sheet. This is because it is merely undistributed profit 'owed' to the shareholders. Nothing has been distributed to the shareholders, so this 'liability' remains. The company may decide to relabel the reserve.

Retaining profit for a particular purpose does not mean that the cash will be available for that purpose when it is required in the future. Although the value of the assets as a whole will have increased as a result of making a profit, the increase is likely to be in the form of extra fixed assets or trading stock, rather than extra cash. Therefore, in order to ensure that the required amount of cash is available, it will be necessary to set aside an equivalent amount of cash in a reserve fund (sometimes called a 'sinking fund') at the same time as profit is retained within the business.

6.8.2.2 Capital reserves

Capital reserves are reserves which, for legal or practical reasons, are not available for distribution by way of dividend. They are part of the long-term capital of the company and therefore not free to be returned to shareholders. The CA 2006 requires some capital reserves to be shown separately on the Balance Sheet.

We have already encountered one type of capital reserve, namely the share premium account (see **6.4.2**). We saw that when a company issues shares at a premium, it is required to record the surplus over the nominal value of the shares on the share premium account (CA 2006, s 610). The share premium account must be shown separately on the Balance Sheet.

A revaluation reserve is an example of a capital reserve. A revaluation reserve is created when a company decides to revalue its assets. As in the case of a partnership, when a company decides to increase the value of an asset to a more realistic amount, the value of assets shown in the Balance Sheet is increased. There must be a corresponding increase in the 'Capital Employed' section of the Balance Sheet. Unlike a partnership, however, it is not the capital accounts which will record this increase; instead, a reserve account will be opened which will be credited with the revaluation increase. A revaluation reserve simply records the fact that asset values have increased.

Example

A company decides to revalue its fixed assets. The revaluation produces a net increase of £100,000 over the assets' previous book value of £140,000. The Balance Sheet will therefore appear as follows:

(Extract) Balance Sheet as at ...

	Before	After
Fixed Assets	140,000	240,000
Net Current Assets	180,000	180,000
	320,000	420,000
CAPITAL AND RESERVES		
Share Capital	100,000	100,000
Revaluation Reserve	–	100,000
Profit and Loss Reserve	220,000	220,000
	320,000	420,000

A new reserve has been created, fixed assets have increased and net current assets remain unchanged.

A capital redemption reserve is required where a company buys back shares out of profits. The company can buy its own shares only if it has the funds available to do so. This usually means distributable profits. To avoid reducing its capital, the company is required to transfer to a capital redemption reserve an amount equivalent to the share capital bought back (CA 2006, s 733).

6.8.2.3   Capitalisation of reserves

The result of retaining part of the net profit in the business is that, after a number of years, a company will have built up substantial reserves of undistributed profit. Although these reserves are in theory 'owed' to the shareholders, in reality they will be represented by fixed assets and net current assets, and there will not be sufficient cash to pay the shareholders everything 'owed'. To recognise this state of affairs, the company may decide to capitalise some of these reserves by making a bonus issue of shares to its members.

The effect of a bonus issue is that each shareholder will own a greater number of shares, but the value of each individual share will be less since the shares as a whole will still be represented by the same total value of assets. In addition, future dividends are likely to be declared at a lower rate because a similar amount of net profit will have to be apportioned among a larger number of shares.

Exercise 6C

Study the following extract from a Balance Sheet.

Balance Sheet as at [date]

Assets	**600,000**
Capital and Reserves	
Share capital	**50,000**
Reserves	**550,000**
	600,000

> **Assume that the company decides to make a 'two for one' bonus issue against reserves. Which one of the following statements is correct?**
> (a) Assets will be reduced by £100,000.
> (b) Reserves will increase by £100,000.
> (c) Reserves will be reduced by £100,000.
> (d) Share capital will be increased by £50,000.

6.9 CONSOLIDATED ACCOUNTS

It is very common for a company which is expanding its business activities either to acquire control of other companies, or to compartmentalise parts of its own organisation so that each part can be run as a separate company (this is sometimes described as 'ring fencing' hazardous parts of the company's business undertaking). The resulting business combinations are referred to as 'groups'. The controlling company is referred to as the 'parent' and the controlled company as the 'subsidiary'.

With some exceptions (mainly for small companies), s 399 of the CA 2006 requires group accounts to be prepared by a 'parent undertaking'. A parent undertaking is essentially a company which holds a majority of the voting rights in a subsidiary, or which has some other significant influence over decision making in the subsidiary, for example by having the power to appoint and remove a majority of the directors.

Shareholders in the parent company need additional financial statements to show the combined results of all the companies in the group if they are to be able to assess performance of their company.

A parent company is normally required to produce:

(a)   a consolidated Profit and Loss Account showing the profit or loss of the group; and

(b)   a consolidated Balance Sheet showing the assets and liabilities of the group as a whole.

Although each company retains its own legal identity and must prepare its own Final Accounts, the requirements as to group accounts reflect the commercial reality that the group as a whole is a single unit.

6.10 DEFERRED TAXATION

A company pays corporation tax on its profits. However, the profit figure on which tax is payable is not the same as the profit figure which is calculated on the Profit and Loss Account. This is because tax legislation is not in the same terms as accounting rules. Some of the expenses which appear on the Profit and Loss Account, such as depreciation, are not deductible from income for tax purposes. In addition, tax legislation allows some deductions which do not feature on the Profit and Loss Account, such as capital allowances. Also, some items of income, such as government grants, are not taxable. The result is that it is often difficult to relate the tax figure to the accounting profit without further information.

6.10.1 The concept

Accountants like to spread expenses evenly over the period to which they relate. Straight line depreciation (see **4.8.1**), where the reduction in value of the assets is spread evenly across the life of the assets, is an example of this.

HMRC is not concerned with matching income and expenses to the appropriate period in the same way. Depreciation is not regarded as a deductible expense for tax purposes, so the tax liability of a company must be calculated on its net profit before deducting depreciation.

Although depreciation is not a deductible expense for tax purposes, the Government wishes to encourage companies to expand and improve. Companies are allowed to deduct part of the cost of some types of assets against their profits for tax purposes under the capital allowance scheme. The rules on the amount which can be deducted in the form of capital allowances vary according to the policies of the current Government.

In some tax years, companies are allowed large 'first year' capital allowances on the cost of purchasing assets. When this is possible, the company obtains a great deal of tax relief in that year, resulting in a low tax bill and consequently large post-tax profits for that year. Once the allowance has been claimed, there will be little or no tax relief for later years, which means larger tax bills and, therefore, smaller post-tax profits for those years.

A distorting effect on a company's post-tax profit is produced by the fact that the benefit of the capital allowance on the purchase of an item of plant or machinery is usually greater initially than the figure treated as an annual accounting expense for depreciation. (Correspondingly, in later years it is generally smaller.) In simple terms, from an accounting point of view, 'too much' tax relief is being allowed initially and, as a result, too much tax will be charged in later years. Accountants would describe such a situation by saying that a timing difference exists.

6.10.2   Object of deferred tax accounting

The object of deferred tax accounting is to redistribute the tax liability shown on the Profit and Loss Account as though timing differences did not exist, and to iron out the distortions which they produce.

The figure for post-tax profits is used by many as a measure of a company's performance. Ordinarily, therefore, a reduction in the post-tax profits from one year to the next would be a cause for concern. However, it may be the case that in the first year the business received large capital allowances, which reduced its tax liability and thus increased its post-tax profit. In the following year, the business may have received lower capital allowances, which increased its tax liability, thus reducing its post-tax profit.

Accountants preparing accounts generally deal with timing differences by creating a provision for tax in a year in which they consider too little tax is being charged. This provision is used in later years to reduce the burden of the tax charged against current profits.

6.10.3   A basic illustration

First, consider how, in the absence of deferred tax accounting, the accounts of the following business (AB Ltd) would appear. For convenience, the example assumes an unchanging corporation tax rate of 30% for all of the years mentioned, and also that 100% capital allowances were available to the company. These assumptions highlight the problems caused by timing differences and make the illustration easier to follow.

Example

AB Ltd is a company which in recent years was making (after depreciation and other overheads) a profit of £15,000 per annum. Assume that in the first year covered by the example, it bought a machine for £15,000. The machine has an expected working life of three years, so that (calculated on the straight line basis) depreciation is for accounting purposes being treated as an annual expense of £5,000.

Since depreciation does not qualify as a deductible expense for tax purposes, the £5,000 will have to be added back to calculate the profit on which tax is payable.

The company took a 100% capital allowance in the year of acquisition in respect of the machine.

You will see from the example that the capital allowance has a distorting effect on the post-tax profit figures because the tax relief is taken in the first year and not spread over the machine's working life.

Year	Taxable profit £	Tax @ 30% £	Post-tax profit £
1	20,000		
less allowance	(15,000)		
	5,000	1,500	13,500
2	20,000	6,000	9,000
3	20,000	6,000	9,000

Over the three-year period, the company pays a total of £13,500 in tax. If this were spread evenly over the three-year period, the company would pay £4,500 pa. This means that in Year 1 the company paid £3,000 too little in tax. In each of the next two years, the company pays £1,500 too much.

To iron out this distortion, AB Ltd should create in Year 1 a provision for deferred tax equal to the amount of tax 'saved' as a result of the excess tax relief (the originating difference). This provision would be shown on the Profit and Loss Account in Year 1, and would have the effect of reducing the post-tax profit for that year. In subsequent years, the provision would be used, and therefore shown on the Profit and Loss Account as a deduction from the taxation figure. This would have the effect of increasing the post-tax profit for subsequent years.

> ## Example
>
> The Profit and Loss Account for Year 1 should show the actual tax paid as well as a provision for the amount of tax saved as a result of the excessive relief.
> (a) Using the figures from the example above, it will be necessary to create a provision of £3,000 for Year 1:
>
> ### Profit and Loss Account for Year 1
>
> | | £ | £ |
> |---|---|---|
> | Net Profit | | 15,000 |
> | Tax | 1,500 | |
> | plus Provision | 3,000 | |
> | | | (4,500) |
> | Post-tax Profit | | 10,500 |
>
> In subsequent years, the accounts will have to show the actual tax paid of £6,000 pa. However, part of the provision created in Year 1 on the Profit and Loss Account will be used to reduce the amount finally shown as charged against profits.
> (b) Each year, £1,500 of the provision will be used to reduce the amount of tax charged in the Profit and Loss Account.
>
> ### Profit and Loss Account for Years 2 and 3
>
> | | £ | £ |
> |---|---|---|
> | Net Profit | | 15,000 |
> | Tax | 6,000 | |
> | less Provision | (1,500) | |
> | | | (4,500) |
> | Post-tax Profit | | 10,500 |

When looking at a set of accounts, you should certainly be concerned if no provision at all has been made, since this may mean that the business will face heavy tax bills in the future. This would mean a dramatic fall in post-tax profits.

SUMMARY

> (1) A company has a separate legal identity from its owners (the shareholders) and the people who run it (the directors).
>
> (2) A company has its own tax liability.
>
> (3) A company's net profit is allocated to:
>
> > (a) payment of tax;
> >
> > (b) dividends;
> >
> > (c) retention within the company.
>
> (4) A company which has a subsidiary must produce consolidated accounts which show the position of the group as a whole.
>
> (5) Because capital allowances may cause fluctuations in post-tax profit, it is usual to make a provision for deferred tax designed to iron out distortions.

SOLUTIONS

Exercise 6A

Shares

Advantages

Dividends need only be paid if profits are sufficient, and the directors will decide on any amount to be paid.

Shares are not normally bought back by the company, so once issued the company has no further capital liability to the shareholder during the lifetime of the company.

Disadvantages

Shareholders have voting power in relation to some company decisions.

Debentures

Advantages

Debenture holders have no voting power.

Disadvantages

The interest under the loan agreement must be paid even if profits are poor.

Cash will have to be available to pay back the debenture in the future.

Exercise 6B

(c) This year's reserved profits will be added to accumulated reserves. As the result is £100,000, last year's reserves must have been £100,000 less £48,000, ie £52,000.

Exercise 6C

(c) Each shareholder will receive two shares for every one share held. Therefore the company will issue 100,000 £1 shares. Share capital will increase by £100,000. Reserves will be reduced by £100,000. Assets will not be affected.

COMPANY ACCOUNTS: REGULATION AND FORMAT

LEARNING OUTCOMES

After reading this chapter you will be able to:

- explain the importance of the regulation of company accounts
- describe the origin of accounts regulation
- describe the different formats of company accounts used in the UK.

7.1 INTRODUCTION

You have seen that the legal nature of a company is reflected in its Final Accounts. In this chapter you will examine how statutory and non-statutory regulations determine the format in which company accounts are presented.

7.2 THE ROLE OF REGULATION

Regulation is means of achieving uniformity. Earlier we highlighted the fact that there is a lot to be said for uniformity in the preparation and presentation of accounts. Uniformity means that accounts can be read and interpreted by anyone who understands the rules, and enables direct comparisons to be made between the accounts of different businesses.

The desirability of uniformity is heightened in relation to companies, where large numbers of individuals, some of who will be financially unsophisticated, become directly involved by investing as shareholders.

Consistency in the preparation of accounts helps to create transparency. It is important that investors and others can trust and rely upon the information contained in the accounts.

Companies are an integral part of the economy. Regulation exists for the protection of the general public. Society generally has an interest in transparency, reliability, equivalence and comparability of published information about companies.

7.3 STATUTORY REGULATION

Companies are themselves a creation of statute. It is not surprising, therefore, that their accounts are also subject to a substantial amount of statutory regulation.

The statutory regulation of company accounts is contained mainly in Part 15 of the CA 2006. Part 15 contains the procedural requirements for company accounts for all UK companies.

The Act imposes slightly different requirements on different kinds of company. The main distinction for this purpose is between companies which are subject to the small companies regime and companies not subject to that regime. A company is subject to the small companies regime if it is a private company which satisfies two or more of the following requirements contained in s 382: its turnover is not more than £10.2 million; its Balance Sheet total is not more than £5.1 million; and it does not employ more than 50 employees. Broadly speaking, for these companies the statutory requirements are more relaxed.

At the most basic level, s 386(1) requires every company to keep 'adequate accounting records'. The directors and other officers of the company commit a criminal offence if they fail to keep such records.

The directors must prepare accounts for the company for each of its financial years (s 394). Section 393 provides that directors of a company must not approve accounts unless they are satisfied that they give a true and fair view of the assets, liabilities, financial position and profit or loss, and auditors must have regard to that obligation when carrying out their functions.

In addition, the CA 2006 requires certain accounts to be filed with the Registrar of Companies. Companies subject to the small companies regime must file a copy of a Balance Sheet drawn up on the last day of the financial year, and a copy of the auditor's report unless the company is exempt from audit. Medium-sized companies may file abbreviated accounts. A company is medium-sized if it satisfies two or more of the following requirements: its turnover is not more than £36 million; its Balance Sheet total is not more than £18 million; and it does not employ more than 250 employees (s 465). All other companies must file full accounts (ss 445–447).

Every company must send a copy of its annual accounts and reports for each financial year to shareholders, debenture holders and anyone entitled to receive notice of general meetings (s 423), although in certain circumstances it may provide a strategic report instead of copies of the accounts (s 426 and Companies (Receipt of Accounts and Reports) Regulations 2013 (SI 2013/1973)). If it is a public company, it must then put the final accounts before the members in general meeting.

Companies normally have to have their accounts audited. Most small companies are exempt from this requirement (s 475). However, shareholders with at least 10% of the nominal issued share capital can always require the company to obtain an audit of its accounts for a financial year (s 476).

7.4 ACCOUNTING PRINCIPLES

For many years company accounts have been subject to statutory regulation under successive Companies Acts. To supplement this statutory regulation, initially the professional bodies of the accounting profession issued recommendations of best practice to their members. By the 1970s it was felt that these to some extent ad hoc arrangements were no longer sufficient to meet the needs of the accounting world. A more formal and centralised system of setting standards and requirements was called for. The professional bodies therefore combined in producing uniform accounting principles to be followed.

7.4.1 UK regulation

The centralised regulation system created in the 1970s required accountants to follow generally accepted accounting principles (GAAP). These principles comprised a combination of statutory requirements, Financial Reporting Standards (FRSs) and a mixture of recommendations of best practice, called collectively 'UK GAAP'.

Over the years, UK GAAP expanded to the point where it was felt to be complex and unwieldy. In January 2015, following a lengthy period of consultation, the UK central regulator, the

Financial Reporting Council, abolished UK GAAP and replaced it with a new accounting regime, the key element of which is FRS 102 The Financial Reporting Standard applicable in the UK and Republic of Ireland. FRS 102 is a comprehensive statement of accounting practice applicable to the majority of UK companies and is aimed at achieving consistency in the preparation of accounts. FRS 102 addresses the accounting principles which must be adopted by, for example, specifying which method of calculation of depreciation should be used and how closing stock is to be valued, as well as dictating some of the detail which must appear on the face of the Profit and Loss Account and Balance Sheet, and specifying what additional documentation should be provided. Some accountants and commentators refer to FRS 102 as 'UK GAAP' or 'New UK GAAP'.

7.4.2 International regulation

It will not surprise you to know that whilst the United Kingdom was developing its own system of accounting regulation, other countries were engaged in the same task. The system of regulation in this country was therefore referred to as UK GAAP in order to distinguish it from the systems of other jurisdictions, such as US GAAP or German GAAP.

The fact of different regulatory systems operating in different countries was of little practical significance until the 1990s when trade and commerce became increasingly international in nature. Individual countries having their own accounting systems was no longer sufficient to meet the needs of a global market. In 2001 the International Accounting Standards Board (IASB) was formed. The IASB issues its own International Financial Reporting Standards (IFRS) which are capable of being adopted in different jurisdictions. The IFRS cover the same aspects of accounts preparation and presentation as FRS 102, but have their own system of rules and regulations.

Since 2005 all EU companies whose shares are traded on a regulated stock market in the EU have been required to use the IFRS for the preparation of their group accounts (Council Regulation 1606/2002/EC). With that exception, an individual company can follow either the IFRS or FRS 102 in preparing its accounts.

7.4.3 Conclusion

The financial reporting rules change rapidly. However, in reality, business transactions are becoming increasingly complex, and accounting standards have to change to accommodate them. This book cannot even begin to address the detail and complexity of accounts regulation. Instead, we are going to focus on the results of this regulation, looking at how regulation affects some of the form and content of the accounts you will encounter in practice.

7.5 ACCOUNTS FORMATS

Section 395 of the CA 2006 requires companies to prepare either 'Companies Act Individual Accounts' or 'International Accounting Standards Individual Accounts'. Essentially, the format of Companies Act Individual Accounts complies with FRS 102 (see **7.5.1**), and that of International Accounting Standards Individual Accounts complies with the IFRS (see **7.5.2**).

Before we look at the differences between these two types of accounts formats, there is one presentation requirement that is common to both but which has been omitted from the examples that follow for the sake of simplicity. This is the requirement that the preceding year's figures must be shown alongside the equivalent figures for the current year. This is very helpful for anyone examining the accounts, as it enables direct year-on-year comparisons to be made, so that changes and trends in the company's performance may be identified.

7.5.1 Companies Act format

Section 395 of the CA 2006 provides that Companies Act Individual Accounts must be prepared 'in accordance with section 396'. Beyond stating that there must be a Profit and Loss

Account and a Balance Sheet, s 396 does not give any indication of the format for the accounts. It does provide, however, that Companies Act Individual Accounts must comply with any relevant regulations. It is in these regulations that the detailed requirements for the format of the accounts may be found.

The main regulations dealing with company accounts formats are the Large and Medium-sized Companies and Groups (Accounts and Reports) Regulations 2008 (SI 2008/410) (and their equivalent for small companies, SI 2008/409). The Regulations contain a small number of format templates showing the way in which both Profit and Loss Accounts and Balance Sheets must be drawn up. These formats are not absolutely mandatory in the sense that some adaptation is permitted, and so you will encounter some variations in practice.

7.5.1.1 Profit and Loss Account

The following is a simple Profit and Loss Account (this may also be referred to as an Income Statement).

Example

Profit and Loss Account for the Year ended . . .

	£000	£000
TURNOVER	250,000	
Cost of Sales	100,000	
GROSS PROFIT		150,000
Distribution costs	15,000	
Administrative costs	20,000	
		(35,000)
OPERATING PROFIT		115,000
Interest Receivable		5,000
PROFIT BEFORE INTEREST		120,000
Interest Payable		(2,000)
PROFIT BEFORE TAXATION		118,000
Tax		(25,000)
PROFIT FOR THE FINANCIAL YEAR		93,000

You will notice immediately that the Profit and Loss Account for a company focuses on 'headline' figures such as 'Administration Expenses' rather than itemising each and every type of expense. This is because company accounts are usually accompanied by a set of Notes which will give a detailed breakdown and explanation of the figures, which avoids the Profit and Loss Account itself looking overly complicated. The way in which the items are grouped together is dictated by accounting standards. There are also some changes in terminology. For example, the sales figure is usually labelled 'Turnover'. You will also see the company's corporation tax liability at the end of the Profit and Loss Account.

The main difference in a company Profit and Loss Account is that it separates the income, expenses and profit from its operating activities from other items such as finance costs. A company's operating profit is simply the profit which it derives from its main trading activities.

With larger companies you will see additional items appearing on the accounts. For example, after the company's ordinary income and tax, you may see reference to 'extraordinary income', which would be a source of income unrelated to the usual business of the company's trade, such as damages received from litigation.

7.5.1.2 Balance Sheet

The following is a simple Balance Sheet (this may also be referred to as the Statement of Financial Position).

Example			
Balance Sheet as at . . .			
	£000	£000	£000
ASSETS			
FIXED ASSETS			
Tangible Assets			200,000
CURRENT ASSETS			
Stock	50,000		
Debtors	50,000		
Cash	45,000		
		145,000	
Amounts Falling Due within 1 Year			
Creditors	20,000		
Provision for Tax	25,000		
		(45,000)	
Net Current Assets			**100,000**
Total Assets less Current Liabilities			300,000
Amounts Falling Due after more than 1 year			
Bank Loan			(20,000)
NET ASSETS			**280,000**
CAPITAL AND RESERVES			
Share Capital			200,000
Profit and Loss Reserve			80,000
SHAREHOLDERS FUNDS			**280,000**

You will notice so far as the first section is concerned the heading is 'Assets' rather than the (by now familiar) employment of capital which appears on a sole trader/practitioner or partnership Balance Sheet. There are some cosmetic differences in that current and long-term liabilities are now labelled as amounts falling due within one year and more than one year respectively. You will also see that an additional figure is shown on the face of the accounts of 'Total Assets less Current Liabilities', which simply shows the value of the business before the long-term liabilities are accounted for. The only point of substance is that the company's liability for tax, which has usually not be paid at the date of the Balance Sheet, is shown.

7.5.2 International format

Accounts presented using the IFRS must comply with international accounting standards, and in particular with IAS 1. International standards tend to be less prescriptive in that, instead of providing templates to follow, they set out minimum requirements for the information which must appear on the face of the accounts.

7.5.2.1 Income Statement

The following is a simple Income Statement (Profit and Loss Account).

Example

Income Statement for the Year Ended . . .

	£000	£000
REVENUE	250,000	
Cost of sales	100,000	
GROSS PROFIT		**150,000**
Distribution expenses	15,000	
Administration expenses	20,000	
		(35,000)
OPERATING PROFIT		**115,000**
Finance Income		
Interest Receivable		5,000
Finance expenses		(2,000)
PROFIT BEFORE TAX		**118,000**
Tax		(25,000)
PROFIT FOR THE FINANCIAL YEAR		**93,000**

You will immediately notice that sales/turnover is now referred to as 'Revenue'. However, beyond that, the content and format are very similar to the Profit and Loss Account we considered earlier.

7.5.2.2 Statement of Financial Position

The following is a simple Statement of Financial Position (Balance Sheet).

Example

Statement of Financial Position as at . . .

	£000	£000	£000
ASSETS			
NON-CURRENT ASSETS			
Property, plant and equipment			200,000
CURRENT ASSETS			
Inventories	50,000		
Receivables	50,000		
Cash	45,000		
		145,000	
CURRENT LIABILITIES			
Payables	20,000		
Tax	25,000		
		(45,000)	
Net Current Assets			**100,000**
Total Assets less Current Liabilities			300,000
NON-CURRENT LIABILITIES			
Bank Loan			(20,000)
NET ASSETS			**280,000**
EQUITY			
Share Capital			200,000
Profit and Loss Reserve			80,000
TOTAL EQUITY			**280,000**

Cosmetically there are a number of differences between this style of presentation and the Balance Sheet which we considered earlier. However, the differences are essentially those of terminology. So, you will see that the term 'non-current assets' is used instead of 'fixed assets' and 'non-current liabilities' instead of 'long-term liabilities'. Similarly, 'debtors' and creditors' have become 'receivables' and 'payables' respectively. Closing stock is referred to as 'inventories', and 'debentures' as 'loan notes'. Once you allow for these simple changes in terminology, again the form and content are familiar. Incidentally, FRS 102 itself adopts this 'international' terminology.

7.6 ANNUAL REPORTS AND ACCOUNTS

Throughout this book we have focused on the Profit and Loss Account and the Balance Sheet produced by the business at the end of its accounting year. However the CA 2006 and both FRS 102 and the IFRS require additional reports and financial statements to be produced. This collection of documents is often referred to as the 'Reports and Accounts'. The quantity of information will vary depending on the size and type of company.

When you are looking at the accounts of a company, particularly those of a company which is required to publish its accounts, in addition to the Profit and Loss Account (or Income Statement) and Balance Sheet (or Statement of Financial Position) you may encounter one or more of the following.

7.6.1 Statement of Cash Flows

As its title indicates, this Statement contains the details of all cash receipts (inflows) and payments (outflows) into and out of the company during the year. Cash can come into the business from a variety of sources: profits, capital, loans. Similarly, cash goes out of the business in a number of ways: dividends, buying fixed assets, loan repayments. In a statement of cash flows, the payments and receipts are grouped into various categories according to whether they are connected to the company's main trading activities, investments or something else.

The net profit figure which is calculated on the Profit and Loss Account is a key indicator of the company's performance. We have seen that when a company sells stock it generates income, which in turn increases the profits. However, if the company sells its stock mainly on credit, it will be generating income, and therefore a healthy profit, but it will not be bringing cash into the business. Cash is in many ways the lifeblood of the business. A company with insufficient levels of cash is likely to be in financial difficulties. In contrast to the profit calculated on the Profit and Loss Account, the Statement of Cash Flows highlights the incoming and outgoing of cash, and is therefore an important tool in assessing the performance of the business.

7.6.2 Statement of Comprehensive Income

This Statement is a FRS 102 requirement. It shows all gains and losses of whatever nature that have arisen during the company's accounting period. It is basically a summary of events which have occurred during the year which have had an immediate effect on the wealth of the business but which are not necessarily reflected in a conventional Profit and Loss Account, for example a revaluation of premises. This Statement can be combined with the Profit and Loss Account.

7.6.3 Statement of Changes in Equity

Once the post-tax profit of a company has been calculated, the directors will decide how much of the profit should be distributed to the shareholders as a dividend. This is an allocation of profit and could in theory be shown in an appropriation account in the same way as a partnership shows how its profit is allocated. However, for companies, in practice dividends are shown in a separate statement called a Statement of Changes in Equity. Dividends are not shown until they have been paid.

This Statement is not confined to dividends. It will also, for example, detail the issue of new shares.

7.6.4 Strategic Report

This is a statutory requirement under s 414A of the CA 2006 (small companies are exempt). It contains a review of the company's business designed to enable the performance of the company to be measured and assessed.

7.6.5 Chairman's Report

This is not a strict requirement, but a Chairman's Report is often produced by quoted companies. The Report usually sets the scene for the accounts, in terms of what has happened in the life of the company during the year. It should be read with a degree of care as the Chairman will inevitably put the best possible gloss on events of the past year.

7.6.6 Directors' Report

This is a statutory requirement under s 415 of the CA 2006. The contents of the Directors' Report are stipulated by the Act, but essentially it comprises factual information about the company, a business review and confirmation that the auditors have been supplied with all relevant information. Small companies are exempt from having to include some of the statutory information.

7.6.7 Auditors' Report

As the name suggests, this is a report given by the auditors. In the report the auditors are required to say whether in their opinion the accounts give a true and fair view of the financial state of the business. There has been criticism of auditors in recent years who have given an unqualified approval certificate to the accounts of companies which have then been revealed as having severe problems.

7.6.8 Notes

Both FRS 102 and the IFRS require the accounts to be accompanied by a set of explanatory notes. The notes often run to many pages, and they are usually the most informative part of the accounts as they expand on the information which appears in the Profit and Loss Account/ Income Statement and Balance Sheet.

SUMMARY

(1) Company accounts are subject to statutory regulation under the CA 2006.

(2) Accountants follow generally accepted accounting principles (GAPP), which comprise standards, regulations and statements of good practice for the preparation and presentation of company accounts.

(3) There are two systems of accounting standards in the UK: FRS 102 and the IFRS.

(4) Those companies whose shares are traded on a regulated stock market in the EU must comply with the IFRS. Other companies may choose to follow either FRS 102 or the IFRS.

ANALYSIS OF ACCOUNTS

> **LEARNING OUTCOMES**
>
> After reading this chapter you will be able to:
>
> - interpret the basic information provided by a set of accounts
> - explain the limitations of accounts
> - employ a range of trends and ratios in order to assess the performance of a business.

8.1 INTRODUCTION

We have now seen how the financial information of a business is first collated and then presented as a set of Final Accounts. In this chapter we turn to the process of analysing those accounts. Through this process of analysis you will be able to assess the present state of any type of business and draw reasoned conclusions about its future.

8.2 THE PURPOSES OF ANALYSING ACCOUNTS

In broad terms, the purposes of analysing the accounts of a business are to assess the business's current performance and to predict its future prospects.

The analysis of accounts can help to answer any number of questions. For example:

- Is the present level of profitability satisfactory?
- Is the profitability likely to improve in the future?
- Can the business meet its current liabilities?
- Will the business be able to meet its liabilities in the future?
- Are investors receiving a satisfactory return on their investment?
- Will the business be doing better or worse in five years' time?

8.3 WHO WILL WANT TO ANALYSE ACCOUNTS AND WHY?

The following people are likely to be interested in reading accounts:

(a) *Investors* – to assess the level of risk and return.

(b) *Managers* – to make sure that the business is performing to its full potential.

(c) *Lenders* – to ensure that the debt will be repaid and that the business can pay interest.

(d) HMRC – to assess the profits for tax.

(e) *Potential purchasers* – to consider whether the business is worth buying.

(f)   *Employees* – to negotiate terms and conditions of employment.

Not all of those interested will be able to get full information about the business they are assessing. Obviously, managers will be able to get all the necessary information, but how much an investor will be able to find out will depend largely on how much of an investment is involved – the larger the amount, the more influence a potential investor will have when demanding information.

8.4   THE LIMITATIONS OF ACCOUNTS

You must be able to understand what is in the accounts, but looking at accounts alone may provide a misleading picture of the state of a business. Accounts are produced only *after* events have occurred. This is an important limitation if you are trying to form a view of the likely performance of the business in the *future*.

Accounts can produce information of a financial nature only. A Balance Sheet is a helpful list of the assets and liabilities of the business; however, it will not indicate the health or otherwise of labour relations, despite the fact that many people would regard good staff relations as a very important asset. Similarly, a poor trade reputation would be regarded by many people as a liability, but it does not appear in the accounts.

The accounts of a business need to be seen in the wider context. There may be commercial or economic issues entirely beyond the control of management, such as a declining market for the firm's products or the general economic climate.

The accounts are an essential tool in the analysis of the position of a business, but they provide only part of the information needed.

8.5   WHAT INFORMATION DO YOU NEED?

It is important to be able to put the accounts that you are looking at in context by gaining a general picture of the business you are investigating:

(a)   It is large or small?

(b)   Is it growing or contracting?

(c)   What is the nature of its business?

(d)   Does it operate in an expanding or a declining market?

(e)   Does it depend heavily on a particular product or products?

The questions you should ask depend on the circumstances and are largely a matter of common sense.

8.5.1   Public companies

We have looked at company accounts from the point of view of the company complying with its statutory obligation to provide certain information. However, for a public company the production of its Annual Report and Accounts gives the company an opportunity to promote itself, to its shareholders, to prospective investors and to analysts.

As you read any company's Annual Report and Accounts, be very aware of the need to question and check everything. If any of the figures in the accounts are unclear you will need to look for explanations, for example in the Notes or the Directors' Report. You may need to take a view on whether the Chairman is expressing overly-optimistic hopes in his Statement. Those hopes may appear unreasonable in the light of the company's current financial position or the general economy.

It is unlikely, although not impossible, that you would find a direct lie in a company's Annual Report and Accounts, but you should always examine the information critically to see whether a particular proposal or intention appears to be justified.

Remember, when you are reading the Annual Report and Accounts, that there are other sources of information as well. Look for newspaper reports, television news, etc.

8.5.2 Partnerships and sole trader/practitioners

There will be no published accounts for partnerships and sole traders/practitioners. Even so, you should obtain copies of the accounts they produce and study them.

You must gather as much information about the business as you can. Find out the following:

(a)   Are its premises in a suitable area?

(b)   Does it seem to be busy?

(c)   Is it dealing in something which is going to provide an income in the long term?

(d)   What sort of reputation does it have locally?

(e)   What can you find out about the proprietors?

You can then look at the accounts in the light of that information. When your analysis raises further questions, you can engage in detailed discussions of the problems with the proprietors or their advisers.

Obviously, the amount of information you can get will depend on what your relationship is, or is to be, with the business.

8.6   PRELIMINARY STEPS

As well as obtaining as much general information about the business as you can, there are a number of preliminary steps you should take before launching into a detailed analysis of the accounts. These involve, in part, checking the accuracy and reliability of the figures presented and, in part, building up a general picture of the business and the market in which it operates. This enables the information extracted to be considered in a proper context. What might be normal for a small business might be very unusual for a large one. A particular level of profitability may be commendable in a time of recession, but disappointing in a period when business generally is 'booming'.

Common preliminary steps are as follows:

(a)   *Obtain the accounts for several years.*

If you are going to make a realistic assessment of a business, it is important that you obtain its accounts for several years rather than for the previous year alone. One year's accounts will reveal important information – the extent of borrowings, the value of fixed assets, the amount of unpaid bills, the value of closing stock – but it is difficult to reach reliable conclusions without making comparisons with earlier years.

(b)   *Check the date of the Balance Sheet.*

A business can choose a Balance Sheet date to suit itself. If the business is seasonal then a Balance Sheet drawn up at one date could include figures which would show the business in a much more favourable light than a Balance Sheet drawn up at another date.

Example

A business manufactures Christmas decorations. It sells the decorations to department stores in September. A Balance Sheet drawn up in September would show a healthy cash balance and probably substantial debtors. By contrast, a Balance Sheet drawn up in July would show substantial closing stock, a high creditors figure and, probably, a large overdraft.

Always consider whether you have to take the date of the Balance Sheet into account when you are analysing the figures:

(i)   Check the method of valuing fixed assets.

(ii) When were the assets last valued? Freehold premises purchased 20 years earlier for £5,000 may still be shown in the Balance Sheet at that value. Their current value will probably be quite different.

(iii) Has provision been made for depreciation? If so, what method has been used?

In the case of a company, you will be looking for the answers to these and other questions in the Notes and the Statement of accounting policies included in the company's published accounts. If you are dealing with a partnership or sole trader, you should ask for that information from the partners or proprietor.

Exercise 8A

What will be the effect on the Profit and Loss Account and on the Balance Sheet if values for fixed assets and depreciation are inaccurate?

(c)   *Check how the closing stock is valued.*

The normal method is to value stock at the lower of cost or current market value. If you want to do the job thoroughly, you should inspect the stock. It may be that it includes items which are no longer readily saleable. For example, in the fashion trade, a business may have purchased items some months ago which are now out of fashion. They could still be appearing in the accounts under 'Closing stock' at cost price, when in fact their current market value is little or nothing.

Exercise 8B

How will the Profit and Loss Account and Balance Sheet be affected if the figure for stock is overstated?

(d)   *Analyse the figure given for debtors.*

Will all the debtors actually pay? Has a provision been made for bad debts? It is quite possible for a business not to write off bad debts, so that the debtors figure appears larger than the amount of cash which the business can readily expect to receive.

Exercise 8C

Why might a business not write off bad debts?
What else is affected apart from the Balance Sheet?
Are there any dangers in a business having a large number of debtors?

(e)   *Look for unusual or exceptional items or major changes.*

The picture given by the Profit and Loss Account and Balance Sheet for a particular year can sometimes be distorted because of some exceptional event or major change either in circumstances or in accounting policy.

Example

A business may have borrowed a substantial amount to invest in new plant or machinery. In the short term, profit may be reduced because there has been no time to use the new machinery to increase profits, yet interest charges will already have been incurred. However, in the long term, there may be prospects of rapid growth in future years.

Fixed assets such as land and buildings may have been revalued for the first time in many years. This will make the Balance Sheet look quite different, but in reality nothing has changed.

You will have to take all these matters into account, particularly if you are going to make comparisons with previous years.

8.7 SOME GENERAL CONSIDERATIONS

8.7.1 Profitability and ability to pay debts

The two main questions which people ask when reading the accounts of a business are:

(a)   Is the business profitable?

(b)   Can the business pay its debts as they fall due?

Profitability is not the same as solvency. The Profit and Loss Account shows whether the business has made a profit. The Balance Sheet shows whether it can pay its debts.

The fact that the accounts reveal that a profit has been made does not necessarily mean that there is money in the bank. The Trading and Profit and Loss Accounts of a business will record sales or levels of professional charges, which in turn will determine the amount of profit; but although the goods may have been sold or bills issued, payment may not yet have been received. Thus, although the Profit and Loss Account may show a large profit, the Balance Sheet may record a high figure under debtors and there may be no cash in the bank.

Alternatively, the business may have sold goods or issued bills and been paid; however, it may have purchased expensive new premises, paying cash. Again, the result is that while the Profit and Loss Account will show a profit, there is no money in the bank.

It is therefore a misconception to think that if a business is profitable, it must be able to pay its debts. This is not so. Obviously, a business which is unprofitable is not likely to be solvent for long, but just because a business is profitable does not necessarily mean that it is able to pay its debts at once.

Liquidity is an important issue for a business. A business can only use current assets to meet its liabilities if it is to continue in business. If it has to sell fixed assets to meet liabilities, it will eventually be unable to continue trading. It is therefore important that the business does not run short of current assets. Cash is the most liquid of current assets. Debts are also liquid as, even if they are not yet due for payment, the business can always turn them into cash quickly by selling them on to someone else to collect. Stock is less liquid as it may be difficult to sell quickly. Some items can only be sold at certain times of year.

Exercise 8D

The accounts of a business show that it has made a large profit but that it has no cash. In fact it has a large overdraft. How many possible factors can you think of to account for the lack of cash?

8.7.2 Treatment of bank overdrafts

It is relatively common for a business to have a bank overdraft. It is necessary to decide how to view the overdraft, particularly if this is substantial. An overdraft will normally appear in the Balance Sheet as a current liability because, in theory at least, it is repayable on demand. The reality may be quite different. The business may maintain a high overdraft indefinitely and finance its activities from it. Unless the business runs into difficulties, the bank will not take steps to call in the money owing.

As a current liability, the bank overdraft will be deducted from the current assets and will therefore reduce the net current assets figure. Ordinarily, a low net current assets figure would raise concerns about the ability of the business to pay its immediate debts. However, in reality the overdraft may be a source of long-term finance for the business, so a misleading picture may emerge if no distinction is made between the bank overdraft and ordinary trade creditors.

8.7.3   The impact of inflation

It is necessary to make allowance for the impact of inflation. If profits are increasing at the rate of 2% pa when inflation is running at 4% pa, in real terms profits are falling.

8.8   TRENDS AND RATIO ANALYSIS

8.8.1   Trends and ratios

Trends and ratios are a useful tool for measuring the performance of a business. In particular, trends and ratios make it easier to compare the figures from two or more sets of accounts, whether these are the accounts for different businesses or the accounts of one business for different years. The task is to calculate the appropriate trend or ratio and then use the result to draw conclusions about the performance of the business.

A trend is simply a comparison of figures from accounts for different years to see whether a pattern is established. For example, the net profit figures for successive years might appear as follows:

2014	2015	2016	2017
£50,000	£75,000	£90,000	£100,000

You will immediately see that the trend is for the net profit to increase year on year.

It can often be more helpful to look at the trend revealed when increases and decreases from year to year are expressed in percentage terms. The percentage change may be calculated using the following formula:

$$\frac{\text{figure for the later year} - \text{figure for the earlier year}}{\text{figure for the earlier year}} \times 100$$

Carrying out the calculation for the above net profit figures for 2013–2014 shows the following increase:

$$\frac{75,000 - 50,000}{50,000} \times 100 = 50\%$$

For the years 2015–2016 the increase is 20% and for the years 2016–2017 the increase is 11%. This shows us that whilst the trend is for the net profit figure to increase year on year, the rate at which net profits are increasing is slowing dramatically. This could be the result of, say, a successful marketing campaign which had a high impact on sales initially, but has now steadied into acceptable growth. Alternatively, it could be cause for concern indicating, perhaps, that whilst there is still demand for the product, interest is beginning to tail off.

Ratios are calculated using the figures from a singles set of accounts. A ratio compares two figures by expressing the relationship of one to the other. The result can be expressed as a percentage or as a ratio. Once you have a percentage or ratio, it is also easy to compare the results of different years or of different businesses to establish the trends.

In reality, any two figures can be compared using a ratio and there is, therefore, any number of different ratios which may be used depending on which aspect of the business's performance you are considering. We shall look at a few of the more common ratios which you may encounter in practice.

8.8.2   Profitability ratios

Whether or not the business is making a profit is a key indicator of its success. Simply looking at the Profit and Loss Account will obviously show you whether the business is making a profit. However, using profitability ratios will help you to assess how effective the business is in generating profits and whether the level of profit is acceptable.

8.8.2.1   Return on capital employed

If you simply look at the net profit figure alone, it is difficult to make comparisons with how profitable the business is when compared with, say, its competitors. Comparisons may more easily be made by relating the profits of the business to the capital invested. This is referred to as the 'return on capital employed' (ROCE). It is normally expressed as a percentage:

$$\frac{\text{Net Profit}}{\text{Capital Employed}} \times 100$$

> **Example**
>
> The balance on the proprietor's capital account at the end of the accounting period is £200,000; net profit for the accounting period was £40,000. The return on capital is:
>
> $$\frac{40,000}{200,000} \times 100 = 20\%$$
>
> The proprietor may consider that this compares very favourably with putting the money in a bank or building society account.

The ROCE shows the profit being made on the resources available to the business. A business with a higher percentage is using its capital more efficiently. A business with a ROCE of, say, 40% is achieving a return of £40 of net profit for very £100 invested, compared with only £15 for a business with a ROCE of 15%.

For a company, the profit figure used in the calculation is usually the figure for operating profit, ie the profit before tax and interest are considered. This concentrates the calculation on the profits made by the company's main trading activity.

It is possible to calculate the return solely on the amount of capital the proprietor has invested. This allows the proprietor to judge whether the return on capital is satisfactory by reference to the return that could be obtained on other investments. As an alternative, long-term loans can be added to the capital employed in order to assess the return across all long-term funding of the business.

When calculating the return, you may choose to take the capital figure at the start of the year, at the end of the year or an average figure. It is normally easiest to take the figure at the end of the year, although arguably it is more accurate to take the figure at the start of the year as that was the amount invested during the relevant trading period.

8.8.2.2   Sales to capital employed

This is a similar calculation to ROCE, which we considered at **8.8.2.1**, in that it focuses on how well the business is using its net assets. However, rather than looking at the net profit generated, this ratio isolates one element of profit and shows the volume of sales produced by the net assets employed in the business.

The calculation is as follows:

$$\frac{\text{Sales}}{\text{Capital Employed}}$$

In simple terms, the more sales that the business is able to generate from its capital employed, the more profitable the business is likely to be. So, the higher the figure, the better.

Isolating the sales figure alone means that the ratio must be used with caution. For example, if the business decides to depreciate its fixed assets, this will have the effect of reducing the capital employed figure and thereby improving the ratio, and yet the business will not have improved its sales. Similarly, a business which owns its premises outright rather than renting them may have a low sales to capital employed ratio because its fixed assets will be high.

However, the business may be more profitable because the income which is produced from its sales is not being used up in paying rent.

8.8.2.3 Gross profit margin percentage

This is a useful ratio to use when assessing the profitability of a trading business. It relates the value of sales made to the gross profit made on them, the so-called 'profit margin'. It can be calculated as follows:

$$\frac{\text{Gross Profit}}{\text{Sales}} \times 100$$

The calculation demonstrates the profit being made on each item sold, so obviously a business is looking to achieve a high percentage figure. A gross profit margin of 35%, for example, shows that for every £1 of sales the business is making 35p in gross profit. This is a fairly basic measure: if a business is not selling its stock for more than it paid for the stock, then it is not going to be viable unless it either raises its prices or finds a cheaper supplier. However, a business with a low gross profit margin should be prompted to focus on its sale and purchase price in order to improve its profitability.

8.8.2.4 Net profit margin ratio

This is the same calculation as discussed in **8.7.2.3** above, but this time using the net profit figure (again, the calculation for a company would use the operating profit figure). The calculation is therefore a little more sophisticated, because it takes into account the effect of the other expenses of the business.

The calculation is as follows:

$$\frac{\text{Net Profit}}{\text{Sales}} \times 100$$

> **Example**
>
> A business has sales of £400,000 and a net profit of £40,000. The net profit percentage is:
> $$\frac{40,000}{400,000} \times 100 = 10\%$$
> This means that out of every £1 of sales, 90p goes in expenses and 10p is profit.

If the net profit margin is unfavourable, particularly compared to the gross profit margin, this helps the proprietor to identify the need to try to increase profitability by reducing expenses.

8.8.3 Liquidity ratios

Liquidity is concerned with whether the business has sufficient finds to pay its creditors on time. Liquidity ratios therefore help to identify whether the business is at risk of insolvency proceedings being initiated by those creditors who have not been paid.

8.8.3.1 Current ratio

The current ratio is a direct comparison of current assets with current liabilities. It is therefore a measure of the assets which can be turned into cash relatively readily in order to meet the liabilities which must be paid within 12 months. The result is normally expressed as a ratio:

$$\frac{\text{Current Assets}}{\text{Current Liabilities}} :1$$

So if the current assets are £40,000 and the current liabilities are £20,000, the current ratio will be:

$$\frac{40,000}{20,000} = 2:1$$

A ratio of 1:1 would mean that the business has exactly £1 of current assets with which to meet every £1 of current liabilities. Most businesses would expect to have a higher ratio, say 1.5:1. However, this depends on the type of business. Supermarkets, for example, will usually have current ratios which are much lower. This is because they buy goods on credit but sell mainly for cash. Each day, they know that large amounts of cash will be injected into the business. In general, therefore, they can meet liabilities due on a particular day from cash received on that day, and need only a small amount of additional available current assets.

8.8.3.2   Acid test

A potential problem with the current ratio is that it takes account of all the current assets. Closing stock, for example, may not be quickly saleable. Indeed, there may be doubt as to whether it is saleable at all. Changes in fashion and technology may make stock obsolete. In the same way, in a non-trading business there will be uncertainty as to how quickly work in progress may be turned into cash. The acid test is the ratio between current liabilities and current assets excluding stock (or work in progress in a non-trading business). The calculation is as follows:

$$\frac{\text{Current Assets} - \text{Closing Stock}}{\text{Current Liabilities}} :1$$

It is common also to exclude any prepayments from the current assets figure. As these represent amounts already paid by the business, their very nature means that they cannot usually be converted back into cash.

Example

The following is an extract from a Balance Sheet:

Current Assets

Stock	65,000	
Debtors	50,000	
Cash	5,000	
		120,000

Current Liabilities

Creditors	40,000	
Accruals	10,000	
		(50,000)

Net Current Assets   70,000

The acid test is: $\dfrac{120,000 - 65,000}{50,000} = 1.1{:}1$

An acid test of 1:1 means that the business has £1 of readily liquid assets for every £1 of current liabilities. The lower the ratio, the greater the risk of the business being unable to meet its debts as they fall due.

However, even a high ratio needs to be considered critically. The business may not be pursuing its debtors rigorously, or may not have written off sufficient bad debts. This would lead to an unrealistic current assets figure and consequently a high acid test ratio.

8.8.4   Efficiency ratios

Efficiency ratios assess how efficient the business is at using the assets available to it. (You should note that as they also deal with elements of liquidity, they are sometimes treated as liquidity ratios – see **8.8.3**.)

8.8.4.1   Stock turnover

This measures how efficient the business is at selling its stock. It is often expressed as a number of days:

$$\frac{\text{Closing Stock}}{\text{Cost of Goods Sold}} \times 365$$

Sometimes an 'Average' Closing Stock figure is used, which simply means an average of the stock held at the beginning and end of the year.

Generally speaking, a business will want to sell its stock quickly in order to generate income and will therefore be aiming at a short stock turnover period. If stock is taking too long to sell, this may be because it is being offered at too high a price or because there is simply no demand.

However, a low stock turnover period will not necessarily always be an indicator of efficiency. It could be a product of the business setting its stock levels too low with the result that it will not be able to respond to any increase in demand.

You must also consider the stock turnover figure in the context of the type of business you re dealing with. A supermarket, for example, would be expected to have a short stock turnover period. In contrast, a dealer in high value fine art would normally have a high stock turnover period.

8.8.4.2   Average settlement period for debtors

This shows the length of time it takes for debtors to pay. A business which is failing to collect its debts is losing out on the opportunity of having ready cash available and is not operating efficiently.

$$\frac{\text{Debtors}}{\text{Sales}} \times 365 = \text{Number of days it takes debtors to pay}$$

If a business is not converting its debtors into cash relatively quickly, it may indicate that its debt collection system is inefficient. It might also suggest that the business is being forced into selling too much on credit because it is not finding ready cash buyers. It could also act as a warning that a major customer is delaying payments because it is in financial difficulties.

An equivalent calculation can be done to see how quickly the business pays its creditors. The two figures may then be compared. A business which is quick to pay its own creditors but slow to secure payment from its debtors is being run inefficiently. It may experience cash flow problems as it is paying cash out faster than it is collecting money in. Such a business may need to improve its debt collection procedures and/or review the contractual terms on which it conducts its business. Conversely, a business which is collecting money from its debtors, but which still cannot pay its creditors promptly, has a cash shortage and may be heading for insolvency.

8.8.5   Gearing

Essentially, gearing is the relationship between the funding which a company derives as capital and the funding which it raises through borrowing. Looking at the how the business is financed in this way is helpful when considering the long-term prospects of the business. Borrowing in itself is not bad, and indeed most businesses will need to borrow money at times in order to fund expansion. However, a business which is too heavily reliant on borrowing may eventually run into difficulties if it cannot meet the loan repayments, perhaps as a result of interest rates rising.

There are many ways of looking at gearing, but at its simplest it may be calculated as follows:

$$\frac{\text{Long-term Liabilities}}{\text{Shareholders Funds}} \times 100$$

If the calculation produces a high percentage figure, the company is said to have high gearing, as it has a high proportion of borrowing compared to its capital. A low percentage figure, or low gearing, shows that the company has a low proportion of borrowing compared to capital.

For a shareholder, investment in a company with high gearing is in a sense more risky. This is because a company with high levels of borrowing will also have high interest payments. Every year the interest will have to be paid, regardless of the level of profit; this may leave little or nothing remaining which can be paid out to the shareholders as a dividend. Even a small reduction in the profits for one year could means that there is nothing left for the shareholders' dividend. If a company has low gearing, on the other hand, this means that the amount available for dividends is less susceptible to fluctuations in profit.

8.8.6 Investment ratios

Investment ratios are used by investors or potential investors to assess the performance of the business. The main investment ratio is the Earnings per Share figure. This is a figure which is arrived at by taking the profit figure after taxation for the year and dividing it by the number of shares in the company. The resulting figure is usually expressed as pence per share.

EXAMPLE

A company has profits of £150,000 and 200,000 issued shares; the earnings per share would be calculated as follows:

$$\frac{150,000}{200,000} = 0.75 \text{ or } 75\text{p per £1 share}$$

The figure shows the amount of profit being generated for each share in the company. In other words, it shows how much each shareholder would receive per share if all the profits for the year were to be paid out in dividends. However, it is important for the investor to remember that this is not the same as the dividend payment per share as a company would not, in practice, pay out all its profits in dividends. However, it is a useful tool for comparing the investment potential between different companies, or between shares and other types of investment.

SUMMARY

(1) It is preferable to look at several years' accounts to get a full picture.

(2) 'One off' events may distort the accounts.

(3) Profitability is not the same thing as an ability to pay debts.

(4) Analysis ratios are a useful tool in assessing the performance of a business in terms of:

    (a) profitability;

    (b) liquidity;

    (c) efficiency;

    (d) gearing;

    (e) investment.

SOLUTIONS

Exercise 8A

Effect on Profit and Loss Account

Depreciation is charged as an expense on the Profit and Loss Account. If the depreciation is understated, the profit will be artificially high.

The reverse will be true if the depreciation is overstated.

Effect on Balance Sheet

Depreciation

The figure for fixed assets will be unreliable if depreciation is inaccurate. The figure for capital owing to the proprietors will also be unreliable as it is increased by the profit calculated on the Profit and Loss Account.

Fixed assets

If assets are overstated, the Balance Sheet will appear healthier than it really is. Fixed assets and capital will both be higher than they should be.

If assets are understated, the business may appear to be producing a high profit from its capital, but since capital is understated this will be misleading.

Exercise 8B

Effect on Profit and Loss Account

Closing stock reduces the figure for cost of goods sold. If cost of goods sold is low, then gross and net profit will appear to be high.

Thus, an overstated closing figure increases profit figures.

Effect on Balance Sheet

Closing stock will be shown as a current asset. An inaccurate figure will improve the relationship between current assets and current liabilities.

Exercise 8C

A business may not write off bad debts because it is taking an unrealistic view of its debtors' ability to pay. Alternatively, it may be a deliberate ploy to give a misleading picture of the financial state of the business.

Debtors are shown in the Balance Sheet as current assets. A high debtors figure will increase the apparent value of the assets. It will affect the balance between current assets and current liabilities.

It is not only the Balance Sheet which will be affected by a failure to write off bad debts. Bad debts appear in the Profit and Loss as expenses. The profit figure will be overstated if insufficient debts are written off as bad.

Whilst a high debtors figure makes the position of the business appear better in the accounts, in practice there are dangers in the business having a large number of debtors. The business could have cash flow problems if the debtors do not pay. The business could be particularly vulnerable if a large proportion of the debts are owed by a single debtor, as that debtor may become insolvent and unable to pay.

Exercise 8D

You should have considered at least the following:

(a) excessive drawings by proprietors/dividends paid to shareholders;

(b) purchase of fixed assets out of cash received;

(c) failure to collect debts;

(d) excessive stock levels;

(e) dishonesty of staff.

PART II

SOLICITORS' ACCOUNTS

THE SRA ACCOUNTS RULES 2011

LEARNING OUTCOMES

After reading this chapter you will be able to:

- explain the principles governing the SRA Accounts Rules and who is bound by them
- identify whether money is office or client money
- identify what money must or can pass through the client bank account
- identify the options available for dealing with money received in a bill
- identify the situations in which a client is entitled to interest and how that interest should be calculated
- recognise the records that a firm providing legal services must maintain.

9.1 INTRODUCTION

A firm providing legal services is a business and must make a profit each year if it is to survive. Like any business, it requires day-to-day records of income, expenses, assets and liabilities, so that at the end of the year it can produce a Profit and Loss Account and Balance Sheet.

Unlike most other businesses, however, law firms frequently hold money that belongs to other people. For example, clients who are buying property or a business will normally give funds to their solicitor in advance of completion of the purchase.

9.1.1 The present

The Solicitors Regulation Authority (the 'SRA') has strict rules about dealing with clients' money. The SRA Accounts Rules 2011 ('the Rules') are examined in some detail in this chapter, which is probably the most important chapter in this part of the book. You are unlikely ever to make entries in your firm's accounts, but you will have to understand the difference between client and office money; and should you become a partner, you will be responsible (with your fellow partners) for ensuring that all SRA requirements are complied with.

This chapter deals with the principles which underpin the SRA Accounts Rules 2011 and with the Rules which impact most significantly on the way in which a firm providing legal services is required to deal with client funds.

9.1.2 The future

On 12 June 2017 the SRA published its Response to a Consultation on amendments to the Accounts Rules, together with new draft Accounts Rules.

Its view is that the length and complexity of the current Accounts Rules makes it difficult for new entrants to the market to understand what is required of them, as well as for consumers to understand what to expect when a firm handles their money. Further, many firms find themselves in technical breach of the Accounts Rules in circumstances where there are no real risks to client money.

The Response states that the SRA proposes to:

- *simplify the Accounts Rules*: by focusing on key principles and requirements for keeping client money safe, including:
    - keeping client money separate from firm money;
    - ensuring client money is returned promptly at the end of a matter;
    - using client money only for its intended purpose;
    - proportionate requirements for firms to obtain an annual accountant's report.

  The Accounts Rules will be supported by an online toolkit which will consist of guidance and case studies to aid compliance;
- *change the definition of client money*: to allow money paid for all fees and disbursements for which the solicitor is liable (for example counsel fees) to be treated as the firm's money. Money held for payments for which the client is liable, such as stamp duty land tax, will continue to be treated as client money and therefore required to be held in a client account. The proposed change in definition is expected to remove the need to have a client account for some firms. The changes may also reduce the number of firms required to obtain an accountant's report through the subsequent reduction in the client account balance;
- *provide an alternative to the holding of client money*: through the introduction of clear and consistent safeguards around the use of third party managed accounts (TPMAs) as a mechanism for managing payments and transactions.

The SRA has stated that the draft SRA Accounts Rules 2018 will not come into effect before the Autumn of 2018. Before then, there will be a further consultation process with the scope for additional amendments to be made before the final version of the SRA Accounts Rules 2018 is presented to the SRA Board for approval.

See further **Appendix 3** to Part II.

9.2 PRINCIPLES GOVERNING THE RULES

In the past the SRA regulated only solicitors. However, the arrival of alternative business structures in October 2011 means that legal services may now also be provided by multi-disciplinary practices and by firms owned by non-lawyers. The SRA hopes to regulate all those providing legal services and has rewritten its Accounts Rules and its Code of Conduct so that they do not refer specifically to solicitors. Anyone who is regulated by the SRA will have to follow the same rules.

The Rules are designed to reduce the risk of accidental or deliberate misuse of client money, and to protect clients from the risks of accidental or deliberate mishandling of their money.

Those regulated by the SRA must follow 10 pervasive Principles, which define the fundamental ethical and professional standards that the SRA expects of all firms and individuals (including non-lawyer owners) it regulates. These Principles apply to all aspects of practice covered in the SRA Handbook, including the regulation of Accounts.

The SRA Handbook Glossary comprises a set of defined terms which are used in the SRA Handbook.

The Rules refer to 'you', which has a lengthy definition (see **9.3**) but broadly speaking means all those running or working in a firm regulated by the SRA and the firm itself.

Rule 1.1 states that the purpose of the Rules is to keep client money safe. Rule 1.2 states that those running firms must comply with the Principles set out in the Handbook and the Outcomes in Chapter 7 of the SRA Code of Conduct in relation to the efficient financial management of the firm. In particular they must:

(a)   keep other people's money separate from money belonging to them or their firm;

(b)   keep other people's money safely in a bank or building society account identifiable as a client bank account, except when the Rules provide otherwise;

(c)   use each client's money for that client's matters only;

(d)   use money held as trustee of a trust for the purposes of that trust only;

(e)   establish and maintain proper accounting systems, and proper internal controls over those systems, to ensure compliance with the Rules;

(f)   keep proper accounting records to show accurately the position with regard to the money held for each client and trust;

(g)   account for interest on other people's money in accordance with the Rules;

(h)   co-operate with the SRA in checking compliance with the Rules; and

(i)   deliver annual accountant's reports as required by the Rules.

In this chapter, we shall look at the way in which the Rules put these principles into practice.

9.3   WHO IS BOUND BY THE RULES?

Rule 4 sets out who is governed by the Rules. They extend very widely.

The practical effect is that the Rules apply equally to solicitors, registered European and foreign lawyers running or working in a firm regulated by the SRA, employees of the firm and to the firm itself.

Note that everyone working in a practice, such as cashiers and non-solicitor fee earners must comply with the Rules. Non-compliance by any member of staff will lead to the principals (defined to include a sole practitioner, a partner, an LLP or company, the principal solicitor or registered European lawyer (REL) employed by a non-solicitor employer (for example a law centre or commercial institution) and, in relation to any other body, a member of the governing body) being in breach of the Rules, since the principals of a practice are required by Rule 6 to ensure compliance. This duty also extends to directors of a company which is a recognised body and members of an LLP. It also extends to the compliance officer for finance and administration ('COFA') of a firm, whether a manager or non-manager.

The case of *Weston v The Law Society* (1998) *The Times*, 15 July is a salutary reminder of how careful those responsible for compliance in a firm must be. The Court of Appeal confirmed that it was appropriate to strike off a solicitor where no dishonesty was alleged. The solicitor in question was liable for breaches of the Rules committed by his fellow partners even though he had been unaware of them. Lord Bingham of Cornhill referred to the 'duty of anyone holding anyone else's money to exercise a proper stewardship in relation to it'.

The Rules do not apply to solicitors employed by bodies such as local authorities or when carrying out judicial functions, such as acting as a coroner (Rule 5).

The 2011 Rules apply (though only to a limited extent) to solicitors acting as:

(a)   liquidators;

(b)   trustees in bankruptcy;

(c)   Court of Protection receivers;

(d)   trustees of occupational pension schemes;

and to solicitors who hold client money jointly with a client, another solicitors' practice or a third party. Solicitors acting in such capacities are bound by some of the record-keeping requirements contained in Rules 29, 31 and 39.

9.4 CATEGORIES OF MONEY

9.4.1 Two categories

Rule 12 divides money into one of two categories:

(a)   client money;

(b)   office money.

The Rules also refer to 'out-of-scope money'. This is money received by a multi-disciplinary practice in relation to activities which are not regulated by the SRA. The SRA is not concerned with such money and the SRA Accounts Rules do not apply to it (except where it is part of a mixed receipt including office or client money). We do not consider it further in this book.

9.4.2 Client money

A client is defined in the Glossary as the person for whom you act.

Client money is money held or received for a client or as trustee *plus* all other money which is not office money (Rule 12.1(a)).

Note that the definition of client money goes beyond holding money for 'a client'. Rule 12.2 gives examples of client money. For instance, money held as a trustee or as stakeholder, bailee, agent, donee of a power of attorney, liquidator, trustee in bankruptcy or Court of Protection deputy, is client money. Money held to the sender's order is client money (Rule 12.3).

In *Challinor and Others v Juliet Bellis & Co and Another* [2013] EWHC 347 (Ch), Hildyard J made the point that a solicitor has a duty to clarify any ambiguity as to whom client money is held for.

Client money includes money received as 'an advance' or 'on account of costs generally' (Rule 12.2(e)), but not money received for costs in payment of a bill or agreed fee (see **12.7**). This is an important distinction.

Exercise 9A

(a)   Solicitor issues a bill to Client A for professional charges of £460. The client sends the solicitor a cheque for £460.
Is the £460 client money or office money?

(b)   Solicitor asks Client B for £200 generally on account of costs. The client sends the solicitor a cheque for £200.
Is the £200 client money or office money?

Where a solicitor receives money to cover disbursements which have not yet been paid, the money will normally be client money (see Rule 12.2(c) and (d)). (There is a limited exception to this; see **9.4.3** at (e).)

9.4.3 Office money

Office money is money which belongs to the solicitor or the practice. Under Rule 12.7 it includes the following:

(a)   Money held or received in connection with running the firm, for example PAYE or VAT on fees charged by the firm.

(b)   Interest earned on client money placed on a general deposit (under the Solicitors Act 1974, solicitors are entitled to keep such interest, although they will probably have to compensate the client – see **Chapter 15** below).

(c) Money received for fees due to the firm (often called profit costs) and VAT where a bill has been sent or a fee agreed (Rule 17.2 and 17.5).

(d) Money received to reimburse the solicitor for disbursements already paid on behalf of clients.

(e) Money received for disbursements which the firm has not yet paid but for which the firm has incurred liability, for example where a firm has an account at Land Registry and pays monthly for searches.

   However, money received for unpaid 'professional' disbursements is not office money, even where the firm has incurred liability. Professional disbursements are fees of counsel or other lawyer, or of a professional or other agent or expert, including the fees of interpreters, translators, process servers, surveyors and estate agents, but not travel agents. Money received in advance for such payments is classified as client money.

   The reason for the special treatment of unpaid professional disbursements is that professional disbursements often amount to large sums of money, whereas items such as search fees are normally small. It would not be right for firms to be allowed to keep large sums in the office bank account which are actually due to other people.

Example

You act for a client in connection with a land dispute. You carry out a Land Registry search. The Land Registry charges the search to the firm's credit account. You also instruct counsel to advise and receive counsel's invoice for the advice.

You send the client a bill showing your profit costs, the Land Registry search fee and counsel's fee. The client sends a cheque in payment.

The amount representing the profit costs and the unpaid Land Registry search fee is office money, but the amount representing the unpaid counsel's fee is client money.

(f) Money held in a client bank account and earmarked under Rule 17.3 for the payment of the firm's professional charges after the firm has sent the client a bill.

(g) Money held or received from the Legal Aid Agency as a regular payment under its contracting arrangements.

One of the principles set out in Rule 1 is the need to keep the money of clients separate from the firm's money. Rule 12.8 deals with a firm providing legal services to a principal of the firm, for example a partner, and states that any money received for the principal is office money. However, if the money is held for the principal *and another person* (eg, a spouse), it will be client money, as will money held for an assistant solicitor or non-solicitor employee.

Exercise 9B

Gemma and Wisan are solicitors in partnership together.

(a) Gemma asks Wisan to deal with the purchase of a house for her. Shortly before completion, Gemma gives Wisan the balance of the purchase price required for completion. Is the firm holding client money?

(b) Gemma is selling her house. Wisan is acting. The buyer pays a deposit to the firm to hold as stakeholder. Is the deposit client money?

9.5 USE OF THE CLIENT BANK ACCOUNT

9.5.1 Requirement for client bank account

Rule 13.1 requires a firm which holds or receives client money to keep at least one client bank account. The account must be in the name of the firm and include the word 'client' in full in the title (Rule 13.3). The omission of the word 'client' in the title is a serious breach of the

Rules. This is because the word 'client' must appear in the title of the account if section 85 of the Solicitors Act 1974 is to apply. Section 85(2) provides that a bank does not have any recourse or right against money in a client bank account in respect of any liability of the solicitor to the bank.

The client bank account must be kept at a bank or building society in England and Wales (Rule 13.4). A firm need have only one client bank account but will often choose to have more than one (eg, a current account and one or more deposit accounts).

Rule 13.5 states that a firm may have two types of client bank account:

(a)   a 'separate designated client account', which is a bank account for money relating to a single client, other person or trust and which includes in its title a reference to the identity of the client, other person or trust; and

(b)   a 'general client account', which is any other client bank account. This will contain money of a number of clients mixed together.

Separate designated accounts are used most frequently where a large amount is being held for a client for an extended period and the firm thinks it will make accounting to the client for interest easier. See **Chapter 15**.

A firm will need a separate bank account to deal with the firm's own money. This is normally referred to as the 'office account'.

9.5.2   Use of client bank account(s)

The primary rule relating to the use of the client bank account is Rule 14.

Rule 14.1 states that client money *must* without delay be paid into the client bank account and held there, except where the Rules provide to the contrary (see in particular Rule 17).

'Without delay' is defined in the Glossary as on the day of receipt or on the next working day.

Rule 14.2 states that only client money may be paid into or held in a client bank account, subject to five exceptions which are set out in Rule 14.2 itself and where it is expressly permitted elsewhere in the Rules (see Rules 17.1(c), 18.2(b) and 19.2(c)(ii)).

9.5.3   Use of client bank account for other money

9.5.3.1   Exceptions contained in Rule 14

The cases where office money may be paid into the client bank account under Rule 14.2 are as follows:

(a)   Rule 14.2(a) allows you to use office money to open a client bank account or to maintain it at an agreed level.

> **Examples**
>
> (1)   Smith and Brown are about to start practising in a partnership. As a preliminary, they need to open a client bank account and an office bank account. As yet, they are holding no client money, so they are allowed to use their own office money to open a client bank account.
>
> (2)   Smith and Brown have agreed with the bank that the balance on the client bank account will not be allowed to fall below £10,000. They will be allowed to pay in office money as and when required to maintain that balance.
>
> A bank might impose such a condition in return for allowing the firm to operate an overdraft on its office bank account.

Guidance note (iii) to Rule 14 makes the point that only a nominal sum is required to open or maintain an account, and that, in practice, banks will usually open (and, if instructed, keep open) accounts with nil balances.

(b)   Rule 14.2(b) allows you to advance money to a client or trust where the firm holds insufficient money in the client bank account and needs to make a payment for that client or trust. The money advanced becomes client money and subject to the ordinary rules applying to such money. (This is not really an example of using the client bank account for other money, as the money advanced becomes client money.)

(c)   Rule 14.2(c) allows you to pay office money into the client bank account to replace money withdrawn improperly.

Example

A junior employee withdraws money from the client bank account on behalf of a client, not realising that the firm is holding no money in the client bank account for that client. This means that money held for other clients has been used to make the payment, and this is a breach of the Rules.

As soon as the mistake is discovered, the firm should rectify it by paying office money into the client bank account.

Note: An efficient firm will organise a system which makes such a mistake impossible.

(d)   Rule 14.2(d) allows you to pay office money into the client bank account in lieu of interest which could have been earned on client money had the money of the client been placed on special deposit.

(e)   Rule 14.2(e) allows a cheque for damages for the client plus your professional charges and disbursements paid pursuant to a Conditional Fee Agreement to be paid into the client bank account.

Rule 14.3 requires firms to return left-over funds to clients promptly once the funds are no longer required. Firms that retain client money after a matter is concluded must inform the client of the amount retained and the reason for the retention (Rule 14.4). Written reminders must be sent at least once every 12 months.

Rule 14.5 says that firms regulated by the SRA 'must not provide banking facilities through a client account. Payments into, and transfers or withdrawals from, a client account must be in respect of instructions relating to an underlying transaction (and the funds arising therefrom) or to a service forming part of your normal regulated activities.' Money launderers who want to hide the illicit source of their funds will often try to pass money through a legitimate business. It is important to be alert to this danger.

EXAMPLE

You are working in your firm's property department. You have a client, Jack, who instructs you regularly to act on his behalf in property transactions which always fail to complete. He gives you large amounts to cover deposits and expenses which you pay into your client bank account and periodically return to him (less your moderate profit costs) using a firm cheque. He never queries your charges.

You should be suspicious of this pattern of behaviour and report the matter to your firm's money laundering officer.

9.5.3.2   SRA warning notice

On 18 December 2014 the SRA issued a warning notice to solicitors about the improper use of client accounts as a banking facility in breach of Rule 14.5. The notice is in response to a rise in breaches of Rule 14.5 and two recent High Court judgments concerning breaches.

The warning notice explained that using a client account as a banking facility increases the risk that solicitors may be assisting clients to launder money or avoid creditors when insolvent. Apart from these risks, using a client account as a bank is objectionable in itself if payments in and out of the account do not relate to any underlying transaction on which the firm is providing advice.

The two judgments dealt with in the SRA Guidance are *Fuglers & Others v SRA* [2014] EWHC 179 (Admin) and *Premji Naram Patel v SRA* [2012] EWHC 3373 (Admin).

In *Fuglers & Others v SRA*, Fuglers acted for a Football Club. The Club's bank account was withdrawn after a winding-up petition was brought by HM Revenue & Customs (HMRC). The Club was insolvent. Over a four-month period, approximately £10 million of the Club's money passed through Fuglers' client account. The Solicitors Disciplinary Tribunal (SDT) fined the firm £50,000 and its two managers £5,000 and £20,000. The High Court dismissed an appeal and confirmed the seriousness of the misconduct that had been found by the SDT, setting out three reasons why client accounts must not be used as banking facilities for clients:

(1) *Objectionable in itself.* It is objectionable in itself for solicitors to be carrying out or facilitating banking activities because they are to that extent not acting as solicitors. If solicitors are providing banking activities which are not linked to an underlying transaction, they are engaged in carrying out or facilitating day-to-day commercial trading in the same way as bankers. This is objectionable because solicitors are qualified and regulated in relation to their activities as solicitors, and are held out by the profession as being regulated in relation to such activities. They are not qualified to act as bankers and are not regulated as bankers. If solicitors could operate a banking facility for clients which was divorced from any legal work being undertaken for them, they would in effect be trading on the trust and reputation which they acquired through their status as solicitors in circumstances where such trust would not be justified by the regulatory regimen.

(2) *Risk of money laundering.* Allowing a client account to be used as a banking facility, unrelated to any underlying transaction which the solicitor is carrying out, carries with it the obvious risk that the account may be used unscrupulously by the client for money laundering. Rule 14.5 was intended to reduce this risk.

(3) *Insolvency or risk of insolvency.* Allowing a client account to be used as a banking facility in an insolvency context allows the client to achieve what would normally be impossible as banks withdraw facilities upon notification that there has been a winding-up petition. The solicitor is therefore giving the client a commercial service which would otherwise be unavailable to it through the device of using a solicitor as if he were a bank. Secondly there is the risk of favouring one creditor over another. A third reason is the risk of s 127 (of the Insolvency Act 1986) applying so as to require creditors to reimburse payments from the client account in a subsequent liquidation. A solicitor who knowingly makes or facilitates such payments may be subject to a personal liability, quite apart from the liability of the payee to reimburse the amount transferred.

In *Premji Naram Patel v SRA*, Mr Patel was a sole practitioner who acted for a company importing high value motor vehicles from Europe at a reduced price, to be sold in the UK for a substantial profit. Two significant investors were unwilling to pay funds directly to the company's owner because of past business failures. Instead investors paid money into the client account operated by Mr Patel. Mr Patel then transferred the relevant funds to the vehicle manufacturers directly.

The SDT imposed a fine of £7,500 on Mr Patel, who appealed to the High Court arguing that the second sentence of Rule 14.5 had to be read disjunctively: payments into and out of a client account have to relate to either (a) an underlying transaction, or (b) a service forming part of the solicitor's normal regulated activities. He submitted that the use of a client account is not in breach of the rule if its use relates to an underlying transaction, albeit not a legal transaction.

The court rejected that argument and upheld the fine imposed by the SDT, commenting that 'movements on client account must be in respect of instructions relating to an underlying transaction which is part of the accepted professional services of solicitors'.

Rule 14(5) has also been considered recently by the Office of the Public Guardian (OPG) in relation to solicitors who act as deputies for people who do not have capacity to manage their own property and financial affairs within the meaning of the Mental Capacity Act 2005. Such people are referred to as 'P' in the legislation.

The OPG was worried that solicitors who used the client bank account for P's funds might be infringing Rule 14(5). Having spoken to the SRA, it issued guidance in the form of *Public Guardian Practice Note 02/2016*, which states:

> We have clarified the purpose of this provision with the SRA and understand that it is intended to prevent client accounts being used for improper or criminal purposes including fraud and money laundering. It does not restrict the use of client accounts where there is a reasonable connection to an underlying legal transaction or recognised professional duties of a solicitor which you are providing.

However, the OPG then stated that it had identified reasons of its own for not using the client bank account for P's money:

(1) The Mental Capacity Act Code of Practice suggests that P's funds should not be 'mixed' with those of other people. If P's funds are placed in the general client bank account, they will inevitably be mixed with funds belonging to the firm's clients. This problem would not arise if the deputy used a separate client bank account designated with P's name and used only for P's funds.

(2) The OPG needs to be satisfied that deputies have proper safeguards in place to protect deputyship funds. Normally only the deputy should authorise payments from P's funds. Within a firm there are likely to be a number of authorised signatories for client bank accounts. It is likely to be more satisfactory to set up a separate bank account separate from the firm's client bank accounts which only the deputy and authorised individuals can draw on.

9.5.3.3 Other exceptions

The most important other Rules allowing non-client money to be paid into the client bank account are Rules 17 and 18. Rule 17 deals with the receipt of money in payment of a bill or agreed fee. It is very important and we look at it in detail at **9.6**.

Rule 18 deals with the receipt of 'mixed payments'. A mixed payment is one which includes client money as well as office money and/or out-of-scope money. Law firms often receive cheques from clients containing a mixture of office and client money. Rule 18 provides that mixed cheques should either be 'split' between the office and client bank account as appropriate, or the whole amount must be paid into the client bank account without delay.

Example

Client X sends a cheque made up of £235 to reimburse the solicitor for expenses paid on X's behalf and £12,000 required to complete the purchase of her house. The whole £12,235 may be paid into the client bank account. The £235 can then be transferred from the client bank account to the office bank account at a later stage.

Note: It would be a breach of the Rules to pay the £12,000 of client money into the office bank account.

Alternatively, it would be permissible to 'split' the cheque and pay £235 into the office bank account and £12,000 into the client bank account.

Although the Rules allow a cheque to be split between two bank accounts, it is rare for banks to agree to do this. Splitting cheques is, therefore, only rarely possible.

Where the cheque is not split, the office money element must be transferred out within 14 days of receipt.

9.5.4 Situations where client money may be withheld from the client bank account (1)

(a)   Rule 15.1(a) provides that client money may be held outside the client bank account (eg, in a safe or in an account in the firm's name which is not a client bank account, such as an account outside England and Wales), but only where this is for the client's own convenience and the client gives written instructions to the firm or the firm confirms instructions given by other means in writing.

Note: Money withheld from a client account under Rule 15.1(a) remains client money, and all the record-keeping provisions of Rule 29 will apply.

(b)   Under Rule 15.1(b), the client may instruct the firm to place the money in a bank or building society account opened in the name of the client or some other person designated by the client. The instruction must again be in writing or confirmed in writing.

Note: Once the money is paid into such an account, it ceases to be client money and is no longer subject to the record-keeping requirements of Rule 29.

(c)   Rule 16 provides that client money may be withheld in the following circumstances:

(i)   cash received and paid without delay in the ordinary course of business to the client or, on the client's behalf, to a third party, or paid in cash in the execution of a trust to a beneficiary or third party – it will be rare for law firms to receive cash in the ordinary course of business, and in fact you should be suspicious of a client who presents large amounts of cash, and should consider whether or not the transaction raises suspicions that it may involve money laundering or the proceeds of crime;

(ii)   a cheque or draft received and endorsed over in the ordinary course of business to the client or, on the client's behalf, to a third party, or without delay endorsed over in the execution of a trust to a beneficiary or third party;

(iii)   money withheld from a client bank account on instructions under Rule 15;

(iv)   money held for a trust which is paid into a non-client bank or building society account (such as an account outside England and Wales) or held in cash for the performance of the trustees' duties;

(v)   money received for unpaid professional disbursements and dealt with under Rule 17.1(b) (see **9.6.2** below);

(vi)   advance payments including client money received from the Legal Aid Agency (LAA), provided the LAA instructs in writing that this can be done (see Rule 19.1(a));

(vii)   money for unpaid professional disbursements received from the LAA and dealt with under Rule 19(1)(b) (see **9.6.4** below);

(viii)   money withheld on the written authorisation of the SRA (only rarely will such authorisation be given). The SRA is able to impose a condition that the firm pays the money to a charity which gives an indemnity against any later legitimate claims to the money.

Note: Even though client money is withheld from the client bank account under Rule 16, dealings with it must be recorded in accordance with Rule 29. See **9.8.2** below.

9.5.5 When can money be taken out of the client bank account? (Rule 20)

9.5.5.1 How much can be spent?

You must not withdraw more money from the client bank account on behalf of a client (or trust) than is being held there for that client (or trust) (Rule 20.6). For example, if you hold

£500 for Client A and £300 for Client B in the client bank account, you can spend only £300 from the client bank account for Client B.

There is one limited exception provided by Rule 20.7. This allows you to make an excessive payment from a general client bank account for a particular client or trust where you hold sufficient money in a separate bank account designated for that client or trust and immediately transfer sufficient money from the separate designated account to the general client bank account.

9.5.5.2   For what purposes can money be withdrawn from the client bank account?

Rule 20.1 provides that *client money* can be withdrawn from the client bank account where it is:

(a)   properly required for a payment to or on behalf of the client (or person for whom the money is held);

(b)   properly required for a payment in the execution of a particular trust;

(c)   properly required for payment of a disbursement on behalf of the client or trust;

(d)   properly required in full or partial reimbursement of money spent on behalf of the client or trust – money is 'spent' when a cheque is dispatched or where payments are charged to a credit account (eg, search fees, taxi fares);

(e)   transferred to another client account (eg, a separate designated account);

(f)   withdrawn on the client's instructions: the instructions must be for the client's convenience and given in writing or be confirmed by you in writing;

(g)   transferred to a non-client bank account or retained in cash by a trustee in the proper performance of the trustees' duties;

(h)   a refund of money advanced by the firm to the client to fund a payment (under Rule 14.2(b));

(i)   money which has been paid into the account in breach of the Rules – it must be withdrawn 'promptly' (Rule 20.5);

(j)   left-over balances not exceeding £500 which are paid to charity in accordance with the requirements of Rule 20.2 (these include making adequate attempts to return the money to its rightful owner);

(k)   money withdrawn on the written authorisation of the SRA.

Left-over client account balances may seem a small matter. However a recent SRA investigation illustrates that this is far from the case. An inspection of a City firm's accounts by the SRA's Forensic Investigation team concluded that there were no less than 2,007 client matters with a client ledger balance totalling £15,230,900 where there had been no movement on the relevant client ledger for a period of at least one year. Subsequent analysis by the firm identified that, of this amount, £7,324,276 related to inactive matters whilst further client ledger balances totalling £1,609,648 remained under review.

In May 2013 the firm circulated its written policy on clearing residual client ledger balances to all of the firm's UK members. A course of action was agreed between the firm and the SRA. An action plan setting out the process and deadlines for clearing the residual balances was approved by the SRA in January 2014.

One partner who became his department's risk manager with responsibility for implementing the action plan failed to do so correctly. Instead, the dormant balances held on the client bank account were transferred to the firm's office bank account after being applied against invoices that had been raised improperly on those matters. In one instance, the partner had transferred time on an unconnected matter, which could not be recovered and was destined to be written off by the firm, to one of the inactive matters before raising an invoice and transferring funds from client to office bank account.

The partner was suspended from practice for a period of three months from 20 November 2017. Additionally, he has agreed to pay the SRA costs of almost £18,000 and faces strict controls on his return to practice for a period of two years, including not being able to act as a sole practitioner, partner, member or director of a firm. He will not be allowed to hold client money or operate a client or office bank account or to authorise payments from a client bank account. Finally, he will not be permitted to act as either a COLP or a COFA for the same period of two years.

Rule 20.3 provides that *office money* may be withdrawn from the client bank account where it:

(a)   was properly paid in to open or maintain an account and is no longer required;

(b)   is properly required to pay the firm's fees and disbursements and the firm has sent a bill or other written notification;

(c)   was paid into the client bank account under Rule 17.1(c) and needs to be withdrawn within 14 days (see below);

(d)   was part of an unsplit cheque;

(e)   was paid into the account in breach of Rules – it must be withdrawn 'promptly' upon discovery (Rule 20.5).

Note: Where a firm wants to transfer money from the client bank account for the firm's own professional charges, the solicitor must send a bill or other written notification. The firm must transfer the money earmarked for costs (which becomes office money after the issue of the bill) within 14 days (Rule 17.2 and 17.3).

9.5.5.3   How is the money withdrawn?

Firms must have appropriate systems and procedures governing withdrawals from the client bank account, in particular as to who should be permitted to sign withdrawals. A withdrawal must be authorised by a suitable person. Rule 21.2 states that a non-manager owner or a non-employee owner of a licensed body is not an appropriate person to be a signatory on client account and must not be permitted by the firm to act in this way. Guidance note (i) states that someone who has no day-to-day involvement in the business of the practice is unlikely to be regarded as a suitable signatory because of their lack of proximity to client matters.

If the money is withdrawn in favour of a solicitor or the firm, the payment from the client bank account must be by cheque or by transfer into the office bank account or a personal account. The withdrawal must not be in cash. This is to ensure that it is easy to see the amount of client money taken by the practice. See Rule 21.4.

> **Example**
>
> A solicitor is owed £100 in professional charges by Client A and owes £100 to a tradesman. The solicitor is holding £500 of A's money in the client bank account.
>
> Provided the solicitor delivers a bill or other written notification of costs, the solicitor may withdraw £100 of the money held for A from the client bank account.
>
> However, it cannot be withdrawn in cash. It must either be a cheque in favour of the solicitor, or a transfer to a personal bank account or the office bank account.

Instructions to the bank or building society to withdraw money from a client account may be given over the telephone, provided a specific authority has been signed in accordance with this Rule before the instructions are given. It is, of course, important that there are appropriate in-built safeguards, such as passwords, to give the greatest protection possible for client money. Suitable safeguards will also be needed for practices which operate a CHAPS terminal or other form of electronic instruction for payment.

A traditional direct debit or standing order should not be set up on a client account because of the need for a specific authority for each withdrawal. The guidance notes to Rule 21 explain that it is possible for firms to authorise the Land Registry to take direct debits because applications for registration are signed; provided the signature complies with the firm's systems and procedures set up under Rule 21, it will constitute the specific authority required by Rule 21.1.

9.6 OPTIONS AVAILABLE FOR DEALING WITH MONEY RECEIVED IN PAYMENT OF A BILL (RULES 17 AND 18)

Rule 17 is quite complicated and you need to study it carefully. It provides that when a firm receives money in payment of a bill or other written notification of costs, there are various options. These are set out below.

9.6.1 Determine the composition of the receipt without delay and deal with it appropriately (Rule 17.1(a))

In order to determine the composition of the receipt, you need to remember Rule 12, which deals with how to classify money:

(a) In particular, remember that money received to repay the solicitor for disbursements already paid is office money.

(b) Money received to cover the cost of unpaid disbursements where the solicitor has incurred liability to pay is office money, unless the disbursements are 'professional disbursements'.

(c) Money received for unpaid professional disbursements, even where the solicitor has incurred liability to pay, is client money.

When proceeding under Rule 17.1(a), a receipt which is:

(a) entirely office money will be paid into the office bank account;

(b) entirely client money (eg, money for unpaid professional disbursements) will be paid into the client bank account;

(c) a mixture of office and client money will be split or all paid into the client bank account under Rule 18.

Rule 17.1(b)–(d) go on to give alternatives.

9.6.2 Receipts consisting of office money (and/or out-of-scope money) and client money in the form of unpaid professional disbursements for which the solicitor is liable (Rule 17.1(b))

You can place the entire amount in the office bank account *provided*, by the end of the second working day following receipt, you either pay the professional disbursements or transfer the amount required for the disbursement to the client bank account.

The effect of this option is to make life a little easier for law firms. Where a receipt consists only of these two elements, the whole amount can be paid into the office bank account and the payment of the disbursement can be made from that account. This reduces the number of transfers made between client and office bank account and the consequent risk of errors.

Note: This option cannot be used if liability for professional disbursements has not yet been incurred, or where the receipt includes other types of client money.

9.6.3 Any receipt irrespective of its composition (Rule 17.1(c))

You can always elect to pay any receipt irrespective of its composition into the client bank account. Any office money element must be transferred out of the client bank account within 14 days of receipt.

Exercise 9C

A firm issues a bill which consists of the following items:

	£
Firm's Professional Charges	200
VAT	40
Court Fees (Paid)	80
Land Charges Search (unpaid)[1]	20
Counsel's Fees (unpaid)[1]	480
	820

[1]The solicitor has incurred liability for these items.

What options are available to the firm when dealing with the receipt of £820?

9.6.4 Receipts from the Legal Aid Agency (Rule 17.1(d))

Rule 17(1)(d) deals with money received from the Legal Aid Agency (LAA) in two situations.

A payment by the LAA for the firm's fees and disbursements can be placed in the office bank account regardless of whether it consists wholly of office money or is mixed with client money in the form of advance payments for fees or disbursements, or money for unpaid disbursements, provided the disbursements are paid or the money for them is transferred to the client bank account within 14 days of receipt (see Rule 19.1(b)).

Note also Rule 19.1(a) which allows an advance payment by the LAA in anticipation of work to be carried out to be placed in the office bank account, even if it includes client money, provided the LAA gives written instructions that it should be done.

9.6.5 Receipts pursuant to a Conditional Fee Agreement (Rule 17.1.(e))

A cheque received in pursuance of a Conditional Fee Agreement which is a mixture of damages, fees and disbursements can be paid into the client bank account under Rule 14.2(e). Rule 17.1(e) requires the money for the fees and disbursements to be transferred out of the client bank account within 14 days of receipt.

9.7 DEPOSIT INTEREST: WHEN MUST INTEREST BE PAID?

Clients are usually – though not always – entitled to interest on client money held for them by solicitors.

Rule 22 provides that firms must account for interest to clients where it is fair and reasonable for them to do so. Rule 23 sets out the basis on which interest should be calculated.

This topic is dealt with in detail in **Chapter 15**.

9.8 WHAT RECORDS MUST A SOLICITOR KEEP?

9.8.1 Importance of records

The SRA is just as concerned that solicitors should keep the correct records as that they should do the correct things. It is impossible to check what is happening if records are inadequate.

9.8.2 The basic records

Rule 29 sets out the basic requirements for everyday transactions:

29.1   You must at all times keep accounting records properly written up to show your dealings with:

(a)   client money received, held or paid by you; including client money held outside a client account under rule 15.1(a) or rule 16.1(d); and

(b)   any office money relating to any client or trust matter.

29.2   All dealings with client money must be appropriately recorded:

(a)   in a client cash account or in a record of sums transferred from one client ledger account to another; and

(b)   on the client side of a separate client ledger account for each client (or other person, or trust).

No other entries may be made in these records.

29.3   If separate designated client accounts are used:

(a)   a combined cash account must be kept in order to show the total amount held in separate designated client accounts; and

(b)   a record of the amount held for each client (or other person, or trust) must be made either in a deposit column of a client ledger account, or on the client side of a client ledger account kept specifically for a separate designated client account, for each client (or other person, or trust).

29.4   All dealings with office money relating to any client matter, or to any trust matter, must be appropriately recorded in an office cash account and on the office side of the appropriate client ledger account.

9.9 OBTAINING AND DELIVERY OF ACCOUNTANTS' REPORTS

Firms which have, at any time during an accounting period, held or received client money must normally obtain an accountant's report for that accounting period within six months of the end of the accounting period; and, if the report has been qualified, deliver it to the SRA within six months of the end of the accounting period (Rule 32A).

Rule 32A(1A) provides that an accountant's report is not required if:

(a)   all of the client money held or received during an accounting period is money held or received from the Legal Aid Agency; or

(b)   in the accounting period, the client money held or received does not exceed an average of £10,000 and a maximum of £250,000, or the equivalent in foreign currency.

Unsurprisingly, the SRA retains power (under Rule 32.2) to require an accountant's report which would not otherwise be required under the Rules if it has reason to believe that it is in the public interest to do so.

SUMMARY

(1) A firm must keep money held for other people separate from the firm's own money (Rule 1).

(2) There are two categories of money (Rule 12):

    (a) client money;

    (b) office money.

(3) Subject to exceptions, client money must be paid into a client bank account without delay (Rule 14).

(4) Subject to exceptions, office money cannot be paid into the client bank account (Rule 14).

(5) Rule 17 gives options for dealing with receipts where a bill has been sent.

(6) A solicitor must never withdraw more client money for a client than is held in the client bank account for that client (Rule 20).

(7) Clients are usually – though not always – entitled to interest on client money held for them by solicitors (Rule 22).

(8) All dealings with client money must be recorded (Rule 29).

SOLUTIONS

Exercise 9A

(a)   Office money. It is a specific payment of a bill.

(b)   Client money. It is generally on account of costs.

Exercise 9B

(a)   No. The only person entitled to the money (until completion) is a partner in the firm.

(b)   Yes. The partner in the firm is not the only person entitled to the money. Stakeholder money is held jointly for both buyer and seller awaiting the event.

Exercise 9C

First identify the composition of the receipt:

- Professional charges and VAT – office money.
- Paid court fees – office money.
- Unpaid search fee – office money (liability has been incurred).
- Unpaid counsel's fee – client money (professional unpaid disbursements).

(1)   Under Rule 17.1(a) and Rule 18, the receipt can be split. The office money element is paid into the office bank account, the client money element into the client bank account.

(2)   Alternatively, under Rule 17.1(c), the whole amount is paid into the client bank account, but the office money element must be transferred out within 14 days.

(3)   The whole amount may be paid into the office bank account under Rule 17.1(b), provided the counsel's fee is paid or the money required for it is transferred to the client bank account by the end of the second working day following receipt.

CHAPTER 10

ENTRIES FOR RECORDING SIMPLE CLIENT TRANSACTIONS

LEARNING OUTCOMES

After reading this chapter you will be able to:

- explain why a firm providing legal services needs two separate sets of accounts
- explain what those accounts look like
- deal appropriately with receipts and payments of both office and client money
- make appropriate entries to deal with professional charges and VAT when issuing a bill.

10.1 INTRODUCTION

The SRA Accounts Rules are primarily concerned with keeping client money safe and ensuring that proper records are kept to allow errors and discrepancies to be picked up on inspection by reporting accountants and the SRA. There are, therefore, detailed rules relating to the handling of money during client transactions and its recording. This chapter looks at the Rules relating to recording a simple client transaction.

10.2 THE TWO SETS OF ACCOUNTING RECORDS

In order to control dealings with client money, a more sophisticated set of day-to-day accounts is needed for a firm providing legal services than for most other businesses. It is essential that all the records of 'client money' dealings are clearly separated from the records of the ordinary 'office money' dealings of the firm. Rule 29 sets out the recording requirements of the Rules.

One way of understanding the system is to think of a law firm as carrying on two separate businesses with two separate sets of accounts. Thus, the law firm would need one set (Set A) for the first business – say the business which handles client money – and another set (Set B) for the second – say the firm's ordinary business accounts. This explains the reason for one of the fundamental bookkeeping rules for firms providing legal services. The two sets of accounts are entirely separate. Thus, you cannot enter a debit on one set of accounts (Set A) and a credit on the other set (Set B).

10.3   THE FORMAT OF THE ACCOUNTS

10.3.1   Requirements as to formats

Law firms may choose any of the various systems on the market which enable the recording requirements of Rule 29 to be satisfied. They all have one thing in common – they are based on the principles of double entry bookkeeping.

10.3.2   The dual cash account

Anyone running a business will need a cash account to record dealings with each bank account. A law firm is *required* by Rule 29.2 to keep a cash account for dealings with the client bank account and by Rule 29.4 to keep a separate cash account for dealings with the office bank account. Thus, the law firm will need (at least) two separate cash accounts. To ease the administrative burden of actually moving from a cash account in one place to another cash account in a different place and back again, the normal format is to have the two individual cash accounts on the same page next to one another. One set of columns for 'Date' and 'Details' will do for both accounts.

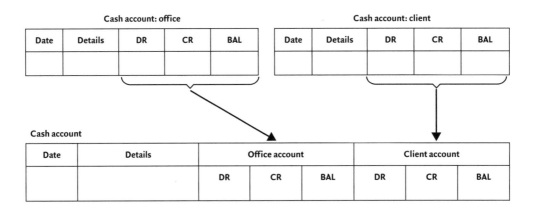

10.3.3   The dual ledger account for each client

To comply with Rule 29.2 and 29.4, there must be two ledger accounts for each client: one to show dealings with office money on behalf of that client, and another to show dealings with client money for that client. As with the two cash accounts, it is usual to combine the two ledger accounts to show them side by side.

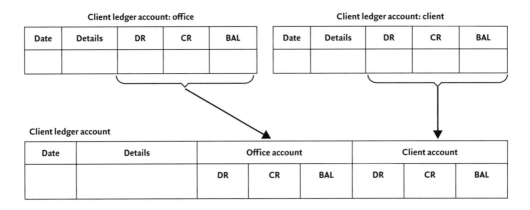

10.4   DEALING WITH RECEIPTS OF MONEY

First decide whether you are receiving office money or client money. The receipt can then be recorded in the correct section.

The entry in the cash account for a receipt is a DR entry.

The corresponding CR entry is in the ledger account of the client from whom, or on whose behalf, the money is received.

Receipts of client money will be held for the relevant client in the client bank account.

Receipts of office money will reduce the indebtedness of the relevant client to the firm.

Note: In the examples that follow the running balances on the cash account are not completed. The amount of the balance depends on the total funds held in the bank at the time. A receipt will increase the balance, and a payment will reduce it. The balance on the cash account is not referable to any one client.

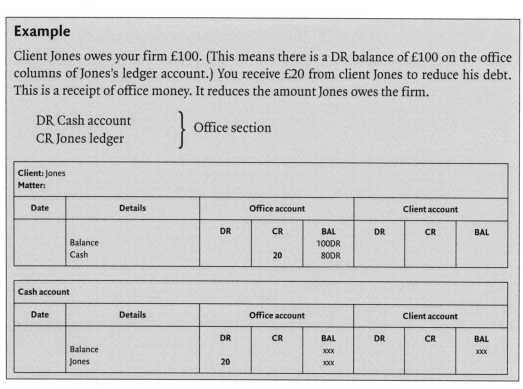

Example

Client Jones owes your firm £100. (This means there is a DR balance of £100 on the office columns of Jones's ledger account.) You receive £20 from client Jones to reduce his debt. This is a receipt of office money. It reduces the amount Jones owes the firm.

DR Cash account
CR Jones ledger } Office section

Client: Jones
Matter:

Date	Details	Office account			Client account		
		DR	CR	BAL	DR	CR	BAL
	Balance			100DR			
	Cash		20	80DR			

Cash account

Date	Details	Office account			Client account		
		DR	CR	BAL	DR	CR	BAL
	Balance			xxx			xxx
	Jones	20		xxx			

Example

You receive £300 from client Brown on account of costs. This is a receipt of client money. The firm will hold the money for Brown.

DR Cash account
CR Brown ledger } Client section

Client: Brown
Matter:

Date	Details	Office account			Client account		
		DR	CR	BAL	DR	CR	BAL
	Cash					300	300CR

Cash account

Date	Details	Office account			Client account		
		DR	CR	BAL	DR	CR	BAL
	Balance						xxx
	Brown				300		xxx

10.5   DEALING WITH PAYMENTS OF MONEY

First, decide whether you are making the payment from the office or client bank account so that the payment can be recorded in the appropriate cash account.

The entry on the cash account for a payment is a CR entry.

The corresponding double entry is a DR in the ledger account of the client on whose behalf the payment is made.

If the payment is made from the office bank account, the resulting DR balance on the office columns of the client ledger will show that the client owes the firm money, ie, is *a debtor*. If the payment is made from the client bank account, it will reduce the amount held for the client (ie, it will reduce the CR balance on the client columns of the client ledger).

Remember that, under Rule 20.6, a payment must not be made from a general client bank account unless the firm is holding sufficient funds in its general client bank accounts for that client.

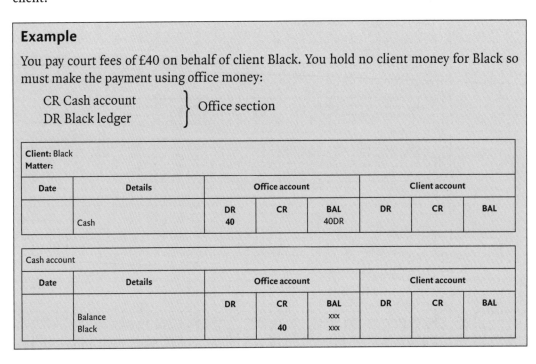

Example

You pay court fees of £40 on behalf of client Black. You hold no client money for Black so must make the payment using office money:

CR Cash account }
DR Black ledger   } Office section

Client: Black
Matter:

Date	Details	Office account			Client account		
		DR	**CR**	**BAL**	**DR**	**CR**	**BAL**
	Cash	40		40DR			

Cash account

Date	Details	Office account			Client account		
		DR	**CR**	**BAL**	**DR**	**CR**	**BAL**
	Balance			xxx			
	Black		40	xxx			

Example

You are holding client money of £500 for client White. You make a payment of £400 for client White.

You hold sufficient client money for White to be able to make the payment using client money.

CR Cash account }
DR White ledger   } Client section

Client: White
Matter:

Date	Details	Office account			Client account		
		DR	**CR**	**BAL**	**DR**	**CR**	**BAL**
	Balance						500CR
	Cash				400		100CR

Cash account							
Date	Details	Office account			Client account		
		DR	CR	BAL	DR	CR	BAL
	Balance White						xxx
						400	xxx

Exercise 10A

You act for Smith. Record the following events on Smith's ledger account and on the cash account.

Note: Assume that the balances on the cash account are: office £2,000 DR, client £20,000 DR. Assume the balances on Smith's ledger account are zero.

June

1 Smith sends £1,000 generally on account of costs.

    Note: This is a receipt of client money because it is not in payment of a bill for profit costs nor in reimbursement of an expense.

2 Firm pays £100 on Smith's behalf.

    Note: This can be paid from the client bank account since sufficient funds are available.

4 Firm pays £900 on Smith's behalf.

    Note: This can be paid from the client bank account since sufficient funds are available.

6 Firm pays £200 on Smith's behalf.

    Note: This must be paid from the office bank account since no funds are held for Smith.

8 Firm pays £400 on Smith's behalf.

    Note: This must be paid from the office bank account since no funds are held for Smith.

10 Smith sends firm £600 in reimbursement of expenses incurred.

    Note: Subject to Rule 17(1)(c), this must be paid into the office bank account since it is a receipt of office money.

10.6 DEALING WITH PROFESSIONAL CHARGES

When the firm issues a bill to the client, it will include an item for professional charges (often called 'profit costs') and VAT on those charges. The solicitor will want to make entries in the accounts to show that the client owes the firm the charges and VAT.

At this stage, there is no movement of cash, so no entry is made in the cash account.

On the client ledger account, the bookkeeper must make DR entries for professional charges and VAT in the office section. The entries must be made in the office section. This is because the purpose of the DR entries is to show that the client owes money to the firm. You are not yet recording the receipt of cash.

The corresponding CR entries are made on the profit costs account and HMRC account respectively. The profit costs ledger account is an income account; at the end of the year, the balance on this account will show the amount the firm has billed for professional charges. The HMRC ledger account shows how much the firm owes HMRC in VAT (see **Chapter 12** for a discussion of the way in which firms account to HMRC for VAT charged to clients).

Example

Firm issues a bill for £400 profit costs plus £80 VAT to client Smith.

DR Smith ledger account £400

DR Smith ledger account £80

CR Profit costs account £400

CR HMRC account £80

(See **Chapter 12** for details of VAT.)

Client: Smith
Matter:

Date	Details	Office account			Client account		
		DR	CR	BAL	DR	CR	BAL
	Costs	400		400DR			
	VAT	80		480			

Profit costs

Date	Details	DR	CR	BAL
	Smith		400	400CR

HMRC

Date	Details	DR	CR	BAL
	Smith		80	80CR

Exercise 10B

Prepare the cash account and client ledger account for Rex to record the following events.

You act for Rex in a litigation matter. The balances on the cash account are office £1,000DR, client £1,000DR. The balances on Rex's ledger account are zero.

June

1   Rex sends you £200 on account of costs.

    Note: This is a receipt of client money because it is not in payment of a bill nor in reimbursement of an expense.

2   You pay court fees £20.

    Note: This can be paid from the client bank account since sufficient funds are available.

5   You pay expert witness £180.

    Note: This can be paid from the client bank account since sufficient funds are available.

7   You pay another expert witness £150.

    Note: There is no client money available. The payment must be made from the office bank account.

10   Matter is settled. You receive a cheque from the defendant for £5,000 in full and final settlement. This cheque is made out to the firm.

    Note: The firm has received client money. (Had the cheque been made out to the client, the firm would simply have forwarded it to the client. It would not have been possible to pay the cheque into a bank account in the firm's name.) You could split the cheque and take £150 in reimbursement of the expense incurred. However, we shall pay it all into the client bank account.

12   You send client a cheque for £5,000.

      Note: This is a payment of client money.

14   You send Rex a bill. Profit costs £200. VAT £40. You ask for the amount necessary to reimburse you for expenses incurred.

16   Rex sends you amount requested on 14 June.

      Note: Rex will send £390 (£240 + £150), and this will be a receipt of office money. Subject to Rule 17.1(c), it must be paid into the office bank account.

SUMMARY

(1) A law firm will have two cash accounts: one for office money and one for client money. They are frequently shown side by side.

(2) A law firm will have two client ledger accounts: one for office money dealings and one for client money dealings. They are frequently shown side by side.

(3) When dealing with cash receipts or payments, decide first whether it involves office money or client money, then record the receipt or payment in the appropriate section of the accounts.

(4) The entries for a receipt are:

- CR on client ledger
- DR on cash account

in the office or client section as appropriate.

The entries for a payment are:

- DR on client ledger
- CR on cash account

in the office or client section as appropriate.

(5) When a bill is sent entries are made:

    (a) to record professional charges with a DR entry in the office section of the client ledger and a CR entry in the profit costs account;

    (b) to record VAT with a DR entry in the office section of the client ledger and a CR entry in the HMRC account.

SOLUTIONS

Exercise 10A

Client: Smith
Matter:

Date	Details	Office account			Client account		
		DR	CR	BAL	DR	CR	BAL
June							
1	Cash. On a/c costs					1,000	1,000CR
2	Cash				100		900
4	Cash				900		–
6	Cash	200		200DR			
8	Cash	400		600			
10	Cash		600	–			

Cash account

Date	Details	Office account			Client account		
		DR	CR	BAL	DR	CR	BAL
June	Balances			2,000DR			20,000DR
1	Smith. On a/c costs				1,000		21,000
2	Smith					100	20,900
4	Smith					900	20,000
6	Smith		200	1,800			
8	Smith		400	1,400			
10	Smith						
	Reimbursement						
	expenses	600		2,000			

Exercise 10B

Client: Rex
Matter: Litigation

Date	Details	Office account			Client account		
		DR	CR	BAL	DR	CR	BAL
June							
1	Cash. On a/c costs					200	200CR
2	Cash. Court fees				20		180
5	Cash. Expert witness				180		–
7	Cash. Expert witness	150		150DR			
10	Cash. Settlement					5,000	5,000
12	Cash. To client				5,000		–
14	Costs	200					
	VAT	40		390			
16	Cash. Amount due		390	–			

Cash account

Date	Details	Office account			Client account		
		DR	CR	BAL	DR	CR	BAL
June	Balance			1,000DR			1,000DR
1	Rex. On a/c costs				200		1,200
2	Rex. Court fees					20	1,180
5	Rex. Expert witness					180	1,000
7	Rex. Expert witness		150	850			
10	Rex. Settlement				5,000		6,000
12	Rex. Amount sent					5,000	1,000
16	Rex. Amount requested	390		1,240			

Note: There will be credit entries on the profit costs account and HMRC account to record the fact that the client was charged £200 profit costs and £40 VAT.

TRANSFERS

> **LEARNING OUTCOMES**
>
> After reading this chapter you will be able to:
>
> - explain the difference between cash transfers and inter-client transfers
> - make appropriate entries to record each kind of transfer.

11.1 INTRODUCTION

The SRA Accounts Rules require firms to show exactly how much money is held for each client at any time. Hence, if money is withdrawn from the client bank account and paid into the office bank account, for example to pay the firm's charges, this must be recorded. This type of transfer is called a cash transfer.

If a firm is holding money in the client bank account for one client and stops holding the money to the order of the first client and starts holding it to the order of a second client, the change in ownership of the money must be recorded. This type of transfer is called an inter-client transfer.

In this chapter you will study the entries required to record cash transfers and inter-client transfers.

11.2 CASH TRANSFERS

11.2.1 Why might such a transfer occur?

11.2.1.1 Reimbursement of an expense incurred

A firm can transfer client money from the client bank account to the office bank account to reimburse the firm for money spent on behalf of the client (Rule 20.1(d)). It is not necessary for the firm to issue a bill of costs before making the transfer. Money is 'spent' for this purpose when the firm sends a cheque to pay an expense or charges an expense, such as taxi fares or search fees, to the firm's account. See guidance note (i)(b) to Rule 20.

The money in the client bank account is client money until the firm decides to make reimbursement, so there is no requirement to make the transfer within 14 days of incurring liability for the expense.

11.2.1.2 Payment of firm's professional fees

A firm can transfer money from the client bank account to the office bank account for its own professional fees, including any VAT element, provided a bill has been issued (or a fee agreed in accordance with Rule 17.5). Once a firm has given a client a bill, the money earmarked for costs becomes office money and must be transferred from the client to the office bank account within 14 days (see Rule 17.3). According to guidance note (viii) to Rule 17, the firm will be regarded as earmarking money in the client bank account for the payment of costs at the time the bill is submitted unless it indicates that the client is to send a separate payment.

11.2.1.3   Other

A firm can transfer office money to the client bank account in the circumstances set out in Rule 14, which include:

(a)   to open or maintain the client bank account;

(b)   to advance money to a client or trust where the solicitor needs to make a payment on behalf of the client or trust and insufficient client money is available (once advanced, the money becomes client money);

(c)   to replace money withdrawn in breach of Rule 20;

(d)   to allow the client a sum in lieu of interest.

11.2.2   Recording a transfer from client to office bank account

This is done in two parts, as follows:

(1)   Record the payment of money from the client bank account:

> CR cash account
> DR client's ledger account   } Client section

(2)   Record the receipt of money into the office bank account:

> DR cash account
> CR client's ledger account   } Office section

Example

You act for Green. On 10 April, you receive £800 from Green on account of costs to be incurred. On 26 April, you send Green a bill for £400 plus £80 VAT. On 28 April, you transfer £480 from the client bank account to the office bank account.

Entries are as follows.

(1)   The £800 is client money. It will be paid into the client bank account and recorded in Green's ledger account and in the cash account.

Client: Green
Matter: Miscellaneous

Date	Details	Office account			Client account		
		DR	CR	BAL	DR	CR	BAL
Apr 10	Cash: From Green. On account					800	800CR

Cash account

Date	Details	Office account			Client account		
		DR	CR	BAL	DR	CR	BAL
Apr 10	Green				800		xxx

(2)   When the bill is issued, the entries for costs and VAT will be DR entries on Green's ledger account (remember that entries for costs and VAT on the issue of a bill are always debited in the *office* section to show that the client owes the firm money).

The CR entries will be on the profit costs and HMRC account which we have not shown.

Client: Green
Matter: Miscellaneous

Date	Details	Office account			Client account		
		DR	CR	BAL	DR	CR	BAL
Apr 10	Cash: From Green. On account					800	800CR
	Costs	400		400DR			
26	VAT	80		480			

Cash account

Date	Details	Office account			Client account		
		DR	CR	BAL	DR	CR	BAL
Apr 10	Green				800		xxx

(3)   The payment from client account will look like this:

DR Green's ledger
CR Cash
}   Client section

Client: Green
Matter: Miscellaneous

Date	Details	Office account			Client account		
		DR	CR	BAL	DR	CR	BAL
Apr 10	Cash: From Green. On account					800	800CR
26	Costs	400		400DR			
	VAT	80		480			
28	Cash. Transfer from client account				480		320

Cash account

Date	Details	Office account			Client account		
		DR	CR	BAL	DR	CR	BAL
Apr 10	Green				800		xxx
28	Green					480	

(4)   The receipt into office account will look like this:

CR Green's ledger
DR Cash
}   Office section

Client: Green
Matter: Miscellaneous

Date	Details	Office account			Client account		
		DR	CR	BAL	DR	CR	BAL
Apr 10	Cash: From Green. On account					800	800CR
26	Costs	400		400DR			
	VAT	80		480			
28	Cash. Transfer from client account				480		320
	Cash. Transfer to office account		480	–			

Cash account

Date	Details	Office account			Client account		
		DR	CR	BAL	DR	CR	BAL
							xxx
Apr 10	Green				800		
28	Green					480	
	Green	480					

Note: For the sake of convenience, the payment from the client bank account and the receipt into the office bank account are often shown on the same line as set out below:

Client: Green
Matter: Miscellaneous

Date	Details	Office account			Client account		
		DR	CR	BAL	DR	CR	BAL
Apr 10	Cash: From Green. On account					800	800CR
26	Costs	400		400DR			
	VAT	80		480			
28	Cash. Transfer from client account to office account		480	–	480		320

Cash account

Date	Details	Office account			Client account		
		DR	CR	BAL	DR	CR	BAL
							xxx
Apr 10	Green				800		
10	Green. Transfer from client to office account	480				480	

11.3 INTER-CLIENT TRANSFERS

11.3.1 What is happening?

Sometimes, a firm which is holding money in the client bank account for Client A stops holding that money for Client A and starts holding it for Client B. An example would be where A owes B money and asks the firm to hold the money for B. No money is taken out of the client bank account. However, the firm must make changes to the firm's internal accounts to record the change in whom the money is held for. This is necessary to comply with the principle set out in Rule 1.2(f) that the firm's accounts must show accurately the position with regard to the money held for each client. This type of transfer is sometimes referred to as a 'paper' transfer or an 'inter-client' transfer.

11.3.2 Requirements

The transfer must comply with Rule 27.1. This means that the solicitor can make the paper entries only if the money could have been:

(a) withdrawn from the client bank account on the instructions of the first client under Rule 20.1; and

(b) paid into the client bank account on the instructions of the second client under Rule 14.

If the transfer is a 'private loan', the firm must have the prior written authority of both clients (Rule 27.2). This is not necessary if the transfer is for other purposes, for example, a gift or in discharge of a debt. A private loan is any loan other than one provided by an institution which provides loans on standard terms in the normal course of its activities.

11.3.3 Recording the transfer

The transfer must be shown in the client ledger accounts of both clients:

> DR Client ledger account of first client
> CR Client ledger account of second client

In addition, Rule 29(2)(a) requires the firm to keep a separate record of all inter-client transfers. This is usually referred to as a 'transfer journal' or a 'transfer sheet'. There are no requirements as to the form of this separate record.

Example

You are instructed by Anne Brown to collect a debt of £10,000 from White & Co. You write to White & Co requesting payment. On 7 August, you receive a cheque from White & Co for £10,000 in payment of the debt.

You already act for Anne's sister, Jane Brown, who is buying a flat. On 9 August, Anne tells you that she is making a gift of £1,000 to Jane and asks you to hold £1,000 of her money to the order of Jane. You make the necessary inter-client transfer.

Entries are as follows.

(1)   When the £10,000 is received, it is client money held to the order of Anne. It will be recorded like this:

Cash account							
Date	Details	Office account			Client account		
		DR	CR	BAL	DR	CR	BAL
Aug 7	Anne Brown				10,000		xxx

Client: Anne Brown Matter: Debt collection							
Date	Details	Office account			Client account		
		DR	CR	BAL	DR	CR	BAL
Aug 7	Cash. From White & Co. Debt					10,000	10,000CR

(2)   When Anne instructs you to hold £1,000 to the order of Jane, there will be no entry on the cash account. There will be the following entries on the ledger accounts of Anne and Jane:

Client: Anne Brown Matter: Debt collection							
Date	Details	Office account			Client account		
		DR	CR	BAL	DR	CR	BAL
Aug 7	Cash. From White & Co. Debt					10,000	10,000CR
9	Jane Brown. Transfer (TJ)				1,000		9,000

Client: Jane Brown Matter: Litigation							
Date	Details	Office account			Client account		
		DR	CR	BAL	DR	CR	BAL
Aug 9	Anne Brown. Transfer (TJ)					1,000	1,000CR

> There will also be a record on the transfer journal. You can include the initials 'TJ' in the details columns of the client ledger, but this is not essential. It is essential to give the name of the ledger account where the other part of the double entry is made.

Exercise 11A

The following events occur:

February

1   You receive £800 generally on account of costs from your client, Dean.

4   You pay a court fee of £100 (no VAT) on behalf of your client, Wade.

5   You receive £7,000 on behalf of your client, Will. It is a debt collected.

8   You agree to act for Simon. You ask for £300 generally on account of costs. Dean tells you that he is prepared to lend Simon the money for this. Dean and Simon instruct you in writing to make the necessary transfer.

11   You issue a bill to Will. Your costs are £400 plus £80 VAT. You transfer the costs from the client bank account to the office bank account.

13   You issue a bill to Wade for £200 plus £40 VAT. Will, who is Wade's uncle, instructs you to transfer an amount sufficient to pay Wade's indebtedness to you from the amount you are holding for Will. It is a gift from Will to Wade.

14   You issue Dean a bill for £600 plus £120 VAT. You transfer the remaining money held for him in the client bank account to the office bank account in part payment of the bill.

Explain the application of the Rules to each transaction, and prepare the clients' ledger accounts and the cash account.

SUMMARY

---

(1)   Cash transfers from one bank account to another involve a cash payment from one bank account and a cash receipt into the other.

(2)   One pair of entries records the payment; one pair of entries records the receipt.

(3)   Inter-client transfers do not involved the movement of cash. The cash remains in the client bank account.

(4)   To record an inter-client transfer there is a DR entry in the client section of the transferor's ledger account and a CR entry in the client section of the transferee's ledger account. There has to be a separate record on a transfer journal or transfer sheet.

SOLUTIONS

Exercise 11A

1 February	The money is client money. You must pay it into the client bank account (Rule 14).
4 February	You are holding no money for Wade, so you must pay the money out of the office bank account (Rule 20.6).
5 February	The money is client money. You must pay it into the client bank account (Rule 14).

8 February	Rule 27 applies. Written instructions are needed for a private loan from one client to another (Rule 27.2). The money could be withdrawn from the client bank account on Dean's instructions (Rule 21.1) and could be received into the client bank account on Simon's instructions (Rule 14). Thus, Rule 27 is satisfied and the inter-client transfer can be made. A record must be made in the transfer journal (Rule 29.2).
11 February	**The bill** DR Will's ledger account office section with profit costs and VAT. CR profit costs account and HMRC ledger account respectively.
	The transfer The payment from the client bank account (CR cash; DR Will – client section) and receipt into the office bank account (DR cash; CR Will – office section) is allowed by Rule 20.3(b).
13 February	**The bill** DR Wade's ledger account office section with profit costs and VAT. CR profit costs account and HMRC ledger account respectively.
	The transfer This is not an inter-client transfer. Rule 27 is not satisfied. The money could be withdrawn from the client bank account on Will's instructions, but it could not be paid into the client bank account on Wade's instructions because it is being received specifically in payment of your bill. It is a receipt of office money and, as such, should be paid into the office bank account. You must therefore record a cash payment from the client bank account on behalf of Will (CR cash; DR Will – client section) and a cash receipt into the office bank account on behalf of Wade (DR cash; CR Wade – office section).
14 February	**The bill** Entries as above.
	The transfer Rule 20.3(b) applies. The entries are the same as those on 11 February.
	Note: When Dean pays the balance, the money received will be office money and must be paid straight into the office bank account (unless it is dealt with under Rule 17.1(c)).

The accounts are shown below.

Client: Dean
Matter: Miscellaneous

Date	Details	Office account			Client account		
		DR	CR	BAL	DR	CR	BAL
Feb 1	Cash. From Dean. Generally on account .					800	800CR
8	Simon. Transfer (TJ)				300		500
14	Costs	600		600DR			
	VAT	120		720			
	Cash. Transfer from client to office account		500	220	500		–

Client: Wade
Matter: Miscellaneous

Date	Details	Office account			Client account		
		DR	CR	BAL	DR	CR	BAL
Feb 4	Cash. Court fee	100		100DR			
13	Costs	200		300			
	VAT	40		340			
	Cash: Transfer from Will		340	–			

Client: Will
Matter: Miscellaneous

Date	Details	Office account			Client account		
		DR	CR	BAL	DR	CR	BAL
Feb							
5	Cash. Debt collected					7,000	7,000CR
11	Costs	400		400DR			
	VAT	80		480			
	Cash. Transfer costs from client to office account		480	–	480		6,520
13	Cash. From client to office account for Wade				340		6,180

Client: Simon
Matter: Miscellaneous

Date	Details	Office account			Client account		
		DR	CR	BAL	DR	CR	BAL
Feb							
8	Dean. Transfer (TJ)					300	300CR

Cash account

Date	Details	Office account			Client account		
		DR	CR	BAL	DR	CR	BAL
				xxx			xxx
Feb							
1	Dean				800		
4	Wade		100				
5	Will				7,000		
11	Will	480				480	
13	Will					340	
	Wade	340					
14	Dean	500				500	

VALUE ADDED TAX

> **LEARNING OUTCOMES**
>
> After reading this chapter you will be able to:
>
> - explain in outline the general principles of VAT
> - explain how, in relation to firms providing legal services, VAT applies to professional charges and disbursements.

12.1 INTRODUCTION

This chapter deals with VAT in so far as it affects firms providing legal services. We begin with a brief outline of the way in which VAT works. We then look at the particular issues that arise in relation to firms providing services. Value added tax is relevant both to the firm's professional charges and to some disbursements paid by the firm on behalf of clients.

12.2 GENERAL PRINCIPLES

Value added tax involves two distinct aspects: output tax (charged by a business to its customers) and input tax (charged to the business by its suppliers). A business registered for VAT charges its customers output tax for which it must then account to HMRC. In other words, it acts as an unpaid tax collector. It will normally be possible for such a business to deduct input tax charged to the business from the amount accounted for to HMRC. See **12.2.2**.

The standard rate of VAT has been 20% since 4 January 2011. There is also a zero rate and a reduced rate which apply to some goods and services. Some goods and services are exempt from VAT. See **12.2.1.3**.

12.2.1 Output tax

Value added tax is chargeable on the supply of goods or services where the supply is a taxable supply and is made by a taxable person in the course or furtherance of a business carried on by him (Value Added Tax Act (VATA) 1994, s 4(1)). Each element of this definition will be considered further below.

The person making the supply is liable to account to the Government for the amount of tax which he charges.

12.2.1.1 Supply of goods

This comprises all forms of supply whereby the whole property in goods is transferred, including a gift of goods.

12.2.1.2 Supply of services

This is anything which is not a supply of goods, but is done for a consideration. Note that a gratuitous supply of services is not a supply for VAT purposes, in contrast to a gift of goods.

12.2.1.3   Taxable supply

This means any supply of goods or services other than an exempt supply. Exempt supplies are listed in Sch 9 to the VATA 1994 and include supplies of land (except for new commercial sales and leases of commercial property where the supplier has opted to be taxable), insurance, some postal services, finance, health services, and burial and cremation.

Taxable supplies may be divided into two main categories:

(a)   those which are chargeable at the standard rate; and

(b)   those which are chargeable at a zero rate. Zero-rated supplies are listed in Sch 8 to the VATA 1994 and include supplies of food, water, books, international services and transport.

A reduced rate of 5% applies, inter alia, to mobility aids, domestic fuel, installation of energy-saving materials, renovation and alteration of dwellings and residential conversions, children's car seats and carrycots with restraint straps.

Zero-rated and exempt supplies are similar in that no VAT is actually charged in either case by the supplier to his customer.

However, they must be carefully distinguished, since only a person who makes taxable supplies is able to recover input tax, ie, the VAT charged to him by his suppliers.

A firm supplying legal services will be making a standard-rated supply. Legal services include profit costs and *some* payments made for clients (see below). A solicitor supplying insurance will be making an exempt supply.

Note that since 1 January 2015 there are special rules which apply to EU businesses providing electronically supplied services, telecoms or broadcasting. These services supplied to any non-VAT registered customer will now be taxable, according to where the consumer is resident.

12.2.1.4   Taxable person

A person is a taxable person if he *is or is required to be* registered under the Act. A person must register if, broadly, the value of his taxable supplies (*not* his profit) in the preceding 12 months exceeded a figure specified in each year's Budget (£85,000 for 2018/19). A firm of solicitors will virtually always have to be registered.

Notice that voluntary registration is permitted. A person may register voluntarily in order to recover input tax charged to him.

12.2.1.5   Business

Value added tax is chargeable by a taxable person only on taxable supplies made in the course or furtherance of a business carried on by him.

'Business' includes any trade, profession or vocation, but the term is not limited to these activities since it also covers, for example, the provision by certain clubs and associations of facilities to members.

Furthermore, although the services of an employee are not generally taxable, the Act provides that, where a person, in the course of carrying on a trade, profession or vocation, accepts any office, any services supplied by him as holder of the office shall be treated as supplied in the course of a business carried on by him and are therefore chargeable with VAT.

A firm supplying legal services which is a taxable person must charge VAT not only on its supplies of legal services but also on any other supplies it makes in the course of its business, eg, the sale of redundant office equipment.

12.2.2 Input tax

Where a taxable person is charged VAT on the supply of goods or services for the purposes of his business, he may deduct the tax charged to him from the amount of output tax which he accounts for to HMRC (s 25(2)). Since input tax charged to a taxable person is recoverable by him, it follows that VAT is not an expense of a person who makes only taxable supplies, whether at the standard or zero rate.

A person who makes only exempt supplies is not a taxable person and so is unable to recover any input tax.

> **Example**
>
> A, an undertaker, and B, a bookseller, each buy stationery for £200 + £40 VAT. The bookseller can recover the VAT; therefore, the expense to be charged to the Profit and Loss Account is only £200. The undertaker cannot recover the VAT and, therefore, the expense to be charged to the Profit and Loss Account is £240.

Where a taxable person makes both taxable and exempt supplies, he is then partly exempt and may recover only a proportion of the input tax charged to him. A solicitor who supplies insurance may find himself in this position.

Where the exempt supplies made by a taxable person fall within certain de minimis limits, they can be ignored, with the result that all his input tax is recoverable.

12.2.3 Value of supply

Where a supply is fully taxable, VAT at the standard rate (20%) is payable on the value of the supply. If the consideration is in money, the value of the supply is such amount as, with the addition of the total tax payable, is equal to the consideration (s 19(2)).

If a price or fee is agreed, this will be deemed to include VAT unless expressly stated to be tax exclusive.

It is important to remember to quote for a fee *plus* VAT. If VAT is not stated to be extra, the customer will only pay the fee quoted; the business will have to pay the VAT from the quoted fee and will end up with less money than it expected.

For example, if a business registered for VAT, and making standard-rated supplies, quotes a fee of £100 and does not stipulate that VAT is extra, the £100 received is deemed to be made up of the fee and VAT at 20%. The total receipt is 120% of the fee so 100/120 will be fee and 20/120 will be VAT.

> **Exercise 12A**
>
> A firm agrees to provide a legal service for client X for £240. How much will be recorded as profit costs and how much as VAT?

12.2.4 Time of supply

The importance of the time of supply (or tax point) is that it decides the quarter at the end of which a taxable person becomes liable to account for output tax on a particular supply. It also determines the quarter in which a taxable person can claim input tax on a taxable supply made to him. The basic tax points are as follows:

(a) *Goods* When the goods are removed or made available to the purchaser (s 6(2)).

(b) *Services* When the services are completed (s 6(3)).

These basic tax points will be varied in the following cases:

(a)   If, within 14 days after the basic tax point, the supplier issues a tax invoice, the date of the invoice will become the tax point unless a longer period has been agreed with HMRC (s 6(5) and (6)). In the case of solicitors, there is a general extension of the 14-day period to three months, so that, provided solicitors deliver their bills within three months of completion of their services, the date of each bill will be the tax point.

(b)   If, before a basic tax point arises, the supplier issues a tax invoice or receives payment, the supply will, to the extent covered by the invoice or payment, be treated as taking place at the date of the invoice or payment (s 6(4)).

12.2.5 Tax invoices

Such invoices are of vital importance to a taxable person since they are evidence of his right to recover the input tax on a supply made to him, ie, without such an invoice, he will generally be unable to claim an input credit, irrespective of whether or not he has made payment to the supplier.

A taxable person making a taxable supply to another taxable person must, within 30 days after the time of supply (or within such longer period as HMRC allows), provide him with a tax invoice, which must state the following particulars:

(a)   an identifying number;

(b)   the date of the supply, ie, the tax point;

(c)   the supplier's name, address and VAT registration number;

(d)   the name and address of the person to whom the supply is made;

(e)   the type of supply, eg, sale, loan, hire;

(f)   the description of the goods or services supplied;

(g)   the quantity of goods or the extent of the services and the amount (excluding VAT) payable for each description;

(h)   the total amount payable (excluding VAT);

(i)   the rate of cash discount;

(j)   the rate and amount of tax charged.

12.2.6 Collection and accounts

Accounting for VAT will generally be by reference to quarterly accounting periods. Within one month after the end of each quarter, a taxable person must send a completed return form to HMRC, together with a remittance for the tax due. The amount payable, ie total output tax charged less deductible input tax, is obtained from a statutory VAT account, which is required to be kept by every taxable person for each tax period. Apart from these details of the tax due, the return form must also contain a list of the tax exclusive value of all outputs, and also the total of all inputs exclusive of tax.

Example

(a)   During an accounting period, a firm providing legal services sends bills charging total profit costs of £200,000 plus output tax of £40,000. In the same period, the firm buys office equipment for £40,000 plus input tax of £8,000.

The firm accounts to HMRC as follows:

	£
Output tax charged	40,000
less input tax suffered	(8,000)
Payable to HMRC	32,000

The firm has to account for the £32,000 due irrespective of whether or not the customers have yet paid the firm the cash. This can sometimes cause a cashflow problem.

(b) During an accounting period, a retailer sells food for £50,000 plus output VAT at the zero rate. In the same period, the retailer buys equipment for £10,000 plus input tax of £2,000.

The retailer accounts to HMRC as follows:

	£
Output tax charged	0
less input tax suffered	(2,000)
Recoverable from HMRC	2,000

Note: In both these examples, the supplier can recover the input tax paid because the supplier is making taxable supplies, even though, in the case of the retailer, they are at the zero rate.

(c) A funeral director sends bills for burial and cremation totalling £150,000. No VAT is charged as these are exempt supplies. During the same period, the funeral director buys equipment for £15,000 plus input tax of £3,000.

The funeral director is not a taxable person and so does not account to HMRC. Therefore, the funeral director cannot recover the input tax paid.

12.3 VAT AND FIRMS PROVIDING LEGAL SERVICES

12.3.1 Professional charges

Firms providing legal services must charge VAT on their supply of services.

Example

	Bill	£
Professional charges		200.00
VAT @ 20%		40.00
Total		240.00

Entries: The firm will need a ledger account in the name of HMRC as well as a profit costs account and a ledger account in the name of the client.

CR   Profit costs account with professional charges
CR   HMRC with VAT
DR   Client ledger account (office section) with professional charges and VAT as

Client:
Matter:

Date	Details	Office account			Client account		
		DR	CR	BAL	DR	CR	BAL
	Costs	200		200DR			
	VAT	40		240			

Profit costs account

Date	Details	Office account		
		DR	CR	BAL
	Client		200	xxx

HMRC account

Date	Details	Office account		
		DR	CR	BAL
	Client		40	xxx

12.3.2   What are disbursements?

As a matter of convenience for the client, firms providing legal services frequently pay expenses (eg, court fees) on behalf of the client. Such expenses are often referred to as 'disbursements'. HMRC does not regard 'disbursements' as part of the supply of legal services and so the firm does not have to charge VAT on them. However, to qualify as a disbursement for this purpose, an item must fulfil certain conditions.

Payments may be treated as disbursements if all the following conditions are satisfied:

(a)   The firm acted as agent for his client when paying the third party.

(b)   The client actually received and used the goods or services provided by the third party to the firm. (This condition usually prevents travelling expenses of firm members, telephone bills, postage, etc, being treated as disbursements for VAT purposes.)

(c)   The client was responsible for paying the third party.

(d)   The client authorised the firm to make payment on his behalf.

(e)   The client knew that the goods or services would be provided by a third party.

(f)   The firm's outlay must be separately itemised when invoicing the client.

(g)   The firm must recover only the exact amount paid to the third party.

(h)   The goods or services were clearly additional to the supplies made to the client by the firm itself.

Thus, only certain payments made by a firm on its client's behalf may be regarded as disbursements for tax purposes. The Law Society issued a Practice Note on 10 March 2011 setting out guidance for the profession on how to identify disbursements.

The guidance refers to the House of Lords decision in *Nell Gwynn House Maintenance Fund Trustees v C&E Commissioners* [1999] STC 79, which confirmed that VAT law draws a clear distinction in principle between:

(i)   expenses paid to a third party that have been incurred by you in the course of making your own supply of services to your client and which are part of the whole of the services rendered by you to your client; and

(ii)   expenses for specific services that have been supplied by the third party to your client and you have merely acted as your client's known and authorised representative in paying the third party.

Only in case (ii) can the amounts of the payments to the third party qualify for treatment as disbursements for VAT purposes.

Items which do not qualify as disbursements are those which are normally and necessarily part of the service supplied to the client, for example, telephone charges, postage and photocopying charges; these are overheads of the business, and HMRC requires the firm to charge VAT on them. As a general rule, travelling expenses incurred by a solicitor are not disbursements and must be included as part of the overall charge. This view was upheld in the case of *Rowe & Maw (A Firm) v Customs and Excise Commissioners* [1975] 1 WLR 1291. The court held that the cost of fares incurred by a solicitor was incurred for the solicitor, not for the client.

Many firms do not include a separate item on the bill for post, fares, photocopying and telephone but include them in the figure charged for profit costs. In such a case, since VAT is charged on profit costs, VAT will inevitably be charged on the post, fares, photocopying and telephone element.

Where a separate mention is made of such elements, the firm must remember to charge VAT on the separate elements.

> **Example**
>
> (1)   You send a bill to your client, Wright. The following is an extract:
>
>   Professional charges ...
>
>   [Details of the work are set out]
>
> | | £ |
> |---|---|
> | Profit costs | 800 |
> | VAT @ 20% | 160 |
> | Post, fares and telephone calls | 40 |
> | VAT @ 20% | 8 |
>
>   In Wright's ledger account, it is simplest to DR £840 as profit costs and £168 as VAT.
>
> (2)   Alternatively, the bill might have appeared as follows:
>
>   Professional charges ...
>
>   [Details of the work are set out]
>
> | | £ |
> |---|---|
> | Profit costs | 840 |
> | VAT | 168 |

The SRA considers that it is not normally appropriate to make a separate charge for such items, although there may be exceptional cases where it is permissible, eg when unusual amounts of photocopying are involved.

The principles of *Nell Gwyn House Maintenance Fund Trustees* and *Rowe & Maw* were applied in *Brabners LLP v HMRC* [2017] UKFTT 0666 (TC) in relation to searches carried out in conveyancing transactions. The searches were carried out by a specialist online search agency engaged by the solicitors. The agency obtained the required property searches from the local authority's digitised or dematerialised files and registers, and passed those results back to the appellant.

In the bundle supplied to the tribunal was a search and a request for official copy entries. The tribunal agreed with HMRC that such searches did not qualify as disbursements. They were part of the overall service provided to clients by the firm enabling it to provide conveyancing services to the client. As part of its conveyancing services, the firm owed its clients a duty to take reasonable care and skill. This required it to make routine property searches to ensure that transactions could safely go ahead; and to identify any risks or other factors adversely affecting the subject property. Payments for searches were therefore part of the overall consideration for that service. The firm was not simply a conduit or post-box for search results.

Historically (since 1 October 1991), and by way of agreement with the Law Society, HMRC had allowed solicitors to treat so-called 'postal' search fees as disbursements. Postal searches are made by the firm to the local authority direct. They are referred to as 'postal' searches because the request was traditionally made by post. The local authority responds using certain standard official forms.

In the *Brabners* case, the Law Society argued that the concessionary treatment of postal searches was correct, and that there was no apparent difference between postal searches and electronic searches. Hence, it argued that it would be inconsistent or anomalous for electronic search fees to be treated differently from postal search fees, and electronic searches should continue to be treated as disbursements.

The tribunal rejected that argument for two reasons.

(1)   The appeal was not concerned with whether the concession in relation to postal search fees was right or wrong.

(2)   In any event, any argument as to consistency would be outside the tribunal's jurisdiction. It was a matter for HMRC.

It remains to be seen whether HMRC will review the concessionary treatment of postal searches as disbursements.

The decision differs from the tribunal's decision in *Barratt, Goff and Tomlinson (a firm) v HMRC (Law Society Intervening)* [2011] UKFTT 71 (TC). In that case the tribunal allowed fees paid by solicitors for medical records and reports obtained in connection with personal injury claims to be treated as disbursements. The difference between the two appears to be that solicitors can only obtain access to patient records with the client's consent. The records are otherwise confidential and are not matters of public record. The client is the subject matter of the records and (at least for certain purposes) could be regarded as the 'owner' of the records and reports. In these circumstances, the solicitor is, arguably, merely an intermediary used to facilitate the obtaining of the service. However, it is possible that HMRC will challenge the treatment of these items again.

Brabners (supported by The Law Society) may appeal. The decision is very significant for conveyancing firms as the vast bulk of searches are now carried out via online agencies. Firms will be required to charge VAT on searches on the basis that they are part of their supply of legal services. The amount in dispute in the Brabners case was £67,776 together with interest.

At the time of writing, the position is that:

- searches conducted on behalf of a firm by a third party agency are not disbursements and must be treated in the same way as postage, fares, photocopying and telephone, that is the firm must increase its professional charges by the amount of the searches and charge its own VAT on the increased figure;
- so-called postal searches are, by concession, disbursements;
- fees for medical records and reports are disbursements.

In addition, HMRC currently accepts that the following are disbursements:

- company search fees;
- company registration fees;
- court fees;
- witness fees;
- oath fees paid to another solicitor.

12.3.3   The treatment of disbursements in the firm's accounts

The firm simply passes on the cost to the client. The payment may be for an item which is non-taxable or which includes its own VAT element.

12.3.3.1   Non-taxable disbursements

These are payments for something not subject to VAT, such as exempt supplies and supplies not in the course of business, for example court fees, stamp duty land tax, Land Registry fees, etc.

The firm can pay these out of the client bank account if there is sufficient money in the client bank account. Otherwise, they are paid out of the office bank account.

In neither case does the firm pay VAT to the supplier or charge the client VAT when obtaining reimbursement.

12.3.3.2   Disbursements including a VAT element

These are payments made by the firm to a taxable person in respect of taxable supplies (eg, counsel, surveyor, accountant, estate agent, etc). The payment made by the firm will include a

VAT element. That VAT element is passed on to the client. The firm does not charge the client any additional VAT.

The difficulty with passing on VAT is that clients who are registered for VAT will want to recover it from HMRC and can do so only if they have a VAT invoice addressed to them. When a firm pays a disbursement that includes VAT on behalf of a client, the supplier may have addressed the invoice to the client or to the firm making the payment. If the invoice is addressed to the client, life is simple. It is rather more complicated if the invoice is addressed to the firm.

There are, therefore, two methods of passing on the VAT. The method to be used depends on whether the original supplier addressed the invoice to the firm or to the client. If addressed to the firm, the '*principal*' method must be used; if addressed to the client, the '*agency*' method must be used.

(1)   *Agency method*

   If the invoice is addressed to the client, the supply is treated as made to the client. The firm simply acts as the agent, handing over the money on behalf of the client. If there is sufficient client money standing to the credit of the client, the payment can be made from the client bank account; otherwise, it must be made from the office bank account.

   The firm does not separate the supplier's fee and VAT in the firm's accounting records; it simply records the total paid.

   The firm must, if asked, send the supplier's tax invoice to the client. If the client is registered for VAT and the supply is in the course or furtherance of a business, the client will use the invoice to recover the input tax.

Example

You pay a surveyor's bill on behalf of a client, ABC Co Ltd. The bill is for £1,000 plus £200 VAT. The invoice is addressed to the client and is paid using the agency method.

You simply pay the total sum of £1,200 and do not distinguish between the fee and the VAT. Whether the payment is made out of office money or client money, you will charge the client £1,200, again without distinguishing between fee and VAT.

Assume that you are holding £2,000 on account of costs and so are able to make the payment from the client bank account. The entries will be as follows:

Client: ABC Co Ltd
Matter: Contract Dispute

Date	Details	Office account			Client account		
		DR	CR	BAL	DR	CR	BAL
							2,000 CR
	Cash – surveyor				1,200		800 CR

Cash account

Date	Details	Office account			Client account		
		DR	CR	BAL	DR	CR	BAL
							xxx
	ABC Co Ltd – surveyor					1,200	xxx

No entries are made on the firm's HMRC ledger account in relation to the payment.

If the client is registered for VAT, and therefore wants the invoice, you must send the client the surveyor's original invoice. The invoice is addressed to the client, and so the client can claim an input.

(2)   *Principal method*

If the invoice is addressed to the firm, the supply is treated as made to the firm in the first instance. The firm can claim the supply as an input. The firm, therefore, must use office money to pay the supplier's fees, together with the input tax.

The firm then resupplies the item to the client at the same price.

The firm will charge the client output tax on both the firm's professional charges *and* the disbursement.

If the client is entitled to a tax invoice, the firm will provide one invoice to cover both the disbursement and the firm's own professional charges.

Example

You receive a surveyor's invoice for £200 plus £40 VAT. You pay:

	£
Surveyor's fee	200
plus input tax	40
	240

You record the fee and the VAT as separate items on the cash account.

The VAT is recorded on the HMRC account. The tax exclusive amount is recorded on the client ledger account.

When you later charge the client your own profit costs of £400, the bill will include:

	£
Surveyor's fee	200
Profit costs	400
plus output tax (£40 + £80)	120

The surveyor's fee and the VAT are separate items on the bill.

Note: A disbursement paid on the principal method must be paid out of the office bank account, even if there is client money available. This is because the supply is treated as made to the firm and not to the client.

So, if we take the same example that we used at (1) above for the agency method, the firm will have to pay the disbursement from the office bank account even though client money is held for the client. The entries will be as follows:

Client: ABC Co Ltd
Matter: Contract Dispute

Date	Details	Office account			Client account		
		DR	CR	BAL	DR	CR	BAL
							2,000 CR
	Cash – surveyor (VAT £200 paid)	1,000		1,000 DR			

HMRC account

Date	Details	Office account		
		DR	CR	BAL
	Cash – surveyor	200		xxx

Cash account

Date	Details	Office account			Client account		
		DR	CR	BAL	DR	CR	BAL
	ABC Co Ltd – surveyor		1,000	xxx			xxx
	– VAT		200	xxx			xxx

When you charge the client for the work done, the VAT on the profit costs is increased by the VAT on the disbursement. Assume you charge profit costs of £600.

Client: ABC Co Ltd
Matter: Contract Dispute

Date	Details	Office account			Client account		
		DR	CR	BAL	DR	CR	BAL
							2,000 CR
	Cash – surveyor (VAT £200 paid)	1,000		1,000 DR			
	Profit Costs	600		1,600 DR			
	VAT (£200 + £120)	320		1,920 DR			

HMRC account

Date	Details	Office account		
		DR	CR	BAL
	Cash – surveyor	200		xxx
	Client		320	xxx

Profit costs

Date	Details	Office account		
		DR	CR	BAL
	Client		600	xxx

PRACTICAL POINT

Students generally find principal method disbursements difficult to deal with. The following summary may be helpful:

(1) Identify that the disbursement is to be treated on the principal basis – if the invoice is addressed to the firm, it will be treated on the principal basis.

(2) CR the disbursement and the VAT on it to cash account office section – it is common, but not essential, to show the two elements separately.

(3) DR VAT to HMRC ledger.

DR VAT exclusive amount to client ledger office section.

Make a memorandum note in the 'Details' column of the client ledger of the amount of VAT which must be added to the VAT charged to the client when an invoice is issued.

(4) When a bill is issued, add the VAT on the principal method disbursement to the VAT on the profit costs and make the normal entries for delivery of a bill.

DR client ledger office section, with VAT and costs as two separate amounts.

CR the costs account with costs.

CR HMRC account with total VAT charged.

12.3.3.3   Counsel's fees – concessionary treatment

Normally, counsel's fee notes are addressed to the firm and therefore would have to be treated on the principal basis. However, a concessionary treatment for counsel's fees was agreed between HMRC, The Law Society and the Bar when VAT was first introduced, and was published in the *Law Society Gazette*, 4 April 1973.

The firm is allowed to alter the fee note so that it is addressed to the client. It is then treated on the agency basis. The firm must give the fee note to the client so that the client can reclaim the input tax. The firm should keep a photocopy of the amended receipted fee note in case the fee note needs to be dealt with in an assessment of costs.

12.3.4   Treatment of search fees in the accounts

Example

You act for Bartok who is buying a house. On 1 May you incur a search fee of £10. You issue a bill on 30 May showing professional charges of £300 plus VAT.

If the search is a 'postal' search, it is, by concession, treated as a genuine disbursement. The cost is passed on to the client and no VAT is charged on it by the firm.

Client: Bartok
Matter: House Purchase

Date	Details	Office account			Client account		
		DR	CR	BAL	DR	CR	BAL
May 1	Search	10		10 DR			
30	Costs	300		310 DR			
	VAT	60		370 DR			

HMRC account

Date	Details	Office account		
		DR	CR	BAL
May 30	Bartok		60	60 CR

If the search is carried out by an online agency, the effect of the *Brabners* decision is that the search fee is not to be treated as a disbursement. Instead, it is part of the firm's supply of legal services and VAT must be charged. The search could be shown on the client ledger account as a separate item or, preferably, added to the profit costs but, either way, VAT must be charged.

If increasing the profit costs to cover the online search, no entry relating to the search will appear on the client ledger. Instead, when the search is paid, the firm will make a credit entry in Cash – Office and a debit entry in an expense account.

Either:

Client: Bartok
Matter: House Purchase

Date	Details	Office account			Client account		
		DR	CR	BAL	DR	CR	BAL
May 1	Search	10		10 DR			
30	Costs	300		310 DR			
	VAT (£60 + £2)	62		372 DR			

HMRC account

Date	Details	Office account		
		DR	CR	BAL
May 30	Bartok		62	62 CR

There will be a credit entry of £10 on Cash made on 1 May.

Or:

Client: Bartok
Matter: House Purchase

Date	Details	Office account			Client account		
		DR	CR	BAL	DR	CR	BAL
May 30	Costs	310		310 DR			
	VAT	62		372 DR			

HMRC account

Date	Details	Office account		
		DR	CR	BAL
May 30	Bartok	62	60 CR	

There will be a credit entry on Cash and a debit entry on a Search Expenses ledger account on 1 May.

Exercise 12B

You act for Barton in connection with a tax dispute. The following events occur:

July

8   You receive £1,000 from Barton on account of costs to be incurred.

10   You pay a court fee of £100 out of client money.

22   You pay an accountant's fee of £400 plus £80 VAT. The invoice was addressed to you.

29   You pay a surveyor's fee of £600 plus £120 VAT. The invoice was addressed to Barton.

August

7   You send Barton a bill and VAT invoice. Your profit costs are £800 plus appropriate VAT.

9   You transfer the £180 remaining in the client bank account to the office bank account in part payment of your costs.

11   You receive from Barton a cheque for the balance of the costs outstanding.

Prepare the cash account and client ledger account for Barton, together with the relevant entries on the ledger account for HMRC.

Exercise 12C

You act for Avis in a boundary dispute. The following events occur:

November

5   You pay a court fee of £100 on Avis's behalf.

7   You receive a cheque from Avis for £1,200 on account of costs. You do not split the cheque.

9   You pay counsel's fee of £400 plus VAT on behalf of Avis. The invoice was addressed to you, but you add the name and address of Avis.

11   You pay a surveyor's fee of £200 plus VAT. The invoice was addressed to you.

13   You send Avis a bill. Your profit costs are £600 plus VAT.

15   You transfer the £720 remaining in the client bank account in part payment of your bill. You receive a cheque from Avis for the balance of £340.

Comment on the application of the SRA Accounts Rules 2011, and explain what steps you will take to deal with the VAT elements involved in this transaction.

Prepare the cash account and client ledger account for Avis, together with the relevant entries on the ledger account for HMRC.

SUMMARY

(1) Persons who are registered for VAT must charge their customers/clients VAT at zero, standard or reduced rate on all taxable supplies of goods and services made in the course or furtherance of the business, and can recover any VAT charged to the business.

(2) Persons who make only exempt supplies do not charge VAT to their customers/ clients, but neither can they recover VAT charged to the business.

(3) Firms must charge VAT on their supply of legal services but do not charge VAT on disbursements paid on behalf of their clients as these are not part of the supply of legal services.

(4) The cost of a disbursement is simply passed on to the client.

(5) If the disbursement includes an element of VAT charged by the original supplier, the firm will treat the disbursement either on the agency basis or on the principal basis. The choice of basis is governed by to whom the invoice is addressed.

(6) If the invoice is addressed to the client, the firm treats the disbursement on the agency basis:

(a) the whole payment is recorded on the cash account and client ledger without distinguishing the VAT;

(b) the firm can use client money to make the payment if there is sufficient available: if not, the firm uses office money;

(c) the firm must give the client the original supplier's invoice if the client is registered for VAT.

(7) If the invoice is addressed to the firm, the firm treats the disbursement on the principal basis:

(a) the whole payment is recorded on the cash account, the VAT is recorded on the HMRC account and the VAT exclusive amount is recorded on the client's ledger account;

(b) the VAT will be charged to the client when the firm bills the client;

(c) the firm must use office money to pay the disbursement even if client money is available;

(d) the firm must give the client a VAT invoice covering both the professional charges of the firm and the VAT on the disbursement;

(e) in the case of counsel's fee note, the firm is allowed to cross out the firm's name and add the client's; the invoice can then be dealt with on the agency basis.

SOLUTIONS

Exercise 12A

The fee is inclusive of VAT. If the profit costs are regarded as 100%, the solicitor may be said to have received 100% plus 20% (profit costs plus VAT). To calculate the profit costs, it is therefore necessary to divide by 120 to give 1% of the receipt and to multiply by 100 to give 100% of the receipt.

$$\text{Receipt} \times \frac{100}{120}$$

$$£240 \times \frac{100}{120} = £200$$

$$\text{VAT} = £40$$

Exercise 12B

Notes

July

8   The money is client money. It will be paid into the client bank account in the usual way pursuant to Rule 14.

10   Rule 20.1(c) permits the payment out of the client bank account. The court fees are exempt from VAT.

22   The invoice was addressed to you, so the disbursement must be paid using the principal method out of office money. Remember that you are responsible for paying the input tax.

At this stage, you only debit the fee, not the VAT, to the client. The cash account records the fee and the total paid, ie the VAT. You debit the VAT to the HMRC ledger account.

[*Note:* You will see a note in the details column of Barton's ledger account that the solicitor has paid input tax. This is a reminder to charge the client output tax later.]

29   The surveyor's invoice was addressed to Barton and is therefore payable using the agency method.

There is sufficient money in the client bank account, and it is sensible to make the payment out of client's money as permitted by Rule 20.1(c).

August

7   You debit Barton's ledger account, office section, with costs and VAT. You must consider carefully how much output tax to charge.

You must charge output tax at the standard rate on the value of the legal services, ie:

(1)   the value of the profit costs of £800; plus

(2)   the value of any general disbursements – there are none in this case; plus

(3)   the value of any taxable disbursements paid on the principal method – in this case the accountant's fee of £400.

Therefore, you must charge VAT on £800 profit costs plus £400 accountant's fee, which makes a total of £1,200. VAT @ 20% is £240.

The double entries for costs and VAT will be in the costs ledger account (not shown) and HMRC ledger account respectively.

[*Note:* There is no entry in the cash account at this point as no movement of money is involved.]

August

9   Rule 20.3(b) permits the withdrawal from the client bank account for payment of costs. Rule 21.4 provides that the withdrawal shall be by way of transfer to the office bank account.

11   This money is received from Barton specifically in payment of the outstanding costs and expenses. The money should be paid straight into the office bank account under Rule 17.1(a) (unless it is paid into the client account in accordance with Rule 17.1(c)).

The accounts will look like this:

Client: Barton
Matter: Tax dispute

Date	Details	Office account			Client account		
		DR	CR	BAL	DR	CR	BAL
Jul							
8	Cash. On account					1,000	1,000CR
10	Cash. Court fee				100		900
22	Cash. Accountant's fee						
	[VAT £80 paid]	400		400DR			
29	Cash. Surveyor's fee				720		180
Aug							
7	Costs	800		1,200			
	VAT (£80 + £160)	240		1,440			
9	Cash. Transfer from client to office		180	1,260	180		–
11	Cash. From Barton. Balance due		1,260	–			

Cash account

Date	Details	Office account			Client account		
		DR	CR	BAL	DR	CR	BAL
Jul	Balance			xxx			xxx
8	Barton				1,000		
10	Barton					100	
22	Barton		400				
	VAT		80				
29	Barton					720	
Aug							
9	Barton	**180**				180	
11	Barton	**1,260**					

HMRC account

Date	Details	Office account		
		DR	CR	BAL
Jul				
22	Cash. Re Barton	**80**		80DR
Aug				
7	Barton		240	160CR

The CR balance shown on HMRC ledger account represents the amount of VAT owed to HMRC.

Exercise 12C

(1)   5 November   You are not holding any money for Avis. Therefore, Rule 20.6 applies and the money cannot be paid out of the client account. The payment is made out of the office account.

Entries:

DR Avis ledger account
CR Cash account ⎱ Office section

7 November   The money is office and client money. You pay it into the client account – Rule 18.2(b).

Entries:

CR Avis ledger account
DR Cash account ⎱ Client section

9 November   The invoice is now treated addressed to Avis, so the payment is made using the agency method. You pay an inclusive sum of £470 with no separate record of VAT. There is sufficient money in the client bank account, so make the payment out of the client bank account – Rule 20.1(c).

Entries:

DR Avis ledger account
CR Cash account ⎱ Client section

11 November   This invoice was addressed to you, so you must pay it using the principal method. You record the fee and VAT separately. You DR the fee to Avis and the VAT to HMRC.

Even though there is enough money in the client bank account, you must make a payment on the principal method out of the office bank account.

Entries:

Fee   DR Avis ledger account
       CR Cash account ⎱ Office section

VAT   DR HMRC ledger account
       CR Cash account ⎱ Office section

13 November   You make entries for costs and VAT separately. The DR entry in the client's ledger account is in the *office* section.

You calculate VAT on the total of profit costs, general disbursements (none in this case) and taxable disbursements paid on the principal method. The surveyor's fee was paid on the principal method. VAT is therefore charged on £600 profit costs plus £200 surveyor's fee, making a total of £800. VAT will be £160.

Entries:

Costs   DR Avis ledger account
         CR Costs account ⎱ Office section

VAT   DR Avis ledger account
         CR HMRC account ⎱ Office section

15 November   You have £720 remaining in the client bank account. Avis owes you £1,060. You will transfer the £720 and receive a cheque for £340 from Avis.

Rule 20.3(b) allows the withdrawal of £720 from the client bank account in payment of your costs. Client money can be withdrawn to reimburse a firm for money already spent under Rule 20.1(d).

The money has been received to repay the disbursements and to pay your costs where a bill has been sent. Subject to Rule 17.1(c), the money must not be paid into the client bank account. It is paid straight away into the office bank account.

Entries:

For transfer

Withdrawal from client account

DR Avis ledger account
CR Cash account } Client section

Receipt into office account

CR Avis ledger account
DR Cash account } Office section

For receipt of money from Avis into office account

CR Avis ledger account
DR Cash account } Office section

Client: Avis
Matter: Boundary dispute

Date	Details	Office account			Client account		
		DR	CR	BAL	DR	CR	BAL
Nov							
5	Cash. Court fee	100		100DR			
7	Cash. From Avis. On account of costs					1,200	1,200CR
9	Cash. Counsel's fee				480		720
11	Cash. Surveyor's fee [VAT £40 paid]	200		300			
13	Costs	600		900			
	VAT (£120 + £40)	160		1,060			
15	Cash. Transfer from client to office account		720	340	720		–
	Cash. From Avis. Balance due		340	–			

Cash account

Date	Details	Office account			Client account		
		DR	CR	BAL	DR	CR	BAL
Nov	Balance			xxx			xxx
5	Avis		100				
7	Avis				1,200		
9	Avis					480	
11	Avis		200				
	C&E		40				
15	Avis	720				720	
	Avis	340					

HMRC account

Date	Details	Office account		
		DR	CR	BAL
Nov				
11	Cash. Re Avis	40		40DR
13	Avis. VAT		160	120CR

CHAPTER 13

Splitting Cheques and Receiving Cheques in Payment of a Bill

LEARNING OUTCOMES

After reading this chapter you will be able to:

- deal with receipts that are a mixture of office and client money
- select the appropriate option to deal with money received in payment of a bill.

13.1 INTRODUCTION

Those providing legal services often receive funds from clients that are a mixture of office and client money. The SRA Accounts Rules 2011 provide options for dealing with mixed receipts. Rule 18 provides two basic options. Rule 17 provides further options which apply only where the firm has issued a bill or agreed a fee.

This chapter looks at Rule 18 and Rule 17 in some detail. There are also further Exercises on the material covered in **Chapters 9–13**.

13.2 RULE 18

13.2.1 Receipts partly of office and partly of client money

You may receive a cheque which is made up partly of office money and partly of client money.

> **Example**
>
> You act for Carollo Ltd. You paid £40 out of the office bank account on its behalf on 1 February. In response to a request by you, it sends a cheque for £100 on 10 February, partly to pay back the £40 and partly to cover future disbursements. The £40 is office money and the £60 is client money.

Under Rule 18.2(a), you can 'split' the cheque. This means paying the different parts of the cheque into different bank accounts. Thus, you might pay the £40 into the office bank account and the £60 into the client bank account.

On splitting the cheque the entries are:

DR Office portion to Cash account } Office section
DR Client portion to Cash account } Client section

CR Office portion to Client ledger } Office section
CR Client portion to Client ledger } Client section

13.2.2 Unsplit cheque

If you do not split the cheque, you must pay it all into the client bank account without delay under Rule 18.2(b). You will then need to transfer the 'office' portion (ie, the £40) to the office bank account within 14 days of receipt (Rule 18.3). It is more common to deal with 'mixed' cheques in this way than it is to split them; banks are usually unwilling to split cheques in practice as it creates administrative problems for them.

You must not pay the whole cheque into the office bank account and transfer the client portion to the client bank account. This would be a breach of the Rules.

If not splitting the cheque, the entries are:

DR whole amount to Cash account } Client section
CR whole amount to Client ledger } Client section

When later transferring office portion:

CR Cash account } Client section
DR Client ledger } Client section

DR Cash account } Office section
CR Client ledger } Office section

Entries (if cheque split):

Client: Carollo Ltd
Matter:

Date	Details	Office account			Client account		
		DR	CR	BAL	DR	CR	BAL
Feb 1	Cash	40		40DR			
10	Cash		40	–		60	60CR

Cash account

Date	Details	Office account			Client account		
		DR	CR	BAL	DR	CR	BAL
Feb							xxx
1	Carollo		40				
10	Carollo	40			60		

Entries (if cheque not split and a transfer is later made of the office money element):

Client: Carollo Ltd
Matter:

Date	Details	Office account			Client account		
		DR	CR	BAL	DR	CR	BAL
Feb 1	Cash	40		40DR			
10	Cash					100	100CR
	Cash transfer		40	–	40		60

Cash account								
Date	Details	Office account			Client account			
		DR	CR	BAL	DR	CR	BAL	
				xxx			xxx	
Feb								
1	Carollo		40					
10	Carollo				100			
	Carollo transfer	40				40		

Exercise 13A

You act for Brian. Complete the ledger accounts to record the following events.

March

7   Pay £30 by cheque on Brian's behalf.

15   You have an interview with Brian. You ask him to reimburse you for the £30 and to give you another £70 in respect of future items. He gives you a cheque for £100. You split the cheque.

21   Pay £50 by cheque on Brian's behalf.

31   Brian instructs you to hold the balance on behalf of Christine and you receive confirmation from Christine to hold this sum for her.

13.3   RULE 17

13.3.1   Cheques received in full or part payment of a bill

As we saw in **Chapter 9**, Rule 17.1 gives various options for dealing with a cheque received in full or part payment of a bill:

(a)   The money can be dealt with in accordance with its nature. Thus, an office money cheque will be paid into the office bank account, a client money cheque will be paid into the client bank account and a mixed cheque will be dealt with under Rule 18.

(b)   Where the money is office money plus client money in the form of unpaid professional disbursements for which the firm has incurred liability, the entire receipt can be paid into the office bank account. However, by the end of the second working day following receipt, you must either pay the disbursement or transfer the money for it to the client bank account.

Note: This option is not available if the cheque received contains client money of any other kind.

(c)   The money, whatever its nature, can be paid into the client bank account. However, any office money must be transferred out of the client bank account within 14 days of receipt. This option means that a firm can give its clients one bank account number which they can use for direct payments into the firm's account.

(d)   Money received from the LAA for professional charges and disbursements can be paid into the office bank account even if it includes client money in the form of money on account and money for unpaid professional disbursements. However, you must either pay the disbursements or transfer the money for them to the client bank account within 14 days of receipt.

(e)   Where there is a Conditional Fee Agreement, a mixed receipt of client money for damages and office money for professional charges and disbursements can be paid into the client bank account under Rule 14.2(e), but the office money element must be transferred out within 14 days of receipt.

13.3.2 Money received for an agreed fee

An agreed fee is a fixed fee which cannot be varied upwards and which does not depend on the transaction being completed. It must be evidenced in writing. It is not necessary under the SRA Accounts Rules to send a bill, provided there is written evidence. However, it is sensible to send a bill even where a fee has been agreed so as to have a record for VAT purposes.

Money received for an agreed fee is office money and should be paid into the office bank account. See Rule 17.5.

13.4 REVISION OF MATERIAL IN CHAPTERS 9–13

Exercise 13B

(1) **Which one of the following items received by a solicitors' partnership is entirely office money?**
  (a) Money received from a client on account of costs.
  (b) A deposit received as stakeholder on the sale of a house by Fred, a partner in the firm, to Joe, an assistant solicitor.
  (c) Money received from a client in payment of a bill comprising profit costs plus VAT and a fee for land charges which is unpaid but for which the firm is liable.
  (d) None of the above.

(2) **Which one or more of the following cannot be paid into the client bank account?**
  (a) The proceeds of sale of a house sold for an assistant solicitor with the firm.
  (b) Office money to open the client bank account.
  (c) A cheque in settlement of the solicitor's bill for profit costs plus VAT.
  (d) A cheque received from Client A with a written request that the money should not be paid in until the client gives the solicitor instructions.

(3) **Client X gives a solicitor a cheque on account of costs. The solicitor endorses the cheque over to an expert witness on X's behalf. Which one of the following statements is correct?**
  (a) Rule 17.1(b) permits the solicitor not to pay the cheque into the client bank account so no entries need be made in the solicitor's accounts.
  (b) Rule 29.2 requires the solicitor to record the receipt and payment on the cash account.
  (c) Rule 29.2 requires the solicitor to record the receipt and payment on the cash account and client ledger account for X.
  (d) Rule 17.1(b) provides that the solicitor must not pay the cheque into the client bank account.

(4) **Client X sends a solicitor a cheque for £240 in satisfaction of the solicitor's bill for profit costs and VAT. Which one of the following statements is correct?**
  (a) The cheque is client money and must be paid into the client bank account without delay.
  (b) The cheque is office money and must be paid into the client bank account.
  (c) The cheque is office money and must not be paid into the client bank account.
  (d) The cheque is office money and can be paid into the client bank account.

(5) **A solicitor is holding £1,000 for Client A. Client A instructs the solicitor to hold £300 of that money to the order of Client B, to whom A owes money. Which one of the following statements is correct?**
  (a) A client bank account cheque for £300 must be sent to B.
  (b) No entries need be made.

(c)   A client bank account cheque for £300 must be drawn, and then the cheque must be paid into the client bank account on B's behalf.

(d)   Entries must be made on the client ledger accounts of A and B and on a record of sums transferred from one ledger account to another.

(6)   **Brown is a bookseller. He sells only books. He does not charge his customers VAT. Is this because:**

(a)   His turnover does not exceed the limit for compulsory registration?

(b)   He makes only exempt supplies?

(c)   He is not carrying on a 'business' for the purposes of the VATA 1994?

(d)   He makes only zero-rated supplies?

(7)   **A solicitor (registered for VAT) agrees to draft a will for Client X for £100. Which of the following statements is correct?**

(a)   He must charge £20 VAT on top of the fee.

(b)   He must not charge VAT.

(c)   The client will pay him £100 plus VAT.

(d)   The client will pay him £100.

(8)   **A solicitor completes the administration of an estate on 31 March and sends a bill on 2 April. When is the tax point?**

(a)   31 March.

(b)   2 April.

(c)   14 April.

(d)   30 June.

(9)   **A solicitor receives an invoice from a surveyor for £200 + VAT in respect of a property transaction being conducted for Client X. The invoice is addressed to the solicitor's firm. The solicitor holds £1,000 in the client bank account for X generally on account of costs. Which one of the following statements is correct?**

(a)   The solicitor can pay the invoice from the client bank account.

(b)   The solicitor must pay the invoice from the office bank account.

(c)   The solicitor must debit the client ledger account immediately with £240.

(d)   All of the above statements are incorrect.

(10)   **On which one or more of the following must a solicitor charge VAT?**

(a)   Postage, fares, telephone.

(b)   'Postal' Land Registry searches.

(c)   Land Registry searches carried out by an online agency.

(d)   Court fees.

(e)   Fees for medical reports.

(11)   **You receive a cheque from the client made up partly of office money and partly of client money. Which one of the following statements is correct?**

(a)   You must split the cheque.

(b)   You may split the cheque.

(c)   You must pay the cheque into the client bank account.

(d)   You must pay the cheque into the office bank account.

SUMMARY

(1) A cheque received from a client which is a mixture of office and client money must either be split between the office and client bank account, or must be paid in its entirety into the client bank account.

(2) If it is all paid into the client bank account, the office money must be transferred to the office bank account within 14 days.

(3) When a cheque is received in payment of a bill there are additional options available under Rule 17.1.

SOLUTIONS

Exercise 13A

Notes

7 March   No client money, so office money must be used.

15 March   This cheque includes office and client money, so can be split under Rule 20. If split, you must record two separate receipts, one for client money and one for office money. If not split, it must be paid into the client bank account.

21 March   Client money is available and can be used.

31 March   This is an inter-client transfer. No entry is made on the cash account although a note must be made in the transfer journal.

DR Brian ledger
CR Christine ledger   } Client section

Client: Brian
Matter:

Date	Details	Office account			Client account		
		DR	CR	BAL	DR	CR	BAL
March							xxx
7	Cash. Payment	30		30DR			
15	Cash. From you		30	–		70	70CR
21	Cash. Payment				50		20
31	Christine. Transfer				20		–

Client: Christine
Matter:

Date	Details	Office account			Client account		
		DR	CR	BAL	DR	CR	BAL
March							
31	Brian. Transfer					20	20CR

Cash account

Date	Details	Office account			Client account		
		DR	CR	BAL	DR	CR	BAL
March				xxx			xxx
7	Brian. Payment		30				
15	Brian. Amount from Brian	30			70		
21	Brian. Payment					50	

Exercise 13B

(1) (c) The money is received partly in payment of professional charges and partly for a disbursement for which liability has been incurred, a bill having been received. In (b), the money is held for a partner in the firm *and someone else*. Therefore, the money is client money.

(2) (d) Note that, although the receipt in (b) and (c) is office money, it can be paid into the client bank account under Rule 17.1(c). However, it must not be left longer than 14 days.

(3) (c) See Rule 29.2.

(4) (d) See Rule 17.1(c).

(5) (d) See Rule 29.

(6) (d)

(7) (d) The solicitor must apportion the fee between the VAT and the VAT exclusive element.

(8) (b) The tax point is the date the bill is issued.

(9) (b) It must be treated on the principal basis and, therefore, must be paid from the office bank account.

(10) (a) and (c)   A solicitor must charge VAT on the supply of legal services but not on items which are additional to the supply and which are supplied to the client and simply paid on behalf of the client by the solicitor. Items (a) and (c) are part of the supply of legal services and so are subject to VAT. Items (b) (by concession), (d) and (e) are disbursements, so the solicitor simply passes on the cost to the client without charging VAT.

(11) (b)

MISCELLANEOUS MATTERS

LEARNING OUTCOMES

After reading this chapter you will be able to deal with the following miscellaneous transactions:

- receipt of a cheque made out to a client or third party
- endorsed cheques
- dishonoured cheques
- abatements
- bad debts
- petty cash
- insurance commission.

14.1 INTRODUCTION

So far you have looked at the treatment of those basic transactions a firm providing legal services will carry out every day. There is a variety of more unusual transactions which will occur from time to time, and this chapter considers how to deal with them. The same principles apply. You will decide whether office or client money is involved and make the appropriate entries to record receipts, payments and transfers.

14.2 RECEIPT OF A CHEQUE MADE OUT TO THE CLIENT OR A THIRD PARTY

If you receive a cheque made out not to the firm but to the client (or a third party), you *cannot* pay that cheque into a firm bank account. The firm is not the payee.

Your only obligation is to forward the cheque to the payee without delay. You have not dealt with client money because the cheque is not 'money' as far as you are concerned; it is a piece of paper which you cannot turn into cash. As you have not dealt with *client money*, there is no obligation under Rule 29 to record the event on the client ledger account and cash account. However, you will want to keep a written record on the correspondence file.

In addition many firms will have a special control account where all cheques received by the firm will be recorded irrespective of the payee. This is not required by the Rules but is a useful precaution to prevent cheques being overlooked. Guidance note (iii) to Rule 29 suggests that it is advisable to record the action taken.

14.3 ENDORSED CHEQUES

You may receive a cheque made out to the firm on behalf of a client. Instead of paying the cheque into the client bank account, you are free under Rule 16.1(b) (assuming the cheque is endorsable, which most are not) to endorse the cheque to the client or to a third party on behalf of the client. However, as this is a *dealing* with client's money, it must be recorded under Rule 29 at the time of receipt on the client ledger account and cash account as a receipt and payment of client money. As the cheque passes in and out of the firm, having no effect on the balances of the accounts, it is common to make the entries for receipt and payment on the same line.

Example

You are acting for Brown in a debt collection and receive a cheque for £1,000 made out to the firm in settlement of a debt due to Brown. You endorse the cheque to Brown.

Client: Brown

Date	Details	Office account			Client account		
		DR	CR	BAL	DR	CR	BAL
	Cash. From debtor Endorsed to Brown				1,000	1,000	–

Cash account

Date	Details	Office account			Client account		
		DR	CR	BAL	DR	CR	BAL xxx
	Brown. From debtor Endorsed to Brown				1,000	1,000	

Note: Rule 16.1(a) allows a firm which receives client money in the form of cash not to pay the cash into the client bank account provided the cash is going to be paid out 'without delay' (that is within two working days). However, as with endorsed cheques, the firm is dealing with client money and must record the receipt and payment in the accounts. It is unusual for a firm to receive cash, and most firms would want an explanation as to why cash was used because of fears of money laundering.

14.4 DISHONOURED CHEQUES

There is nothing in the rules to prevent a solicitor drawing against a cheque which has been paid into the client bank account but which has not yet been cleared. However, if that cheque is then dishonoured, there will be a breach of Rule 20.6, and the solicitor will have to transfer money from the office bank account to the client bank account to make up the deficiency.

Example

On 1 March, you receive a cheque for £500 on account of costs from your client, Smith.

On 2 March, you pay a court fee of £100 out of the client bank account on behalf of Smith.

On 4 March, the bank informs the solicitor that Smith's cheque for £500 has been dishonoured.

First you must make entries to reverse the apparent receipt on 1 March. Then you must deal with the consequences of the payment from the client bank account.

Because it turns out that you had no money for Smith when you made the £100 payment, you must have used £100 belonging to another client for the benefit of Smith. You must, therefore, transfer £100 from the office bank account to the client bank account to remedy your breach of the rules.

On 7 March, Smith tells you that there are now sufficient funds to meet the cheque. He asks you to re-present it. You do so on 7 March and it is met.

When you re-present the cheque, the client now owes you £100. This means you can either split the cheque, or pay the whole amount into the client bank account and transfer the £100 to the office bank account at a later stage.

Notes:

March

1   The money is client money and is paid into the client bank account (Rule 13).

          Entries:

               CR Smith ledger account } Client section
               DR Cash account

2   Rule 20 allows the money to be paid out of the client bank account even though the cheque from Smith has not yet been cleared.

          Entries:

               DR Smith ledger account } Client section
               CR Cash account

4   You must make entries reversing those made when you received the cheque.

          Entries:

               DR Smith ledger account } Client section
               CR Cash account

This results in a DR balance of £100 on Smith's ledger account and you are in breach of Rule 20.6. Effectively, you have used client money on behalf of a client for whom you were not holding any.

4   You must make an *immediate* transfer of £100 from the office bank account to the client bank account to rectify the breach.

          Entries:

          Withdrawal from office account

               DR Smith ledger account } Office section
               CR Cash account

          Receipt into client account

               CR Smith ledger account } Client section
               DR Cash account

7   When the cheque is re-presented you can, under Rule 18, either pay the whole amount into the client bank account, or, as in this example, split it so that £100 goes into the office bank account and £400 into the client bank account.

          Entries if split:

          £100 Office money

               CR Smith ledger account } Office section
               DR Cash account

£400 Client money

CR Smith ledger account
DR Cash account

} Client section

The accounts look like this:

Client: Smith
Matter: Miscellaneous

Date	Details	Office account			Client account		
		DR	CR	BAL	DR	CR	BAL
March							
1	Cash. From Smith						
	On account					500	500CR
2	Cash. Court fee				100		400
4	Cash. Smith's cheque – returned				500		100DR
	Cash. Transfer from office account						
	to rectify breach	100		100DR		100	–
7	Cash. Smith's cheque re-presented		100	–		400	400CR

Cash account

Date	Details	Office account			Client account		
		DR	CR	BAL	DR	CR	BAL
							xxx
March							
1	Smith				500		
2	Smith					100	
4	Smith					500	
	Smith		100		100		
7	Smith	100			400		

A well-run firm will operate a system which makes it impossible to draw against a client bank cheque before it has cleared. Guidance note (iii) to Rule 20 recommends 'discretion' when drawing against uncleared cheques.

14.5 ABATEMENTS

Clients may complain that the amount of their bill is too high. Sometimes, the firm may decide to reduce, or abate, the costs. HMRC allows the output tax charged on the bill to be reduced proportionately.

In order to record the abatement, you reverse the entries made on the profit costs and HMRC account when the bill was sent to the extent of the abatement. You also send the client a VAT credit note.

Entries:

DR Profit costs account
DR HMRC account

} with the reduction

CR Client ledger account (office section) with the reduction in your professional charges and VAT.

Example

You send your client Jones a bill for £600 plus VAT on 4 May. On 6 May, after discussion with Jones, you agree to reduce the bill by £100 plus VAT.

The accounts will look like this:

Client: Jones
Matter: Miscellaneous

Date	Details	Office account			Client account		
		DR	CR	BAL	DR	CR	BAL
May 4	Costs	600		600DR			
	VAT	120		720			
6	Costs – Abatement		100	620			
	VAT – Abatement		20	600			

Profit costs account

Date	Details	Office account		
		DR	CR	BAL
May 4	Jones		600	600CR
6	Jones	100		500

HMRC account

Date	Details	Office account		
		DR	CR	BAL
May 4	Jones		120	120CR
6	Jones	20		100

If preferred, the firm may debit abatements to a separate abatements account. At the end of the accounting period, the debit balance on the abatements account is transferred to the debit side of the costs account.

14.6 BAD DEBTS

14.6.1 The general rule

From time to time, a firm will realise that a client is not going to pay the amount owing to the firm. The firm will have to write off the amount owing for profit costs and VAT and for any disbursements paid from the office bank account. The general rule for VAT used to be that there was no VAT relief, and VAT had to be accounted for to HMRC even if the debt was written off. Thus, the VAT was an additional element of the bad debt and increased the amount which had to be written off.

Entries:

> CR Client's ledger account, office section } with the whole amount
> DR Bad debts account

14.6.2 VAT relief

However, VAT relief is available once the debt has been outstanding for at least six months since the date payment was due. In this case, the solicitor will be entitled to a refund from HMRC.

Entries:

When debt is written off:

> CR Client's ledger account, office section, with the full amount owing
> DR Bad debts account with the full amount owing

When VAT relief becomes available:

CR Bad debts account with amount of VAT

DR HMRC with amount of VAT

Example

On 9 April, you send Green a bill for £400 plus VAT. On 6 June, you write off Green's debt. Six months after the due date of payment of Green's bill (31 October), you become entitled to VAT bad debt relief.

The accounts will look like this:

Client: Green
Matter: Miscellaneous

Date	Details	Office account			Client account		
		DR	CR	BAL	DR	CR	BAL
Apr 9	Costs	400		400DR			
	VAT	80		480			
June 6	**Bad debts**		480	–			

Profit costs account

Date	Details	Office account		
		DR	CR	BAL
Apr 9	Green		400	400CR

HMRC account

Date	Details	Office account		
		DR	CR	BAL
Apr 9	Green		80	80CR
Oct 31	**Bad debts. VAT relief**	80		–

Bad debts account

Date	Details	Office account		
		DR	CR	BAL
June 6	**Green**	480		480DR
Oct 31	**HMRC. VAT relief**		80	400

14.7 PETTY CASH

14.7.1 Need for petty cash account

Any firm will need some petty cash on the premises to meet small cash payments. When cash is withdrawn from the bank for petty cash, the entries will be:

CR Cash – office section

DR Petty cash account

When a payment is made, for example a roll of sticky tape is bought, the entries will be:

CR Petty cash account

DR appropriate ledger account, for example Sundries

14.7.2 Petty cash payments for clients

A firm will sometimes make a payment from petty cash on behalf of a client. The CR entry will be made on the petty cash account, not on the main cash account. The firm will want to DR the client ledger account to show that the client now owes the firm for the expense incurred. The DR entry must be made on the office section of the client ledger even if client money is held for the client. This is because petty cash is office money. Thus, by deciding to use petty cash, the firm has elected to use office money on behalf of the client.

Example

You hold £200 in the client bank account for Smith. You pay £20 expenses to an expert witness from petty cash.

Smith's client ledger account will look like this:

Client: Smith Matter:		Office account			Client account		
Date	Details	DR	CR	BAL	DR	CR	BAL
	Cash. Received on account					200	200CR
	Petty cash. Expert witness	20		20DR			

The corresponding credit entry will be on the petty cash account, not on the cash account. Notice that the 'Details' section of Smith's ledger account refers to 'petty cash', not to cash.

14.8 INSURANCE COMMISSION

Firms providing legal services may be offered commission from insurance companies or sellers of financial products. Where the firm is entitled to retain the commission, it represents an additional source of income; the firm will have a commission received account to which receipts are credited and a ledger account in the name of each company paying commission.

However, it will be relatively rare for the firm to be entitled to retain commission. Outcome 1.15 of the SRA Code of Conduct requires those regulated by the SRA to 'properly account to clients for any financial benefit' received as a result of client instructions.

What does 'properly account' mean? Indicative Behaviour IB(1.20) suggests that proper accounting where a financial benefit has been received as a result of acting for a client is:

- paying it to the client;
- offsetting it against fees; or
- keeping it only where you can justify keeping it, you have told the client the amount of the benefit (or an approximation if you do not know the exact amount) and the client has agreed that you can keep it.

There is a further reason for not retaining commission. Firms that wish to take advantage of the exemption allowing professional firms to avoid regulation by the Financial Reporting Council in relation to investment business must account for all commission to clients.

Exercise 14A

You act for Forsyth.

March

1	Forsyth sends £100 on account of costs.
2	You pay court fees of £40 from the client bank account.
3	The bank informs you that Forsyth's cheque has been dishonoured.
15	You re-present the cheque, instructing the bank that, assuming the cheque is honoured, you want £40 to be paid into the office bank account and £60 into the client bank account.
16	You pay accountant's fee of £200 plus £40 VAT. The invoice is addressed to Forsyth.
18	You issue a bill for £400 plus £80 VAT.
19	Forsyth complains, and you reduce the bill by £40 plus £8 VAT.
31	You write off Forsyth's debt as bad, having transferred any balance in the client bank account to the office bank account.

Make the necessary entries in Forsyth's client ledger account and the cash account. Do not complete the balances on the cash account.

SUMMARY

---

(1) Cheques which are not made out to the firm cannot be paid into the firm's bank account. The cheque does not represent money in the firm's hands. The firm must forward the cheque to the payee, and does not need to record the receipt and payment in the accounts as there is no dealing with client money.

(2) Instead of paying a cheque made out to the firm into the client bank account, a firm can endorse the cheque over to the client or to someone else on the client's behalf. The firm is dealing with client money, and must record the receipt and payment of client money on the cash account and the client's ledger account. (The firm can treat cash receipts in the same way so long as the cash is paid out within two working days.)

(3) A firm can draw against a client's cheque before it has cleared. However, this is not advisable. If the client's cheque is dishonoured, the firm will have breached the Rules and will have to remedy the breach by transferring sufficient cash from the office to the client bank account to cover the payment.

(4) If the firm reduces the amount charged for profit costs, the VAT is also reduced.

(5) If a client's debt is written off as bad, the firm will lose the amount charged for profit costs plus any disbursements paid from the office bank account. VAT bad debt relief can be obtained once the debt has been outstanding for six months.

(6) Petty cash is office money, so any payment made for a client using petty cash is a payment of office money.

(7) A firm will normally account to a client for commission received as a result of acting for a client.

SOLUTION

Exercise 14A

Notes:

March

1   This was received generally on account of costs and is client money.

2   You appear to have client money available and so can make the payment from the client bank account.

3   Drawing against an uncleared cheque is not in itself a breach of rules. However, as the cheque has been dishonoured, there has been a breach which must be remedied by transferring £40 from the office to the client bank account.

15   The re-presented cheque is split between the office and the client bank account. The portion representing reimbursement of the expense incurred for court fees is office money; the balance is client's money.

16   As the invoice is addressed to the client, the agency basis is used. Office money is used as you do not have sufficient client money.

19   This is an abatement. Simply make the opposite entries you would make if delivering a bill.

31   There is £60 in the client bank account which can be transferred to the office bank account. The rest of Forsyth's indebtedness, including VAT, must be written off as a bad debt.

No VAT relief is available at present. The debt has not been outstanding for six months since the due date for payment.

Client: Forsyth
Matter:

Date	Details	Office account			Client account		
		DR	CR	BAL	DR	CR	BAL
March							
1	Cash. On account					100	100CR
2	Cash. Court fees				40		60
3	Cash. Dishonoured cheque				100		40DR
3	Cash. To remedy breach	40		40DR		40	–
15	Cash. Re-presented cheque		40	–		60	60CR
16	Cash. Accountant	240		240			
18	Costs	400		640			
	VAT	80		720			
19	Costs – abatement		40	680			
	VAT – abatement		8	672			
31	Cash. Transfer		60	612	60		–
31	Bad debts		612	–			

Cash account

Date	Details	Office account			Client account		
		DR	CR	BAL	DR	CR	BAL
March							
1	Balances						
1	Forsyth. On account				100		
2	Forsyth. Court fees					40	
3	Forsyth. Dishonoured cheque					100	
3	Forsyth. To remedy breach		40		40		
15	Forsyth. Re-presented cheque	40			60		
16	Forsyth. Accountant		240				
31	Forsyth. Transfer	60				60	

ACCOUNTING TO THE CLIENT FOR INTEREST

LEARNING OUTCOMES

After reading this chapter you will be able to:

- explain the circumstances in which a client is entitled to be paid interest on client money
- identify the two methods of accounting for interest
- explain the advantages and disadvantages of each method
- explain how interest is calculated.

15.1 INTRODUCTION

Solicitors may hold money belonging to other people for substantial periods of time. Inevitably some of those people will wonder whether they are entitled to be paid a sum in lieu of the interest they might otherwise be earning on that money. Given that Principles 2 and 4 require those providing legal services to act with integrity and in the best interests of the client, it is hardly surprising that the answer is that clients are usually entitled to interest on client money held.

This chapter covers:

(a) the circumstances in which a client is entitled to be paid interest on client money;

(b) the use of separate designated client accounts; and

(c) the use of a general client bank account.

15.2 CIRCUMSTANCES IN WHICH A CLIENT IS ENTITLED TO BE PAID INTEREST ON CLIENT MONEY

15.2.1 When must a firm allow interest?

Rule 22.1 provides that firms must account to clients for interest on money held in a client bank account where it is fair and reasonable to do so in all the circumstances. The obligation to pay interest extends to client money held outside a client account under Rule 15(1)(a) or Rule 16(1)(d) (for example, in the firm's safe in the form of cash, or in a non-client bank account such as an account outside England and Wales).

Rule 22.3 requires firms to have a written policy on the payment of interest which seeks to provide a fair outcome. The terms of the policy must be drawn to the client's attention at the start of the retainer unless it is inappropriate to do so, for example where the client has a continuing relationship with the firm.

Rule 22.2 says that there is no need to allow interest:

(a) on money held for the payment of a professional disbursement, once counsel etc has requested a delay in settlement;

(b) on money held for the Legal Aid Agency;

(c) on an advance from the office bank account made under Rule 14.2(b) to cover a disbursement for which insufficient client money was available; or

(d) if there is an agreement that interest shall not be paid.

15.2.2 How is interest calculated?

Under Rule 13(5), firms are free to choose to pay client money either into a general client bank account or into a separate bank account designated for money of that particular client (a 'separate designated client account'). Whichever they choose to do, the requirement under the Rules is the same: Rule 23 provides that the interest paid must be a 'fair and reasonable' sum.

Firms will usually open a separate designated bank account for a particular client's money when they recognise that they will be holding a substantial amount for a significant time and simply want to pass on to the client all the interest allowed by the bank. In the past, the income tax rules applying to bank interest made it impracticable for firms to retain any part of the interest earned. This was because, for tax years before 2016/17, banks deducted basic rate tax at source from interest earned on separate designated client accounts (subject to the tax status of the individual clients) and credited the net amount to the separate designated account. For tax years 2016/17 onwards, banks and building societies pay all interest gross. It is likely, however, that firms will continue to account to clients for all interest earned on money in specially designated accounts given the obligation to act in the client's best interests.

Where a client's money is left in the general client bank account, the firm has to decide by reference to its policy whether to allow interest and how to calculate it. The sum decided upon will be allowed from the office bank account and is, in effect, an expense of the business – a well-run firm will cover the expense by earning interest on client money and having that interest paid into its office bank account (see **15.2.3**).

Guidance note (i)(e) to Rule 22 suggests that firms may choose to apply a *de minimis* policy, for example providing that no interest is payable to clients if the amount calculated on the balance held is £20 or less. The amount which is regarded as *de minimis* will need to be set at a reasonable level and regularly reviewed in the light of current interest rates.

Where interest is to be allowed, guidance note (ii) to Rule 23 deals with how to decide on a fair and reasonable sum. It says:

> The sum paid by way of interest need not necessarily reflect the highest rate of interest obtainable but it is unlikely to be appropriate to look only at the lowest rate of interest obtainable. A firm's policy on the calculation of interest will need to take into account factors such as:
>
> (a)   the amount held;
>
> (b)   the length of time for which cleared funds were held;
>
> (c)   the need for instant access to the funds;
>
> (d)   the rate of interest payable on the amount held in an instant access account at the bank or building society where the client account is kept;
>
> (e)   the practice of the bank or building society where the client account is kept in relation to how often interest is compounded.

15.2.3 Factors affecting choice of method

When the firm opens a separate designated client bank account, the bank calculates the amount and pays the amount of interest earned. If such an account is not opened, the firm has to pay an appropriate amount in lieu of interest from the office bank account. It might seem, therefore, that it is always preferable to open a separate designated client account. However, this is not so.

A firm which opened a separate designated client bank account for every client for whom money was held would end up with an enormous number of different bank accounts, and this would be administratively inconvenient.

Moreover, solicitors are allowed under the Solicitors Act 1974 to put client money held in a general client bank account on deposit and keep any interest earned over and above what is required to be paid under the Rules. In general, the more money placed on deposit, the higher the rate of interest earned. The firm only has to pay the client the rate that is fair and reasonable on the amount held *for that client*. The result is that the firm may earn more interest on client money than is paid out to clients. This is likely to encourage the firm to use the second method.

15.3 USE OF SEPARATE DESIGNATED BANK ACCOUNT

15.3.1 What is involved?

Rule 13.5 defines a 'separate designated client account' as an account for money of a single client, other person or trust, which includes in its title a reference to the identity of the client, other person or trust.

The firm simply opens a separate account at the bank designated with the name of the client or trust and pays the client money into it. The firm will account to the client for the interest allowed by the bank.

Separate designated client accounts do not have to be deposit accounts. In principle, a firm can open a designated current account but, in practice, it will only bother where it wants to earn interest.

Rule 29.3 provides that where a firm opens separate designated client accounts, it must keep:

(a) a combined cash account to show the total amount held in separate designated client accounts; and

(b) a record of the amount held for each client either in a deposit column of a client ledger account, or on the client side of a client ledger account kept specifically for a separate designated client account, for each client.

The disadvantage of this method (as explained at **15.2.3** above) is that the firm loses the opportunity to benefit from interest earned by client money.

15.3.2 Accounting entries

The firm will instruct the bank to open a deposit bank account – the separate designated client bank account – and to transfer the appropriate amount from the (current) client bank account into it. The firm will record the receipt into the separate designated client bank account by making a DR entry on the combined cash account (required by Rule 29.3).

Entries are also needed on the client ledger accounts to show what has happened to the money. You may prefer not to worry about the bookkeeping entries, in which case you can go straight to **15.4**.

Rule 29.3(b) requires that where a firm opens a separate designated client account, entries must be made either in an additional 'client-deposit' column on the ordinary client ledger account, or on a separate client ledger account opened for that client. When a separate ledger account is used, the office columns are normally redundant as you already have a client ledger account showing dealings with office money. We have, therefore, shaded the office columns on separate ledger accounts to indicate that they will not be used.

When transferring money from the general client bank account to a separate designated bank account, there are two stages:

(1)   To record a payment out of the general client bank account:

Entries:

> CR Cash
> DR Client ledger account (1)   } Client section

(2)   To record a receipt into the separate designated client bank account:

> CR Client ledger account (2) (or additional deposit column on Client ledger account (1))
> DR Combined cash account

Note: If money is received and paid straight into a separate designated bank account step 1 is not required.

The bank will pay interest earned into the separate designated bank account. You will record the interest as a CR on the client's new ledger account and as a DR on the combined cash account.

Banks often do not allow payments directly from deposit accounts. Where this is the case, you must transfer the total sum including interest from the separate designated deposit bank account to the general client bank account so that a cheque can be drawn on the general client bank account.

Example

You act for Dash Ltd, which is owed £2,200 by Bingley. You write to Bingley, and you receive a cheque from him for the money owed on 3 April. On 4 April, Dash Ltd tells you to hold the money for five weeks until 9 May. You put the money on deposit in a separate designated client bank account. On 9 May, you tell the bank to close the account. They tell you that they have allowed £18 interest. The £2,218 is transferred to the general client bank account. You send Dash Ltd the £2,218.

Notes:

April

3   The money is received as client money and paid into the general client bank account.

> *Entries:*

> CR Dash Ltd (debt collection) ledger account   } Client section
> DR Cash account

4   The bank will transfer the cash from your general client bank account to the separate designated client bank account. You will need an entry on your combined cash account (CCA) to record the additional funds held in separate designated client bank accounts, and a new client ledger account (or additional deposit section on the old client ledger) to show that funds are held for Dash in a separate designated deposit account.

> *Entries:*

> CR Cash account   } Client section
> DR Dash Ltd (debt collection) ledger account

> DR Combined cash account (CCA)
> CR Dash Ltd (money held on deposit) ledger account

Note:

Had you known on 3 April that you would want to put the money on deposit, you could have paid the money straight into the separate designated client bank account without passing it through the general client bank account.

Entries:

> DR CCA
> CR Dash Ltd (money held on deposit) ledger account

May

9   Deal with the interest first. The interest has been earned on behalf of Dash Ltd and belongs to it. It is client money and the bank will pay it into the separate designated client bank account.

Entries:

> DR CCA with interest
> CR Dash Ltd (money held on deposit) ledger account with interest

Then pay out the total from the separate designated client bank account.

Entries:

> CR CCA
> DR Dash Ltd (money held on deposit) ledger account

Then receive the total into the general client bank account.

Entries:

> DR Cash account   } Client section
> CR Dash Ltd (debt collection) ledger

You can now pay Dash Ltd the total sum you are holding on its behalf.

Entries:

> CR Cash account   } Client section
> DR Dash Ltd (debt collection) ledger

The completed accounts look like this:

Client: Dash Ltd (1)
Matter: Debt collection

Date	Details	Office account			Client account		
		DR	CR	BAL	DR	CR	BAL
April							
3	Cash. Bingley					2,200	2,200CR
4	Cash. On deposit				2,200		–
May							
9	Cash. Off deposit					2,218	2,218
	Cash. Returned				2,218		–

Client: Dash Ltd (2)
Matter: Money held on deposit

Date	Details	Office account			Client account		
		DR	CR	BAL	DR	CR	BAL
April							
4	Deposit cash. A/C opened					2,200	2,200CR
May							
9	Deposit cash interest					18	2,218
9	Deposit cash. A/C closed				2,218		–

Cash account

Date	Details	Office account			Client account		
		DR	CR	BAL	DR	CR	BAL
				xxx			xxx
April 3	Dash Ltd (1). Bingley				2,200		
4	Dash Ltd (1). On deposit					2,200	
May 9	Dash Ltd (1). Off deposit				2,218		
9	Dash Ltd (1). Returned to client					2,218	

Combined cash account (CCA)

Date	Details	Office account			Client account		
		DR	CR	BAL	DR	CR	BAL
April 4	Dash Ltd (2). A/C opened				2,200		xxx
May 9	Dash Ltd (2). Interest				18		xxx
9	Dash Ltd (2). A/C closed					2,218	–

You may choose to have a separate deposit section on the existing client ledger account instead of a separate client ledger account. In this case, the Dash Ltd example would appear as follows.

Client: Dash Ltd
Matter: Debt collection

Date	Details	Office	Client			Client – Deposit		
			DR	CR	BAL	DR	CR	BAL
April 3	Cash. Bingley			2,200	2,200CR			
4	Cash. On deposit		2,200					
4	Deposit cash. A/C opened						2,200	2,200CR
May 9	Deposit cash. Interest						18	2,218CR
9	Deposit cash. A/C closed					2,218		–
9	Cash. Off deposit			2,218	2,218CR			
9	Cash. Returned		2,218		–			

Cash account

Date	Details	Office account			Client		
		DR	CR	BAL	DR	CR	BAL
April	Balance						xxx
3	Dash Ltd (1). Bingley				2,200		
4	Dash Ltd (1). On deposit					2,200	
May 9	Dash Ltd (1). Off deposit				2,218		
9	Dash Ltd (1). Returned					2,218	

Combined cash account (CCA)

Date	Details	Office account			Client		
		DR	CR	BAL	DR	CR	BAL
April	Balance						xxx
4	Dash Ltd. A/C opened				2,200		xxx
May 9	Dash Ltd. Interest				18		xxx
9	Dash Ltd. A/C closed					2,218	–

15.4 USE OF GENERAL CLIENT BANK ACCOUNT

15.4.1 What is involved?

The firm must bear in mind the requirement to allow a fair and reasonable sum under Rule 23.

Assume that you hold £1,600 of client money for nine weeks on behalf of your client, Smith, in the general client bank account. Taking into account the factors set out in guidance note (ii), the firm must calculate a fair and reasonable amount and allow it to the client.

The disadvantage of this method is that the firm has to calculate how much would have been earned in respect of each individual client to whom the rules apply. Also, at first sight, it appears that the firm will be out of pocket. However, as explained at **15.2.3**, this is not necessarily the case.

A well-organised firm will always put a proportion of its client money on deposit in a general deposit bank account. It will then be entitled to keep the interest earned on that general deposit bank account. Provided the firm organises its bank accounts sensibly, it should earn more interest on its general deposit bank account than it has to pay to individual clients. A firm can never put all of its client money on deposit since it must ensure that it has sufficient client money readily available to meet all day-to-day expenses for clients.

Often, the amount allowed in interest will simply reduce the amount that the client has to pay the firm for the services provided. However, if the client has already paid, the firm may actually send a cheque.

15.4.2 Accounting entries

You may prefer to skip the detail of the bookkeeping entries, in which case you may proceed straight to the Summary at the end of this chapter.

Using this method, the interest payment is an expense of the business and will be recorded on an interest payable account. It is equivalent to the firm paying any other business expense, such as electricity or wages.

To comply with Rule 29.4, the office money dealing must be recorded in an office cash account and on the office section of the client ledger account. If the money is transferred from the office bank account to the client bank account and held for the client, as permitted by Rule 14.2(d), entries must be made on the client ledger and cash account to record the cash transfer from the office to client bank account.

Example

To enable you to make a direct comparison, we shall use the same basic facts as in the previous example, except that the money is not put into a separate designated client bank account.

Notes:

April

3   You receive the £2,200 on behalf of Dash Ltd and pay it into the general client bank account. Entries as before:

Entries:

CR Dash Ltd ledger account } Client section
DR Cash account

May

9   You have to allow Dash Ltd £18 interest, and therefore have to account to Dash Ltd for £2,218. You can do this in one of two ways.

Method 1   Send two cheques: one drawn on the office bank account for the £18 interest, and the other drawn on the client bank account for the £2,200.

Entries must be made on the client ledger office section to record the dealing with office money.

Entries:

To record £18 owed to client in interest

DR Interest payable ledger account   } Office section
CR Dash Ltd ledger account

To record £18 office cash sent to client

DR Dash Ltd ledger account   } Office section
CR Cash account

To record £2,200 client cash sent to client

DR Dash Ltd ledger account   } Client section
CR Cash account

The accounts will look like this:

Client: Dash Ltd
Matter: Debt collection

Date	Details	Office account			Client account		
		DR	CR	BAL	DR	CR	BAL
April 3	Cash. Bingley					2,200	2,200CR
May 9	Interest payable		18	18CR			
9	Cash. Interest	18		–			
9	Cash. Returned				2,200		–

Cash account

Date	Details	Office account		Client account		
		CR	BAL	DR	CR	BAL
April 3	Dash Ltd. Bingley			2,200		
May 9	Dash Ltd. Interest	18				
9	Dash Ltd. Returned				2,200	

Interest payable account

Date	Details	Office account		
		DR	CR	BAL
May 9	Dash Ltd.	18		18DR

Method 2   Transfer the £18 from the office bank account to the client bank account, and then send Dash Ltd one cheque drawn on the client bank account for £2,218. In this case, additional entries must be made on the client section of the client ledger and on the client section of the cash account to show that money has been held for the client in the client bank account.

Entries:

To record £18 owed to client in interest

> DR Interest payable ledger account
> CR Dash Ltd ledger account   } Office section

To record £18 office cash paid out of office bank account

> DR Dash Ltd
> CR Cash   } Office section

To record £18 received into client bank account

> CR Dash Ltd ledger account
> DR Cash account   } Client section

Payment to Dash Ltd of £2,218 from client bank account

> DR Dash Ltd ledger account
> CR Cash account   } Client section

The accounts will look like this:

Client: Dash Ltd
Matter: Debt collection

Date	Details	Office account			Client account		
		DR	CR	BAL	DR	CR	BAL
April 3	Cash					2,200	2,200CR
May 9	Interest payable		18	18CR			
9	Cash. Interest	18		–		18	2,218
9	Cash. Returned				2,218		–

Cash account

Date	Details	Office account			Client account		
		DR	CR	BAL	DR	CR	BAL
April 3	Dash Ltd. Bingley			xxx	2,200		xxx
May 9	Dash Ltd. Interest		18	xxx			
	Dash Ltd. Interest				18		xxx
9	Dash Ltd. Returned					2,218	xxx

Interest payable account

Date	Details	Office account		
		DR	CR	BAL
May 9	Dash Ltd.	18		18DR

Exercise 15A

You act for the executor of Swan, deceased, and for Cygnet, the residuary beneficiary of Swan's estate. You complete the administration and ask Cygnet for instructions on what to do with the money due to him (£200,000). Cygnet tells you to hold the money pending his instructions as he is hoping to buy a house in the near future.

March

20   You transfer Cygnet's residuary entitlement of £200,000 from the executor's ledger account to Cygnet's ledger account.

April

15   You realise that Cygnet will be entitled to interest on the money held for him. You calculate that he is entitled to £100 for the period from 20 March. You pay the sum from the office bank account into the client bank account.

16   You tell the bank to open a separate deposit bank account designated with Cygnet's name and to pay all the money held for Cygnet into that separate designated client account.

30   Cygnet tells you to send him the amount to which he is entitled. The bank credits £120 interest. You close the separate designated client account, transfer the money to the general client bank account and send Cygnet a cheque for the whole amount.

May

6   Cygnet tells you he thinks he is entitled to more interest for the period 20 March–15 April.

You agree and send him an office bank account cheque for £30.

Show relevant cash accounts and client ledger entries for Cygnet.

SUMMARY

(1) Clients are normally entitled to interest on client money held by firms providing legal services (although there are some exceptional cases where there is no such entitlement).

(2) The firm can use one of two methods to meet the obligation to account for interest.

(3) The firm can open a separate deposit bank account designated with the name of the client and account to the client for all the interest earned on the account.

(4) Alternatively, the firm can pay the client interest from the office bank account. The amount due is calculated by reference to the amount of interest that would have been earned had a separate designated deposit account been opened.

(5) A firm which pays interest from the office bank account will be out of pocket unless it puts a proportion of the money in the client bank account on deposit. The Solicitors Act 1974 allows solicitors to keep the interest earned on client money placed on general deposit.

SOLUTION

Exercise 15A

Notes:

March

20   This is an inter-client transfer from the ledger account of the executor to the ledger account of Cygnet. No entries will be made on the cash account as the money remains in the client bank account. A note would be made in the transfer journal.

April

15   To record the payment of interest from the office bank account:

DR Interest payable
CR Cygnet (1) – Office section

$\left.\begin{array}{l} \text{CR Cash} \\ \text{DR Cygnet (1)} \end{array}\right\}$ Office section

Since the interest is going to be held by the firm for Cygnet, it must be received into the client bank account:

$\left.\begin{array}{l} \text{DR Cash} \\ \text{CR Cygnet (1)} \end{array}\right\}$ Client section

16   To record the transfer of the money into a separate designated client account:

$\left.\begin{array}{l} \text{CR Cash} \\ \text{DR Cygnet (1)} \end{array}\right\}$ Client section

DR Combined cash account (CCA)
CR Cygnet (2)

30   To record the bank's payment of £120 interest:

DR CCA
CR Cygnet (2)

To record the transfer of £200,220 back to the general client bank account:

CR CCA
DR Cygnet (2)

$\left.\begin{array}{l} \text{DR Cash} \\ \text{CR Cygnet (1)} \end{array}\right\}$ Client section

To record the payment of £200,220 to Cygnet:

$\left.\begin{array}{l} \text{CR Cash} \\ \text{DR Cygnet (1)} \end{array}\right\}$ Client section

May

6   To record the payment of £30 interest from office money:

DR Interest payable
CR Cygnet (1) – Office section

$\left.\begin{array}{l} \text{CR Cash} \\ \text{DR Cygnet (1)} \end{array}\right\}$ Office section

As the £30 is paid out to Cygnet directly and is not held by the firm in the client bank account, no entries need be made on the client section of Cygnet's ledger account or on the client section of the cash account.

Client: Cygnet (1)
Matter: House purchase

Date	Details	Office account			Client account		
		DR	CR	BAL	DR	CR	BAL
March 20	Executor of Swan Residuary entitlement (TJ)					200,000	200,000CR
April 15	Interest payable		100	100CR			
15	Cash. Interest	100		–		100	200,100
16	Cash. On deposit				200,100		–
30	Cash. Off deposit					200,220	200,220
30	Cash. Returned				200,220		–
May 6	Interest payable		30	30CR			
6	Cash. Interest	30		–			

Client: Cygnet (2)
Matter: Money held on deposit

Date	Details	Office account			Client account		
		DR	CR	BAL	DR	CR	BAL
April 16	Deposit cash. A/C opened					200,100	200,100CR
30	Deposit cash. Interest					120	200,220
30	Deposit cash. A/C closed				200,220		–

Cash

Date	Details	Office account			Client account		
		DR	CR	BAL	DR	CR	BAL
April 15	Balance			xxx			xxx
15	Cygnet (1). Interest		100		100		
16	Cygnet (1). On deposit					200,100	
30	Cygnet-deposit (1). Off deposit				200,220		
30	Cygnet (1). Returned to client					200,220	
May 6	Cygnet (1). Interest		30				

Combined Deposit Cash

Date	Details	Office account			Client account		
		DR	CR	BAL	DR	CR	BAL
April 16	Cygnet (2). A/C opened				200,100		xxx
30	Cygnet (2). Interest				120		
30	Cygnet (2). A/C closed					200,220	

Interest payable

Date	Details	Office account		
		DR	CR	BAL
Apr 15	Cygnet (1).	100		100DR
May 6	Cygnet (1).	30		130

FINANCIAL STATEMENTS

> **LEARNING OUTCOMES**
>
> After reading this chapter you will be able to:
>
> - prepare a simple Financial Statement showing how much money is required from or due to a client.

16.1 INTRODUCTION

If you handle money for a client, you should always prepare a written statement explaining how the client's money held has been dealt with and how much, if anything, is due to or from the client.

The statement is particularly important in property transactions where it is likely to be sent to the client part-way through the transaction to inform the client how much he will have to provide or how much will be available to the client at the end of the transaction.

Errors made in such statements are a common cause of complaint from clients.

In this chapter you will learn how to prepare a simple Financial Statement.

16.2 LAYOUT

There is no set layout but the statement must be clear and easy for the client to follow.

A common layout is to show the statement in the form of a sum, starting with the purchase price, adding expenses and deducting receipts (or in the case of a sale, starting with the sale price, deducting expenses and adding receipts).

Note: Items to be deducted are frequently shown in brackets.

Example

FINANCIAL STATEMENT [date]
TO: MR AND MRS BOUNDS
PURCHASE OF 3 WICKET STREET

		£	£
Purchase price			300,000
less: Prepaid deposit	(30,000)		
Mortgage advance net of legal fees	(222,340)		
			(252,340)
			47,660
add: Stamp duty land tax	5,000		
Land Registry fees	100		
Professional charges (including online searches)	420		
VAT	84		
			5,604
less: Received on account of costs			(400)
DUE FROM YOU			52,864

Where a simultaneous sale and purchase are involved, it is good practice to show separate subtotals for the sale and for the purchase so that the client can see how much the purchase cost and how much is available from the sale. The statement may then show in a summary the total amount due to or from the client in respect of both transactions.

Exercise 16A

You act for Clara, who is selling 6 High Street for £165,000 to Priscilla and buying 'The Cedars' for £180,000 from Viola.

The Bayswater and District Building Society, for whom you act, is granting a mortgage on 'The Cedars' of £120,000, and there is a mortgage to redeem on 6 High Street of £140,000.

June

1   Clara gives you £200 on account of costs.

3   You pay postal search fees of £10 by cheque on 'The Cedars'.

5   You receive a cheque from Clara for £18,000 (the deposit agreed on 'The Cedars') made out to Viola's solicitors.

7   You send the cheque for £18,000 to Viola's solicitors to hold as stakeholders. You receive a cheque for £6,000 from Priscilla's solicitors which you are to hold as stakeholders.

16   You send a Financial Statement to Clara which shows the total required from her to complete both transactions. You also present your bill which includes £200 costs on sale and £300 costs on purchase plus VAT. Your charges to the building society, which Clara is to pay by way of indemnity, are £40 on the mortgage advance and £20 on the mortgage redemption, plus VAT in each case.

18   You receive from Clara the amount requested on 16 June and you receive the mortgage advance from the building society.

20   You complete the sale and purchase.

21   You pay Land Registry fees of £100 and stamp duty land tax of £1,100 on 'The Cedars' and transfer the amount due to you for costs, etc.

Prepare the financial statement sent to Clara on 16 June.

PRACTICAL POINT

You need to be clear which items relate to the sale and which to the purchase. The following is a breakdown:

Sale	Purchase
Official Copies of title from Land Registry	Pre-contract searches and enquiries, eg local authority search, environmental search
Mortgage Redemption	Land Registry search
Estate Agent's Fees	Mortgage Advance
Bankruptcy Search if also acting for Mortgagee	Land Registration Fees
	Stamp Duty Land Tax
	Bankruptcy Search

SUMMARY

(1) If you handle client money, you must prepare a Financial Statement showing how the money has been dealt with.

(2) There is no required form for Financial Statements, but they must be clear, accurate and easy for clients to understand.

(3) Where a transaction involves the sale of one property and the purchase of another, it is good practice to show separate subtotals for the amount available from the sale and the amount required for the purchase.

SOLUTION

Exercise 16A

FINANCIAL STATEMENT 16 JUNE
TO: CLARA
PURCHASE OF 'THE CEDARS'

		£	£
Purchase price			180,000.00
less	Prepaid deposit	(18,000.00)	
	Mortgage advance	(120,000.00)	
			(138,000.00)
			42,000.00
add	Our professional charges	300.00	
	VAT	60.00	
	Professional charges to building society and VAT payable by you	48.00	
	Land Registry fees	100.00[1]	
	Stamp duty land tax	1,100.00[1]	
	Postal search fees	10.00	
			1,618.00
Required for purchase			**43,618.00**

SALE OF 6 HIGH STREET

Sale price			165,000.00
less	Mortgage redemption	(140,000.00)	
	Our professional charges	(200.00)	
	VAT	(40.00)	
	Professional charges to building society costs and VAT payable by you	(24.00)[2]	
			(140,264.00)
Available on sale			**24,736.00**
SUMMARY			
	Required for purchase		43,618.00
less	Available on sale		(24,736.00)
			18,882.00
less	Received on account		(200.00)
DUE FROM YOU			**18,682.00**

[1] Although you have not paid these on 16 June, you know that they will be required and will therefore include them on the Financial Statement.

[2] The VAT on the fees charged to the building society is not itemised separately as the invoice is addressed to the building society, not the client.

ACCOUNTING PROBLEMS FOR SOLICITORS

LEARNING OUTCOMES

After reading this chapter you will be able to:

- identify how many ledger accounts are required in particular transactions
- understand how to deal with instructing another firm to act as your agent in a client transaction
- identify the circumstances in which client money may be withheld from the client bank account and whether entries need to be made.

17.1 INTRODUCTION

In this chapter you will look at some unusual situations that present particular accounting complexities, including the number of ledger accounts required, agency transactions and the question of withholding funds from a client bank account.

17.2 NUMBER OF LEDGER ACCOUNTS REQUIRED

17.2.1 The problem

You must show the amount of client money held for each client. This requires a separate ledger account for each client for whom money is held. (There is one exception contained in Rule 29.10 – see **17.2.5**.) You must consider carefully which client the firm is holding money for, and whether money ceases to be held for one client and becomes held for someone else as this will require an inter-client transfer.

17.2.2 Funds originally held for one client being held for another

This can happen in a number of different types of transaction.

Example

You act for the executors of a deceased person. You complete the administration of the estate and inform the residuary beneficiary of the amount of his entitlement. The residuary beneficiary asks you to hold the money for him pending completion of a transaction on his behalf.

The money will stay in your client bank account, so no entries are made on your cash account. However, you must mark the fact that the money is no longer held for the executors but is now held for the residuary beneficiary. You do this by an inter-client transfer.

> *Entries:*
>
> DR executors' ledger
> CR residuary beneficiary's } Client section
>
> You must make a note in a transfer journal.

Exercise 17A

You act for George and for George & Co Ltd. George is a director of George & Co. George is selling land to George & Co for £120,000. The sale is to be completed on 5 June.

On 1 June, George tells you that he will be investing in a venture capital trust and asks you to hold the proceeds of sale of the land until he gives you further instructions.

On 4 June, the company gives you the funds to complete the purchase. On 5 June, you complete the sale. On 7 June, George tells you to pay the sale proceeds to the Gallymead Venture Capital Trust.

How will you deal with the sale proceeds of the land?

17.2.3 Stakeholder money

You may receive a deposit to hold as stakeholder. This is clearly a receipt of client money and so must be held in the client bank account. Who is it held for?

You are holding it jointly for the buyer and the seller. It will not become the property of the seller unless and until completion takes place. Therefore, you cannot simply record the stakeholder money as held for the seller alone. Note, however, that it is normal for conditions of sale to provide that sellers who are buying a residence in England and Wales may use all or any part of a deposit to fund the deposit on the property being purchased. See Standard Conditions of Sale, 5th edn, SC 2.2.5.

The Guidance to Accountants issued by The Law Society on 16 December 2005 said that stakeholder money may be shown on the seller's ledger but must be clearly labelled as stakeholder money held for both buyer and seller.

> *Entries:*
>
> DR Cash
> CR Seller's ledger, noting money held as stakeholder } Client section

The alternative is to open a separate ledger account in the name of the client and the buyer and credit the stakeholder money to that account.

> *Entries:*
>
> DR Cash
> CR Separate stakeholder ledger } Client section

As soon as the completion takes place, you start to hold the money for the seller alone. You must record this by making an inter-client transfer from the stakeholder ledger account to the seller's ledger account.

> *Entries:*
>
> On the day of completion:
>
> DR Separate stakeholder ledger
> CR Seller's ledger } Client section

This is much more trouble than following the procedure suggested in the Guidance to Accountants. However, it has the advantage of keeping the entries relating to the stakeholder funds entirely separate from those relating to the money held for the seller alone. It therefore avoids the risk of making a payment from the client bank account for the seller using funds which are not yet available to the seller.

It is not acceptable to credit all stakeholder money to one general stakeholder ledger account, because this does not comply with the requirement in Rule 29.2 that all dealings with client money are to be recorded on the client side of a *separate* client ledger account for each client.

A deposit received as agent for the seller belongs to the seller alone and is credited directly to the seller's ledger account.

> *Entries:*
>
> DR Cash   } Client section
> CR Seller's ledger

17.2.4 Bridging finance

A deposit received as stakeholder is not available to the seller until completion without agreement (see, for example, Standard Conditions of Sale (5th edn), SC 2.2.5). A seller who is purchasing a replacement property may have insufficient cash available to pay the deposit on the purchase. Where a deposit is not available or is insufficient, it is possible to take a bridging loan from a bank to cover the period from exchange of contracts on the purchase to completion of the sale, when cash will become available.

A bridging loan is a personal loan to the borrower and, once received, belongs to the borrower and not the bank. Hence, when a solicitor receives the cash (whether direct from the bank or via the borrower), it will be held to the order of the borrower and must be credited to the borrower's ledger account, not to a ledger account in the name of the lending bank.

On completion of the sale, the loan, together with interest, must be repaid to the bank.

17.2.5 Mortgages

17.2.5.1 Introduction

Many clients who buy property need to borrow money on mortgage. A client who sells property which is subject to a mortgage will have to redeem, ie repay, that mortgage after completion.

If you act for a client who is buying a property, you may also act for the lender, provided that there is no conflict of interest.

Where you are instructed to act for both the borrower and the lender, you must bear in mind that there are two separate clients. You must consider carefully for which client you are holding client money.

17.2.5.2 Mortgage advances – solicitor acting for buyer and lender

When you receive a mortgage advance, you hold it for the lender until the day of completion, when it becomes available to the borrower. The client ledger accounts must clearly distinguish money held for one client from money held for every other client. This normally requires a separate ledger account for each client, so that there would have to be a separate ledger account for the lender. However, Rule 29.10 provides a limited exception to the rule that money held for each separate client must be shown on a separate ledger account.

The exception in Rule 29.10 applies only to institutional lenders which provide mortgages on standard terms in the normal course of their activities. Banks and building societies are examples of such lenders.

Where a mortgage advance is provided by an *institutional lender* which provides mortgages in the normal course of business, you need not have a separate ledger account for the lender. Instead, the advance can be credited to the ledger account of the borrower. However, Rule 29.10 requires the funds belonging to each client to be 'clearly identifiable'. This is done by including the name of the lender in the details column of the borrower's ledger account and describing the funds as 'mortgage advance'. It is not enough to state that the money was received from the ABC Building Society without specifying the nature of the payment, or vice versa. See guidance note (v) to Rule 29.

Example

The Southern Cross Building Society advances £50,000 to Brown on 6 June for his house purchase.

Client: Brown
Matter: House Purchase

Date	Details	Office account			Client account		
		DR	CR	BAL	DR	CR	BAL
June 6	Cash. Mortgage advance held for Southern Cross Building Society					50,000	50,000CR

It is important to remember that Rule 29.10 applies only to loans from institutional lenders. A loan from a private lender must be dealt with in the ordinary way. A separate client ledger account is required in the name of the lender (see **17.2.5.6**).

Note: Frequently, the money advanced by way of mortgage will be paid direct to the seller's solicitor by the lender. In such a case, as the buyer's solicitor does not handle the mortgage advance, there will be no entries relating to the money in the accounts of the buyer's solicitor.

17.2.5.3 Profit costs on mortgage advance

You are entitled to charge the lender for work done in connection with the mortgage advance as well as to charge the buyer for the work done in connection with the purchase. The buyer will frequently have agreed with the lender to pay the costs charged to the lender. The normal rule is that costs and VAT *must* be debited to the ledger account of the person (Person A) to whom the legal services were supplied. If another person, B, is discharging the debt by way of indemnity, the debt can be transferred from A's ledger account to B's ledger account.

In the case of a mortgage advance from an institutional lender, the normal rule has to be varied because you will probably not have a ledger account for the lender. Thus, the mortgage costs will have to be debited from the beginning to the ledger account of the buyer/borrower. The costs of the purchase and the costs of the mortgage with appropriate VAT will be shown separately in the ledger account kept for the buyer/borrower, making it clear which relate to the purchase and which to the loan.

Entries:

DR Buyer's ledger account, office section, with purchase costs and VAT
CR Profit costs account and HMRC account, with costs and VAT

DR Buyer's ledger account, office section, with mortgage costs and VAT
CR Profit costs account and HMRC account, with mortgage costs and VAT

17.2.5.4 Mortgage redemption – acting for both lender and seller

Many sellers have a balance left on their mortgage at the date of sale. The balance has to be paid off from the proceeds of sale.

It is uncommon to act for both lender and seller. However, it is possible. Rule 29.10 applies only to mortgage advances, not to mortgage redemptions. This means that, on a redemption, you will need one ledger account to show dealings with the seller's money and a separate ledger account to show dealings with the lender's money.

When you receive the balance of the sale price from the buyer, it is client money and must be paid into the client bank account. The whole receipt is initially credited to the seller's ledger account to give a full picture of amounts handled for the seller.

Entries:

CR Seller's ledger account
DR Cash account } Client section

However, part of the receipt is required to redeem the mortgage. That money belongs to the lender, and it must be shown as such in the lender's ledger account. It must be immediately transferred from the seller's ledger account to the lender's ledger account.

Entries:

DR Seller's ledger account
CR Lender's ledger account } Client section

You will then send the lender a cheque for the mortgage redemption money out of the client bank account.

Entries:

DR Lender's ledger account
CR Cash account } Client section

Note 1: It is permissible to argue that you receive part of the proceeds for the seller and part for the lender, so that it is correct to split the credit entries at the time of receipt. If this is done, you will credit part of the proceeds to the seller's ledger account and part to the lender's ledger account. The whole amount is debited to the cash account client section.

Note 2: Frequently, the money due for the mortgage redemption will be paid direct to the lender's solicitor. In such a case, as the seller's solicitor does not handle that money, there will be no entries relating to the money in the solicitor's accounts.

17.2.5.5 Legal fees on mortgage redemption

The seller may have agreed to pay the legal fees of the lender. The seller's solicitor will address a bill to the lender. As there is a separate ledger account for the lender, the legal fees on the mortgage redemption must initially be debited to the lender's ledger account. The debt will then be transferred to the seller's ledger account to show that it is the seller who will discharge it, not the lender.

Entries:

DR Seller's ledger account, office section, with fees charged on the sale and VAT
CR Costs account and HMRC account with fees charged on the sale and VAT

DR Lender's ledger account, office section, with fees charged on the mortgage and VAT
CR Costs account and HMRC account with fees charged on the mortgage and VAT

Transfer debt from Lender's ledger account to Seller's ledger account as follows:

CR Lender's ledger account with fees charged on the mortgage and VAT
DR Seller's ledger account with fees charged on the mortgage and VAT

17.2.5.6   Private lenders

Rule 29.10 does not apply to private lenders so the solicitor must open a separate ledger account for each client.

(a) *Legal fees.* The legal fees charged on the mortgage will be charged to the lender; the legal fees charged on the purchase/sale will be charged to the buyer/seller. The buyer/seller is likely to be responsible for the lender's legal fees, which may be transferred as a debt from the lender's ledger account to the buyer/seller's.

(b) *Receipt of mortgage advance for purchase.* The buyer's solicitor receives this on behalf of the lender. It is shown in the lender's ledger account. It is transferred to the buyer's ledger account immediately before completion of the purchase to show that it is now available to the buyer.

(c) *Redemption of mortgage on sale.* The seller's solicitor receives the proceeds of sale on behalf of the seller and then deals with the redemption in the same way as for the institutional lender.

Below are examples of transactions involving two clients.

Example 1

Purchase – with mortgage advance

Your firm is instructed by Eliot, who is purchasing 'The Willows' for £157,000 with the aid of an £85,000 mortgage from Gravesend Building Society for whom you also act. The following events occur:

August

4   Eliot tells you that he has paid £500 preliminary deposit to the estate agents, Coomb & Co.

5   You order online local search (£5) from a commercial provider who takes payment by direct debit.

12   You receive £15,200 from Eliot being the balance of the 10% deposit required.

15   You receive and pay surveyor's invoice in Eliot's name of £164 including VAT.

20   You exchange contracts and pay the balance of the deposit.

29   You order bankruptcy search (£5) from a commercial provider who takes payment by direct debit.

30   You send financial statement and bill of costs to Eliot. (Professional charges on purchase amount to £400 plus searches (£10) plus VAT and on mortgage to £80 plus VAT.)

September

1   You receive mortgage advance of £85,000 from Gravesend Building Society.

1   You receive sum due for completion from Eliot.

2   You complete purchase of 'The Willows'.

8   You pay Land Registry fees of £200 and stamp duty land tax of £640 and transfer all sums due to the firm to close the account.

Show the entries necessary to record the above transaction in the client ledger and cash account, together with the financial statement sent on 27 August.

Notes:

August

4   You do not need to make any entries – but remember that, when contracts are exchanged and the 10% deposit is payable, £500 of the deposit has already been paid.

5   The money for the search is paid from the office bank account. It will not appear on the client ledger as you will CR Cash – Office and DR Searches. You will increase your professional charges.

12   The money is client money and is paid into the client bank account.

> Entries:
>
> CR Eliot ledger account ⎫
> DR Cash account   ⎬ Client section
>   ⎭

Remember that £500 has already been received. This money makes up the balance of £12,700.

15   The invoice is addressed to Eliot, and so you must pay it using the agency method. The money in the client bank account is specifically for payment of the deposit. It cannot therefore be used for payment of this bill. The bill must be paid out of office money as you have no client money available.

> Entries:
>
> DR Eliot ledger account ⎫
> CR Cash account   ⎬ Office section
>   ⎭

20   The payment can be made out of the client bank account as you have client money available.

> Entries:
>
> DR Eliot ledger account ⎫
> CR Cash account   ⎬ Client section
>   ⎭

29   As with the local search, this is paid from the office bank account. No entries appear on the client ledger. You will increase your professional charges.

30   Sending the Financial Statement does not require any entries in the accounts. The Statement simply shows the client how much is required. A suitable Financial Statement is shown at the end of this example.

Professional charges and VAT: A bill is sent so the usual entries are made for profit costs and VAT. Remember to charge the profit costs on the mortgage advance as well as those on the purchase to Eliot. They should, however, be shown on separate lines. Remember to increase your professional charges to cover the searches.

> Entries:
>
> Profit costs   DR Eliot ledger account ⎫
> CR   Profit costs account   ⎬ Office section
>   ⎭
>
> VAT   DR Eliot ledger account ⎫
> CR   HMRC ledger account   ⎬ Office section
>   ⎭

(Profit costs and HMRC accounts are not shown.)

September

1   The money is client money. It is paid into client bank account. You are receiving the money on behalf of your client, Gravesend Building Society. However, Rule 29.10 allows you to credit the money to Eliot's ledger account provided it is labelled as held for the Gravesend Building Society and described as a mortgage advance.

Entries:

> CR Eliot ledger account
> DR Cash account   } Client section

1   This is the amount shown in the Financial Statement. The money is a mixture of office and client money. We have not split the cheque but have paid it all into the client bank account (Rule 18).

Entries:

> CR Eliot ledger account
> DR Cash account   } Client section

2   On completion, the balance of the purchase price owing is paid out of the client bank account.

Entries:

> DR Eliot ledger account
> CR Cash account   } Client section

8   The Financial Statement took into account the amount which would be payable for Land Registry fees and stamp duty land tax. There is therefore enough money in the client bank account to cover them, so the payment can be made from the client bank account.

Entries:

> DR Eliot ledger account
> CR Cash account   } Client section

The transfer from the client to office bank account is recorded in the usual way.

Entries:

Withdrawal from client bank account

> DR Eliot ledger account
> CR Cash account   } Client section

Receipt into office bank account

> CR Eliot ledger account
> DR Cash account   } Office section

The *completed* accounts look like this:

Client: Mr Eliot
Matter: Purchase of 'The Willows'

Date	Details	Office account			Client account		
		DR	CR	BAL	DR	CR	BAL
Aug							
12	Cash. From Eliot. Balance of deposit					15,200	15,200CR
15	Cash. Surveyor's fee	164		164			
20	Cash. Vendor's solicitor. Balance of deposit				15,200		–
30	Profit costs on purchase	410		574			
	VAT	82		656			
	Profit costs on mortgage	80		736			
	VAT	16		752			
Sep							
1	Cash. From Gravesend Building Society. For mortgage advance					85,000	85,000
1	Cash. From Eliot					57,892	142,892
2	Cash. Vendor's solicitor. Completion				141,300		1,592
8	Cash. Land Registry fee				200		1,392
	Cash. Stamp duty land tax				640		752
	Cash. Transfer costs and disbursements		752	–	752		–

Cash account

Date	Details	Office account			Client account		
		DR	CR	BAL	DR	CR	BAL
	Balances			xxx			xxx
Aug							
5	Online searches		5				
12	Eliot. Balance of deposit				12,200		
15	Eliot. Surveyor		164				
20	Eliot. Payment of deposit					12,200	
29	Online searches		5				
Sep							
1	Eliot. Mortgage advance. Gravesend B Society				85,000		
	Eliot. Balance purchase price				57,892		
1	Eliot. Payment purchase price					141,300	
2	Eliot. Land Registry fee					200	
8	Eliot. Stamp duty land tax					640	
	Eliot. Costs and disbursements	752				752	

FINANCIAL STATEMENT 27 AUGUST

TO: ELIOT
PURCHASE OF 'THE WILLOWS'

			£	£
	Purchase price			157,000
less:	Prepaid deposit			(15,700)
				141,300
less:	Mortgage advance			(85,000)
				56,300
add:	Professional charges on purchase including searches (£10)		410	
	VAT on professional charges and searches		82	
	Professional charges on mortgage (inc VAT)		96	
	Surveyor's fee (inc VAT)		164	
	Land Registry fee		200	
	Stamp duty land tax		640	
				1,592
	DUE FROM YOU			57,892

Example 2

Sale and purchase – mortgage redemption and advance

You are acting for Laura, who is selling 'Obrion' for £140,000 and buying 'The Towers' for £200,000. There is an existing mortgage of £20,000 on 'Obrion' in favour of Brighton Building Society. This is to be redeemed following completion of the sale. Brighton Building Society has also agreed to a new mortgage to Laura of £50,000 for the purchase of 'The Towers'. You have been instructed to act for Brighton Building Society in connection with the redemption and the new advance. Laura has agreed to pay the building society's legal fees in connection with the advance and redemption.

The following events occur:

May

17   You order from a third party provider official copy entries relating to 'Obrion' (£5) and a local land charges search in respect of 'The Towers' (£5). The agency takes payment by direct debit.

24   You receive £20,000 from Laura to use as the deposit on 'The Towers'.

28   You exchange contracts on sale and purchase. Receive a £14,000 deposit on 'Obrion' as stakeholder. You pay deposit on 'The Towers'.

31   You send a completion statement in respect of 'Obrion' showing the balance due (£126,000).

June

1   You receive a completion statement in respect of 'The Towers' showing the balance due (£180,000).

2   You order a bankruptcy search from a third party provider. The agency takes payment (£5) by direct debit.

3   You send a bill of costs and a financial statement to Laura. Professional charges on sale are £400 plus VAT; on purchase £600 plus VAT; on mortgage redemption £40 plus VAT; and on the new mortgage advance £80 plus VAT.

8   You receive £13,692 from Laura, being the amount shown due in the financial statement.

9   You receive the mortgage advance of £50,000 from the building society.

10	You complete the sale and purchase.
11	You send the building society a cheque to redeem the mortgage. You pay stamp duty land tax (£1,100) and Land Registry fee (£250) in respect of 'The Towers'.
12	You pay the estate agent's commission of £980 including VAT. The invoice was addressed to Laura. You transfer all costs and disbursements owing to you.

Show the entries necessary to record the above transaction in the client ledger and the cash account, together with the financial statement sent on 3 June.

Notes:

May

17	These payments for searches are made from the office bank account. They will not appear on the client ledger as you will CR Cash – Office and DR Searches account.
24	Client money must be paid into client bank account.

Entries:

CR Laura ledger account
DR Cash account } Client section

28	The £4,000 deposit received is client money so is paid into the client bank account, but CR stakeholder ledger account, not Laura ledger account.

Entries:

CR Stakeholder account
DR Cash account } Client section

The £10,000 due for the deposit will be paid out of client money.

Entries:

DR Laura ledger account
CR Cash account } Client section

31	No entries are required. There are no additional items referred to, so at completion only the balance of the sale price (£36,000) will be received.

June

1	This confirms that only the balance of the purchase price (£90,000) will be payable at completion.
2	The search is dealt with in the same way as on 17 May.
3	The usual entries for profit costs and VAT are made. You will increase your charges to cover the cost of the searches.
	Remember that Laura is responsible for your charges to her and for your charges to the Brighton Building Society. You must debit the legal fees on the mortgage redemption and VAT to the building society's ledger account and then transfer the debt to Laura's ledger account. The legal fees on the mortgage advance and VAT will be debited directly to Laura's ledger account.
	A financial statement is given at the end of this example.
8	The cheque is a combination of office and client money. We have not split it but have paid it into the client bank account (Rule 18).

Entries:

CR Laura ledger account
DR Cash account } Client section

9	The money is received on behalf of your client, Brighton Building Society, but Rule 29.10 applies and the mortgage advance can be shown immediately as a CR in Laura's ledger account.

10   **Completion of sale:**

£36,000 is received from the purchaser's solicitor. It is client money and paid into the client bank account.

Entries:

CR Laura ledger account
DR Cash account   } Client section

Then transfer the deposit, which now belongs to Laura, from stakeholder account.

Entries:

DR Stakeholder ledger account
CR Laura ledger account   } Client section

There will be a record of the transfer made in the transfer journal (Rule 29.2).

Redemption of mortgage:

Part of the sale proceeds (the portion required to redeem the mortgage) is held for the building society. Transfer the redemption money from Laura to Brighton Building Society. Keep a record in the transfer journal.

Entries:

DR Laura ledger account
CR Brighton Building Society ledger account   } Client section

Completion of purchase:

Send the seller's solicitor the balance required of £90,000 from the client bank account.

Entries:

DR Laura ledger account
CR Cash account   } Client section

11   Send Brighton Building Society a cheque for £20,000 from the client bank account.

Entries:

DR Brighton Building Society ledger account
CR Cash account   } Client section

The Land Registry fees and stamp duty land tax can be paid from the client bank account.

DR Laura ledger account
CR Cash account   } Client section

12   The estate agent's bill is paid from the client bank account using the agency method.

Entries:

DR Laura ledger account
CR Cash account   } Client section

Transfer money from the client to the office bank account in the usual way.

Entries:

Withdrawal from the client bank account

DR Laura ledger account
CR Cash account   } Client section

Receipt into the office bank account

CR Laura ledger account } Office section
CR Cash account

The *completed* accounts look like this:

Client: Laura
Matter: Sale of 'Obrion'; Purchase of 'The Towers'

Date	Details	Office account			Client account		
		DR	CR	BAL	DR	CR	BAL
May							
24	Cash. From Laura. For deposit on 'The Towers'					20,000	20,000CR
28	Cash. To Vendor's solicitor. Deposit on 'The Towers'				20,000		–
June							
3	Profit costs. Sale	405		405			
	VAT	81		486			
	Purchase	610		1,096			
	VAT	122		1,218			
	Costs. Mortgage advance	80		1,298			
	VAT	16		1,314			
	Brighton BS. Transfer mortgage redemption costs and VAT	48		1,362			
8	Cash. From Laura					13,692	13,692CR
9	Cash. From Brighton Building Society. For mortgage advance					50,000	63,692
10	Cash. Purchaser's solicitor. Complete sale					126,000	189,692
	Laura and Buyer, Transfer deposit (TJ)					14,000	203,692
	Cash. Vendor's solicitor. Complete purchase				180,000		23,692
	Brighton Building Society. Transfer mortgage redemption (TJ)				20,000		3,692
11	Cash. Stamp duty land tax. 'The Towers'				1,100		2,592
	Cash. Land Registry fee. 'The Towers'				250		2,342
12	Cash. Estate agent. 'Obrion'				980		1,362
	Cash. Transfer costs and disbursements from client to office account		1,362	–	1,362		–

Client: Brighton Building Society
Matter: Mortgage redemption re Laura

Date	Details	Office account			Client account		
		DR	CR	BAL	DR	CR	BAL
June							
3	Profit costs	40					
	VAT	8		48DR			
	Laura. Transfer mortgage redemption costs and VAT		48	–			
10	Laura. Transfer mortgage redemption (TJ)					20,000	20,000CR
11	Cash. To Brighton Building Society				20,000		–

Cash account

Date	Details	Office account			Client account		
		DR	CR	BAL	DR	CR	BAL
				xxx			xxx
May							
17	Online search		5				
	Online search		5				
24	Laura. For deposit				20,000		
28	Stakeholder				14,000		
	Laura. Deposit to vendors					20,000	
June							
2	Online search		5				
8	Laura. Balance for purchase				13,692		
9	Laura. Mortgage advance. Brighton Building Society				50,000		
10	Laura. Purchaser's solicitors				126,000		
	Laura. Complete purchase					180,000	
11	Brighton Building Society. Mortgage redemption					20,000	
	Laura. Stamp duty land tax					1,100	
	Laura. Land Registry fee					250	
12	Laura. Estate agent					980	
	Laura. Professional charges and disbursements	1,362				1,362	

Client: Laura (and buyer)
Matter: Stakeholder

Date	Details	Office account			Client account		
		DR	CR	BAL	DR	CR	BAL
May							
28	Cash. Deposit on 'Obrion' re Laura					14,000	14,000CR
June							
10	Laura. Transfer deposit (TJ)				14,000		–

FINANCIAL STATEMENT 3 JUNE

TO: LAURA
SALE OF 'OBRION'

		£	£
	Sale price		140,000
less:	Mortgage redemption		(20,000)
			120,000
	Professional charges on sale (including search £5)	405	
	VAT on professional shares plus searches	81	
	Professional charges on mortgage redemption (inc VAT)	48	
	Estate agent's commission (inc VAT)	980	(1,514)
	Available on sale		**118,486**

PURCHASE OF 'THE TOWERS'		
Purchase price		200,000
less: Prepaid deposit		(20,000)
		180,000
Mortgage advance		(50,000)
		130,000
add: Professional charges on purchase (including searches £10)	610	
VAT on professional charges and searches	122	
Professional charges on mortgage advance (inc VAT)	96	
Stamp duty land tax	1,100	
Land Registry fees	250	2,178
Required for purchase		132,178
SUMMARY		
Required for purchase		132,178
less: Available from sale		(118,486)
DUE FROM YOU		13,692

17.3 AGENCY TRANSACTIONS

A firm providing legal services may decide to use another firm as its agent. This may occur in any type of transaction, but probably happens most often in the context of a litigation matter.

17.3.1 The agent firm

The agent firm treats the instructing firm like any other client. There will be a client ledger account in the name of the instructing firm, and the normal entries will be made to deal with any client money and the delivery of the bill.

17.3.2 The instructing firm

The professional fees charged by the agent are not a disbursement paid by the instructing firm on behalf of the client. The instructing firm is providing legal services to the client using an agent. The professional fees of the agent are, therefore, an expense of the instructing firm. The firm will charge more for its legal services in order to cover the expense of using an agent. Any true disbursements (eg court fees, counsel's fees) will be charged to the client as usual, and it is irrelevant whether the agent or the instructing firm pays them.

When the instructing firm pays the agent's bill, he sends one office bank account cheque for the total amount. There can be three different elements of that total: the agent's professional fees, VAT on those fees and any disbursements paid by the agent. The different elements will be recorded separately in the instructing firm's accounts.

Entries:

Agent's professional charges	CR Cash account DR Agency expenses account	} Office section
Agent's VAT	CR Cash account DR HMRC account	} Office section
Agent's disbursements	CR Cash account DR Client's ledger account	} Office section

When the instructing firm sends its own client a bill, it adds the agent's professional charges to its own professional charges and passes on the agent's disbursements to the client.

Example

You act for Williams. You instruct Gibsons LLP, a firm of solicitors, as your agents. On 17 May, you receive their bill showing their professional charges of £200 plus VAT and a court fee of £70. You pay their bill on the same day. On 18 May, you send Williams a bill. Your own professional charges are £400 plus VAT.

Notes:

May

17   When you pay the agent's bill, you will pay a total of costs £200 plus £40 VAT and the court fee of £70, ie, a total of £310. However, you will make three separate pairs of DR and CR entries to record the three separate elements of the bill.

The accounts will look like this:

Cash account

Date	Details	Office account			Client account		
		DR	CR	BAL	DR	CR	BAL
				xxx			xxx
May 17	Agency expenses		200				
	VAT		40				
	Williams		70				

Client: Williams
Matter: Miscellaneous

Date	Details	Office account			Client account		
		DR	CR	BAL	DR	CR	BAL
May 17	Cash, Gibsons. Court fee	70		70DR			

Agency expenses account

Date	Details	Office account		
		DR	CR	BAL
May 17	Cash. Williams	200		200DR

HMRC account

Date	Details	Office account		
		DR	CR	BAL
May 17	Cash	40		40DR

18   When you issue your bill, you add the agent's professional charges to your own and make the usual entries for costs and VAT.

The accounts will look like this:

Cash account

Date	Details	Office account			Client account		
		DR	CR	BAL	DR	CR	BAL
				xxx			xxx
May 17	Agency expenses		200				
	HMRC		40				
	Williams		70				

Client: Williams
Matter: Miscellaneous

Date	Details	Office account			Client account		
		DR	CR	BAL	DR	CR	BAL
May 17	Cash, Gibsons.	70		70DR			
	Court fee						
18	Profit costs (400 + 200)	600		670			
	VAT (80 + 40)	120		790			

Profit costs account

Date	Details	Office account		
		DR	CR	BAL
May 18	Williams		600	600CR

Agency Expenses account

Date	Details	Office account		
		DR	CR	BAL
May 17	Cash. Williams	200		200DR

HMRC account

Date	Details	Office account		
		DR	CR	BAL
May 17	Cash. Williams	40		40DR
18	Williams		120	80CR

17.4 WITHHOLDING FUNDS FROM THE CLIENT BANK ACCOUNT

17.4.1 Rule 15 and Rule 16 exceptions from the need to pay money into client bank account

As we saw in **Chapter 9**, there are situations where client money does not have to be paid into a client bank account.

Under Rule 15, client money may be held outside the client bank account, for example, in the firm's safe or in an account outside England and Wales.

However, the client must have instructed the firm to this effect and the instructions must have been either given in writing or confirmed by the firm in writing.

Under Rule 16, the firm can withhold money from the client bank account without written instructions or written confirmation of instructions in seven situations, for example where cash is received and is without delay paid in the ordinary course of business to the client or on the client's behalf.

17.4.2 Rule 29.2 – the need to record dealings

Whenever the solicitor is dealing with client money, the dealing must be recorded on the cash account and on the client ledger account.

17.4.3 Non-recording

The only receipts which will not be recorded are those which are not regarded as 'money' in the firm's hands, for example a post-dated cheque (until the post date arrives) and a cheque which is made out not to the firm but to someone else. Such cheques could not be paid into the firm's bank account and are not regarded as 'money' for this purpose.

Exercise 17B

Which of the following receipts must be paid into the client bank account? Which must be recorded as a receipt of client's money?

(1) You act for the executor of Alan. The executor gives you £250 cash which he found in Alan's house. You authorise the executor to take back the cash in partial payment of a debt due from Alan to the executor.

(2) You act for Brian in a debt collection. You receive a cheque for £5,000 from the debtor. The cheque is in part payment of the debt due to Brian and the cheque is made out to Brian.

(3) You act for Clay. Clay gives you a cheque for £500 on account of costs. He is unsure whether or not he has sufficient funds to cover the cheque and, in his accompanying letter, asks you not to pay the cheque in until he instructs you to do so.

(4) You act for the executors for Diana. You have negotiated a loan from Diana's bank of £3,841 to cover the inheritance tax due on application for a grant of probate. The bank sends you a cheque made out to HMRC.

SUMMARY

---

(1) If a firm has been holding client money for one client and then starts to hold some or all of it for another client, the firm must open a client ledger account for the transferee and record an inter-client transfer of the money.

(2) A deposit received as stakeholder is client money and must be paid into the client bank account. It is held for the buyer and seller jointly so it must either be credited to a joint ledger account (usually called 'stakeholder') or credited to the seller's ledger account and identified as stakeholder money held jointly for both buyer and seller.

On the day the sale is completed the cash becomes the seller's. If a stakeholder ledger account was opened, the firm must make an inter-client transfer to show that the deposit is now held for the seller alone. If the deposit was credited to the seller's ledger account, the note identifying the sum as stakeholder money held jointly for buyer and seller must be removed.

(3) Where a mortgage advance is received from an institutional lender which makes loans on standard terms in the normal course of its activities, the money is client money and must be paid into the client bank account. It is held for the client but Rule 29.10 permits the firm to credit it to the ledger account of the borrower. The money must be clearly identifiable as belonging to the lender.

(4) When one firm providing legal services instructs another to act as its agent, the professional charges of the agent firm are an office expense of the instructing firm, not a client disbursement. The instructing firm will increase its own professional charges to cover the costs of the agent.

---

(5)   Rule 29.2 requires all dealings with client money to be recorded on a client cash account and a client ledger account. This includes situations where client money is kept outside the client bank account under Rules 15 and 16.

SOLUTIONS

Exercise 17A

When the company gives you funds on 4 June, you must record a receipt of the company's money.

> *Entries:*
>
> DR Cash
> CR George & Co Ltd   } Client section

When the sale is completed on 5 June, you must show that the money is now held for George. You show this by doing an inter-client transfer.

> *Entries:*
>
> DR George & Co Ltd
> CR George   } Client section

When you complete the investment for George on 7 June, you must record a payment of George's money.

> *Entries:*
>
> DR George
> CR Cash   } Client section

Exercise 17B

(1)   This is a receipt of client money. It need not be paid into the client bank account under Rule 16.1(a). However, you are dealing with client money and must *record* the receipt (and payment) on your client ledger for the executor and on your cash account.

(2)   Because the cheque is not made out to the firm, this is not a receipt of money so the question of 'office or client' does not arise. No entries need be made to record the receipt. The cheque could not be paid into the firm's client bank account.

(3)   This is a receipt of client money. You will not pay this cheque in as the client has given you written instructions not to (Rule 15). However, as in (1) above, you must record the receipt on your client ledger for Clay and on your cash account.

(4)   As in (2) above, this is not a receipt of money so no entries need be made. The cheque could not be paid into the firm's client bank account.

COMPLIANCE

> **LEARNING OUTCOMES**
>
> After reading this chapter you will be able to:
>
> - explain the investigative powers of the SRA
> - explain the need to deliver accountants' reports.

18.1 INTRODUCTION

There is absolutely no point in the SRA having rules governing how client money is treated if it is unaware of breaches. Some years ago therefore, the Rules were tightened to ensure that only accountants with auditor status inspected solicitors' accounts and that they were under an obligation to report breaches to the SRA. The rules on compliance were stringent.

In 2015 the SRA announced that it was making accountants' reports more targeted and relevant for firms and accountants alike. Solicitors' practices that present little or no risk – such as those firms that do not hold much client money – are now exempt from obtaining a report from their accountant.

The form that solicitors' accountants complete each year was also changed to give accountants more opportunity to exercise their professional judgement when preparing and finalising reports. Only qualified reports are now required to be submitted to the SRA, instead of all reports, as was previously the case.

18.2 INVESTIGATIVE POWERS OF THE SRA

Any firm or sole practitioner must, at a time and place fixed by the Solicitors Regulation Authority (SRA), produce to any person appointed by the SRA any papers, files, financial accounts, documents and other information requested in writing (Rules 31.1 and 31.2). The regulatory powers override any solicitor/client confidentiality or privilege. See guidance note (i) to Rule 31.

Anyone regulated by the SRA must be prepared to explain and justify any departures from the guidelines for accounting procedures and systems published by the SRA (Rule 31.6).

Any report produced by the SRA may be sent to the Crown Prosecution Service or the Serious Fraud Office and/or used in proceedings before the Solicitor's Disciplinary Tribunal (Rule 31.7).

18.3 ACCOUNTANTS' REPORTS

Subject to Rule 32A.1A, every firm that has handled client money must obtain an accountant's report for that accounting period within six months of the end of the accounting period (Rule 32A.1).

If the report has been qualified, the firm must deliver it to the SRA within six months of the end of the accounting period.

A qualified accountant's report is a report where the reporting accountant forms the judgement that the rules have not been complied with in such a way that the safety of client money is at risk.

Firms are not required to obtain or deliver an accountant's report if:

(a)   all of the client money held or received during an accounting period is money held or received from the Legal Aid Agency (or subsequently recovered from third parties as set out in Rule 19.3); or

(b)   in the accounting period, the client money held or received does not exceed an average of £10,000 and a maximum of £250,000, or the equivalent in foreign currency.

The SRA may require a firm to obtain or deliver an accountant's report at any time if it has reason to believe that it is in the public interest to do so (see Rule 32A.2).

Rule 34 requires that reporting accountants must have registered auditor status, together with membership of one of the major accountancy bodies. So that the SRA can maintain accurate records, firms must inform the SRA of any change in the reporting accountant (Rule 36). Frequent changes will alert the SRA to the possibility that a firm is trying to conceal matters.

Firms have to produce a letter of engagement for accountants, incorporating the terms set out in Rule 35. These cannot be amended. The letter has to be kept for six years and produced to the SRA on request (Rule 35.2).

Rule 43A.1 requires the accountant to exercise his or her professional judgement in determining the work required in order to assess risks to client money in relation to the firm on which he or she is reporting.

Guidance note (i) says that the purpose of the report is to enable a proportionate degree of oversight by the SRA over risks to clients' funds, but that it may also help the firm identify any improvements in its control systems that are required. The form of the report that the accountant is required to complete is intended to provide assurance that client funds are properly safeguarded. If the accountant forms the judgement that non-compliance with the Rules has put the safety of client money at risk, then the accountant is required to 'qualify' the report and set out details of the areas where risks have been identified.

Guidance note (ii) states that the types of work the accountant is required to undertake will depend on a number of factors, including the size and complexity of the firm, the nature of the work undertaken, the number of transactions and amount of client funds held. The accountant may also want to consider the firm's existing systems and, for example, the numbers and types of breaches of the Rules that the firm's compliance officer for finance and administration (COFA) has recorded under his or her reporting obligations. Separate guidance as to the work that might be considered as part of a work programme has been issued by the SRA and is updated from time to time; see the SRA's *Guidance to Reporting Accountants and firms on planning and completion of the annual Accountants' Reports, under Rule 32A of the SRA Accounts Rules 2011*.

The accountant must complete and sign his or her report in the form published from time to time by the SRA. The current form of the accountant's report under Rule 44 requires the accountant to confirm if he or she has found it necessary to qualify the report. If so, the report must be delivered to the SRA – as required by Rule 32A.1(b).

SUMMARY

(1)   The accounts of all firms regulated by the SRA have to be inspected by an accountant with auditor status once a year.

(2)   Solicitors have to inform the SRA each time the reporting accountant is changed.

SOLICITORS' ACCOUNTS

Topic	Summary
Why does the SRA regulate accounts?	The SRA wishes to ensure that the highest possible standards are maintained by those providing legal services. Law firms will usually hold money belonging to their clients and the SRA Accounts Rules impose strict requirements.
	Firms must keep other people's money separate from money of their own; they must keep other people's money safely in a bank or building society account and use each client's money only for that client's matters; they must keep proper accounting records to show how much money is held for each client.
The SRA Accounts Rules 2011	The Rules define client money and office money, and require firms regulated by the SRA to have separate bank accounts used for client and office money. Rules 17 and 18 contain special provisions for dealing with receipts as a result of which office money can sometimes be paid into the client bank account and client money can sometimes be paid into the office bank account. However, there are strict requirements as to how long money may be left in the 'wrong' account.
	Rule 20 sets out the circumstances in which money may be withdrawn from the client bank account. The most important is Rule 20.6 which provides that money withdrawn for a particular client must not exceed the amount held for that client.
Need to record client transactions	Rule 29 deals with the need for accurate records of dealing with client money. The effect of Rule 29 is that a firm regulated by the SRA must have a cash account for the office and client bank accounts, and a ledger account for each client showing office and client money transactions for that client. Every dealing with client money must be recorded in the client cash account and on the particular client's ledger account. The SRA Accounts Rules 2011 are fully dealt with in Chapter 9.
Types of entry	There are really only four things that firms providing legal services ever record: the amount of professional charges and VAT owing when a bill is issued, a receipt of cash, a payment of cash and an inter-client transfer – this is where a firm which is holding client money for one client stops holding it for that client and starts holding it for another. The entries for the four events are set out in Chapter 11.

Topic	Summary
VAT and disbursements	When a firm makes a payment on behalf of a client which includes a VAT element, the treatment of the payment in the firm's records will depend on whether the invoice is addressed to the firm or the client. If it is addressed to the firm, the principal method must be used and the payment must be made from office money. If the invoice is addressed to the client, the agency method must be used and the payment can be made from office or from client money if any is available. See Chapter 12 for a full discussion of VAT.
Accounting to clients for interest	Rule 22 provides that clients are entitled to receive interest earned on client money where it is fair and reasonable for them to do so. If the money is left in the general client bank account, the firm must pay the client a sum from the office bank account equal to the amount that would have been earned had a separate designated deposit account been opened. Where a firm chooses to put money in a separate designated deposit account, it will account to the client for all interest allowed by the bank. This is because of the income tax treatment of interest allowed by banks. Deposit interest is dealt with in Chapter 15.
Particular points in relation to property transactions	Money received as stakeholder is held for the buyer and seller jointly. It must either be recorded on a ledger account opened for the buyer and seller jointly, or, be shown on the seller's ledger but labelled as stakeholder money.

Money received as a mortgage advance is normally held for the lender. However, Rule 29.10 allows the advance to be shown on the borrower's client ledger account in certain circumstances, provided it is labelled as held for the lender. |
| Particular points in relation to probate transactions | The client in a probate transaction is the personal representative. The administration of the estate is complete when the residuary beneficiary approves the estate accounts and is sent a cheque for the amont due. If the beneficiary asks the firm to continue holding the money, the firm must make an inter-client transfer to a new ledger account opened for the beneficiary. |

MULTIPLE CHOICE QUESTIONS

This Appendix contains multiple choice questions designed to test your knowledge of the material contained in Part II. Always read multiple choice questions carefully, and be particularly alert to words like 'always', 'must' and 'never'. Most (although not all) of the Rules contain exceptions, so any statement containing one of these words is likely to be wrong.

Questions

1. **Which ONE of the following receipts CANNOT be paid into the client bank account?**

    A   A deposit on the sale of a property for a partner in your firm, to be held as stakeholder.

    B   A deposit on the sale of a property for a partner in your firm, to be held as agent for the seller.

    C   The sale proceeds of a property sold by an assistant solicitor in the firm.

    D   The sale proceeds of a property sold jointly by a partner in the firm and her husband who is not a partner.

2. **Which ONE of the following statements is WRONG?**

    A   Money held for a trust can be paid into the client bank account.

    B   Client money need not always be paid into the client bank account.

    C   You must always send a client a bill before transferring money from the client to the office bank account.

    D   Any dealing with client money must be recorded under Rule 29.

3. Arthur, your client, pays £900 on account of costs. He telephones to ask you not to pay in the cheque until the following week, as he needs to transfer funds to his bank account to meet the cheque.

    Which ONE of the following statements is CORRECT?

    A   The money is client money and you must pay the cheque into the client bank account without delay.

    B   The money is office money.

    C   Arthur's instruction is sufficient to authorise you to withhold the money from the client bank account.

    D   The money is client money, and the receipt must be recorded on the client ledger and client column of the cash account without delay.

4. You pay a surveyor's fee of £300 + VAT on behalf of a client, registered for VAT, for whom you hold £500 on account of costs.

    Which ONE of the following statements is CORRECT?

    A   If the invoice is addressed to the client, the invoice must be paid from the client bank account.

    B   If the invoice is addressed to the firm, the invoice can be paid from the client bank account.

    C   If the invoice is addressed to the client, the invoice cannot be paid from the office bank account.

    D   If the invoice is addressed to the firm, the invoice must be paid from the office bank account.

5.   **Which ONE of the following statements is CORRECT?**

A   A firm can never make a payment from a client bank account on behalf of a client if the firm does not hold sufficient money in that account on behalf of the client.

B   A client account for a firm regulated by the SRA must be in the firm name and must include the word 'client' in full; an abbreviation is not acceptable.

C   There is no VAT relief on bad debts.

D   It is a breach of the SRA Accounts Rules 2011 to make a payment from the client bank account on behalf of a client before receiving confirmation that the client's cheque for money on account of costs has cleared.

6.   **Which ONE of the following statements is CORRECT?**

A   A firm regulated by the SRA must account to a client for interest where it is fair and reasonable to do so.

B   It is a breach of the SRA Accounts Rules 2011 not to open a separate designated client account when holding more than £10,000 for a client.

C   When paying interest, a firm must calculate the rate by reference to the best rate it is possible to get on the amount held.

D   Clients are always entitled to receive interest on client money.

7.   You are holding £400 client money for a client and need to make a payment of £600 for that client. There is no time to ask the client for additional funds.

      Which ONE of the following statements is CORRECT?

A   You can pay £600 from the client bank account without breaching the SRA Accounts Rules 2011, provided you transfer money from the office bank account within two days after making the payment.

B   You must pay the £600 from the office bank account.

C   You can transfer £400 from the client to the office bank account and then make the payment from the office bank account.

D   You can pay £600 from the client bank account without breaching the SRA Accounts Rules 2011, provided you transfer £200 from the office to the client bank account before doing so.

8.   You hold £500 on account of costs for the client. You pay a surveyor's fee of £200 + £40 VAT for the client. The invoice is made out to you.

      Subsequently you send the client a bill for £400 in professional charges. The client is registered for VAT.

      Which ONE of the following statements is CORRECT?

A   You could use client money to pay the surveyor's fee.

B   You will send the client two VAT invoices: the surveyor's and the solicitor's.

C   You will make no entries in the firm's VAT records in relation to the surveyor's fee.

D   You will send the client one VAT invoice covering the VAT on both the survey and the profit costs.

Answers

1.   B
2.   C
3.   D
4.   D
5.   B
6.   A
7.   D
8.   D

SRA ACCOUNTS RULES 2011

[Extracts]

Part 1 – General

Rule 1 – The overarching objective and underlying principles

1.1 The purpose of these rules is to keep *client money* safe. This aim must always be borne in mind in the application of these rules.

1.2 *You* must comply with the Principles set out in the Handbook, and the outcomes in Chapter 7 of the *SRA Code of Conduct* in relation to the effective financial management of the *firm*, and in particular must:

(a) keep other people's money separate from money belonging to *you* or *your firm*;

(b) keep other people's money safely in a *bank* or *building society* account identifiable as a *client account* (except when the rules specifically provide otherwise);

(c) use each *client's* money for that *client's* matters only;

(d) use money held as *trustee* of a *trust* for the purposes of that *trust* only;

(e) establish and maintain proper accounting systems, and proper internal controls over those systems, to ensure compliance with the rules;

(f) keep proper accounting records to show accurately the position with regard to the money held for each *client* and *trust*;

(g) account for *interest* on other people's money in accordance with the rules;

(h) co-operate with the SRA in checking compliance with the rules; and

(i) deliver annual accountants' reports as required by the rules.

Rule 2 – Interpretation

2.1 The guidance notes do not form part of the rules.

2.2 The SRA Handbook Glossary 2012 shall apply and, unless the context otherwise requires:

(a) all italicised terms shall be defined; and

(b) all terms shall be interpreted,

in accordance with the *Glossary*.

2.3 References to the Legal Aid Agency are to be read, where appropriate, as including the Legal Services Commission.

Guidance notes

(i) The effect of the definition of 'you' is that the rules apply equally to all those who carry on or work in a firm and to the firm itself. See also rule 4 (persons governed by the rules) and rule 5 (persons exempt from the rules).

(ii) The general definition of 'office account' is wide. However, rule 17.1(b) (receipt and transfer of costs) and rule 19.1(b) and 19.2(b) (payments from the Legal Aid Agency) specify that certain money is to be placed in an office account at a bank or building society. Out-of-scope money can be held in an office account (which could be an account regulated by another regulator); it must not be held in a client account.

(iii)   For a flowchart summarising the effect of the rules, see Appendix 1. For more details of the treatment of different types of money, see the chart 'Special situations – what applies' at Appendix 2. These two appendices do not form part of the rules but are included to help solicitors and their staff find their way about the rules.

Rule 12 – Categories of money

12.1   These rules do not apply to *out-of-scope money*, save to the limited extent specified in the rules. All other money held or received in the course of practice falls into one or other of the following categories:

(a)   'client money' – money held or received for a *client* or as *trustee*, and all other money which is not *office money*; or

(b)   'office money' – money which belongs to *you* or your *firm*.

12.2   'Client money' includes money held or received:

(a)   as *trustee*;

(b)   as agent, bailee, stakeholder, or as the donee of a power of attorney, or as a liquidator, trustee in bankruptcy, *Court of Protection deputy* or trustee of an occupational pension scheme;

(c)   for payment of unpaid *professional disbursements*;

(d)   for payment of stamp duty land tax, Land Registry registration fees, telegraphic transfer fees and court fees (but see also guidance note (i));

(e)   as a payment on account of *costs* generally;

(f)   as a financial benefit paid in respect of a *client*, unless the *client* has given *you* prior authority to retain it (see Chapter 1, outcome 1.15 and indicative behaviour 1.20 of the SRA *Code of Conduct*);

(g)   jointly with another person outside the *firm*.

12.3   Money held to the sender's order is *client money*.

(a)   If money is accepted on such terms, it must be held in a *client account*.

(b)   However, a cheque or draft sent to *you* on terms that the cheque or draft (as opposed to the money) is held to the sender's order must not be presented for payment without the sender's consent.

(c)   The recipient is always subject to a professional obligation to return the money, or the cheque or draft, to the sender on demand.

12.4   An advance to a *client* which is paid into a *client account* under rule 14.2(b) becomes *client money*.

12.5   A cheque in respect of damages and *costs*, made payable to the *client* but paid into a *client account* under rule 14.2(e), becomes *client money*.

12.6   Endorsing a cheque or draft over to a *client* or employer in the course of practice amounts to receiving *client money*. Even if no other *client money* is held or received, *you* must comply with some provisions of the rules, e.g.:

(a)   rule 7 (duty to remedy breaches);

(b)   rule 29 (accounting records for client accounts, etc.);

(c)   rule 31 (production of documents, information and explanations);

(d)   rule 32A (obtaining and delivery of accountants' reports).

12.7   'Office money' includes:

(a)   money held or received in connection with running the *firm*; for example, PAYE, or VAT on the *firm's fees*;

(b)   *interest* on *general client accounts*; the *bank* or *building society* should be instructed to credit such *interest* to the *office account* – but see also rule 14.2(d); and

(c)   payments received in respect of:

(i) *fees* due to the *firm* against a bill or written notification of *costs* incurred, which has been given or sent in accordance with rule 17.2;

(ii) *disbursements* already paid by the *firm*;

(iii) *disbursements* incurred but not yet paid by the *firm*, but excluding unpaid *professional disbursements*;

(iv) money paid for or towards an *agreed fee*; and

(d) money held in a *client account* and earmarked for *costs* under rule 17.3;

(e) money held or received from the Legal Aid Agency as a *regular payment* (see rule 19.2).

12.8 If a *firm* conducts a personal or office transaction – for instance, conveyancing – for a *principal* (or for a number of *principals*), money held or received on behalf of the *principal(s)* is *office money*. However, other circumstances may mean that the money is *client money*, for example:

(a) If the *firm* also acts for a lender, money held or received on behalf of the lender is *client money*.

(b) If the *firm* acts for a *principal* and, for example, his or her spouse jointly (assuming the spouse is not a *partner* in the practice), money received on their joint behalf is *client money*.

(c) If the *firm* acts for an assistant solicitor, consultant or non-solicitor employee, or (if it is a *company*) a director, or (if it is an *LLP*) a member, he or she is regarded as a *client* of the *firm*, and money received for him or her is client money – even if he or she conducts the matter personally.

Guidance notes

(i) Money held or received for payment of stamp duty land tax, Land Registry registration fees, telegraphic transfer fees and court fees is not office money because you have not incurred an obligation to HMRC, the Land Registry, the bank or the court to pay the duty or fee; (on the other hand, if you have already paid the duty or fee out of your own resources, or have received the service on credit, or the bank's charge for a telegraphic transfer forms part of your profit costs, payment subsequently received from the client will be office money);

(ii) Money held:

(a) by liquidators, trustees in bankruptcy, Court of Protection deputies and trustees of occupational pension schemes;

(b) jointly with another person outside the practice (for example, with a lay trustee, or with another firm);

is client money, subject to a limited application of the rules – see rules 8 and 9. The donee of a power of attorney, who operates the donor's own account, is also subject to a limited application of the rules (see rule 10), although money kept in the donor's own account is not 'client money' because it is not 'held or received' by the donee.

(iii) If the SRA intervenes in a practice, money from the practice is held or received by the SRA's intervention agent subject to a trust under Schedule 1 paragraph 7(1) of the Solicitors Act 1974, and is therefore client money. The same provision requires the agent to pay the money into a client account.

(iv) Money held or received in the course of employment when practising in one of the capacities listed in rule 5 (persons exempt from the rules) is not 'client money' for the purpose of the rules, because the rules do not apply at all.

(v) The receipt of out-of-scope money of an MDP which is mixed with other types of money is dealt with in rules 17 and 18.

(vi)   See Appendices 1 and 2 (which do not form part of the rules) for a summary of the effect of the rules and the treatment of different types of money.

Part 2 – Client money and operation of a client account

Rule 14 – Use of a client account

14.1   *Client money* must *without delay* be paid into a *client account*, and must be held in a *client account*, except when the rules provide to the contrary (see rules 8, 9, 15, 16, 17 and 19).

14.2   Only *client money* may be paid into or held in a *client account*, except:

(a)   an amount of the *firm's* own money required to open or maintain the account;

(b)   an advance from the *firm* to fund a payment on behalf of a *client* or *trust* in excess of funds held for that client or trust; the sum becomes *client money* on payment into the account (for *interest* on *client money*, see rule 22.2(c));

(c)   money to replace any sum which for any reason has been drawn from the account in breach of rule 20; the replacement money becomes *client money* on payment into the account;

(d)   *interest* which is paid into a *client account* to enable payment from the *client account* of all money owed to the *client*; and

(e)   a cheque in respect of damages and *costs*, made payable to the *client*, which is paid into the *client account* pursuant to the Society's Conditional Fee Agreement; the sum becomes *client money* on payment into the account (but see rule 17.1(e) for the transfer of the *costs* element from *client account*);

and except when the rules provide to the contrary (see guidance note (ii) below).

14.3   *Client money* must be returned to the *client* (or other person on whose behalf the money is held) promptly, as soon as there is no longer any proper reason to retain those funds. Payments received after *you* have already accounted to the *client*, for example by way of a refund, must be paid to the *client* promptly.

14.4   *You* must promptly inform a *client* (or other person on whose behalf the money is held) in writing of the amount of any *client money* retained at the end of a matter (or the substantial conclusion of a matter), and the reason for that retention. *You* must inform the *client* (or other person) in writing at least once every twelve months thereafter of the amount of *client money* still held and the reason for the retention, for as long as *you* continue to hold that money.

14.5   *You* must not provide banking facilities through a *client account*. Payments into, and transfers or withdrawals from, a *client account* must be in respect of instructions relating to an underlying transaction (and the funds arising therefrom) or to a service forming part of *your* normal regulated activities.

Guidance notes

(i)   Exceptions to rule 14.1 (client money must be paid into a client account) can be found in:

(a)   rule 8 – liquidators, trustees in bankruptcy, Court of Protection deputies and trustees of occupational pension schemes;

(b)   rule 9 – joint accounts;

(c)   rule 15 – client's instructions;

(d)   rule 16 – cash paid straight to client, beneficiary or third party;

(A)   cheque endorsed to client, beneficiary or third party;

(B)   money withheld from client account on the SRA's authority;

(C)   money withheld from client account in accordance with a trustee's powers;

(e)   rule 17.1(b) – receipt and transfer of costs;

(f)   rule 19.1 – payments by the Legal Aid Agency.

(ii)   Rule 14.2(a) to (e) provides for exceptions to the principle that only client money may be paid into a client account. Additional exceptions can be found in:

(a)   rule 17.1(c) – receipt and transfer of costs;

(b)   rule 18.2(b) – receipt of mixed payments;

(c)   rule 19.2(c)(ii) – transfer to client account of a sum for unpaid professional disbursements, where regular payments are received from the Legal Aid Agency.

(iii)   Only a nominal sum will be required to open or maintain an account. In practice, banks will usually open (and, if instructed, keep open) accounts with nil balances.

(iv)   If client money is invested in the purchase of assets other than money – such as stocks or shares – it ceases to be client money, because it is no longer money held by the firm. If the investment is subsequently sold, the money received is, again, client money. The records kept under rule 29 will need to include entries to show the purchase or sale of investments.

(v)   Rule 14.5 reflects decisions of the Solicitors Disciplinary Tribunal that it is not a proper part of a solicitor's everyday business or practice to operate a banking facility for third parties, whether they are clients of the firm or not. It should be noted that any exemption under the Financial Services and Markets Act 2000 is likely to be lost if a deposit is taken in circumstances which do not form part of your practice. It should also be borne in mind that there are criminal sanctions against assisting money launderers.

(vi)   As with rule 7 (Duty to remedy breaches), 'promptly' in rule 14.3 and 14.4 is not defined but should be given its natural meaning in the particular circumstances. Accounting to a client for any surplus funds will often fall naturally at the end of a matter. Other retainers may be more protracted and, even when the principal work has been completed, funds may still be needed, for example, to cover outstanding work in a conveyancing transaction or to meet a tax liability. (See also paragraphs 4.8 and 4.9 of the Guidelines for accounting procedures and systems at Appendix 3.)

(vii)   There may be some instances when, during the course of a retainer, the specific purpose for which particular funds were paid no longer exists, for example, the need to instruct counsel or a medical expert. Rule 14.3 is concerned with returning funds to clients at the end of a matter (or the substantial conclusion of a matter) and is not intended to apply to ongoing retainers. However, in order to act in the best interests of your client, you may need to take instructions in such circumstances to ascertain, for instance, whether the money should be returned to the client or retained to cover the general funding or other aspects of the case.

(viii)   See rule 20.1(j)–(k) for withdrawals from a client account when the rightful owner of funds cannot be traced. The obligation to report regularly under rule 14.4 ceases to apply if you are no longer able to trace the client, at which point rule 20.1(j) or (k) would apply.

Rule 15 – Client money withheld from client account on client's instructions

15.1   *Client money* may be:

(a)   held by *you* outside a *client account* by, for example, retaining it in the *firm's* safe in the form of cash, or placing it in an account in the *firm's* name which is not a *client account*, such as an account outside England and Wales; or

(b)   paid into an account at a *bank*, *building society* or other financial institution opened in the name of the *client* or of a person designated by the *client*;

but only if the *client* instructs *you* to that effect for the *client's* own convenience, and only if the instructions are given in writing, or are given by other means and confirmed by *you* to the *client* in writing.

15.2   It is improper to seek blanket agreements, through standard terms of business or otherwise, to hold *client money* outside a *client account*.

15.3   If a *client* instructs *you* to hold part only of a payment in accordance with rule 15.1(a) or (b), the entire payment must first be placed in a *client account*, before transferring the relevant part out and dealing with it in accordance with the *client's* instructions.

15.4   A payment on account of *costs* received from a person who is funding all or part of *your fees* may be withheld from a *client account* on the instructions of that person given in accordance with rule 15.1.

Guidance notes

(i)   Money withheld from a client account under rule 15.1(a) remains client money, and all the record-keeping provisions of rule 29 will apply.

(ii)   Once money has been paid into an account set up under rule 15.1(b), it ceases to be client money. Until that time, the money is client money and, under rule 29, a record is required of your receipt of the money, and its payment into the account in the name of the client or designated person. If you can operate the account, rule 10 (operating a client's own account) and rule 30 (accounting records for clients' own accounts) will apply. In the absence of instructions to the contrary, rule 14.1 requires any money withdrawn to be paid into a client account.

(iii)   Rule 29.17(d) requires clients' instructions under rule 15.1 to be kept for at least six years.

Rule 16 – Other client money withheld from a client account

16.1   The following categories of *client money* may be withheld from a *client account*:

(a)   cash received and *without delay* paid in cash in the ordinary course of business to the *client* or, on the *client's* behalf, to a third party, or paid in cash in the execution of a *trust* to a beneficiary or third party;

(b)   a cheque or draft received and endorsed over in the ordinary course of business to the *client* or, on the *client's* behalf, to a third party, or *without delay* endorsed over in the execution of a *trust* to a beneficiary or third party;

(c)   money withheld from a *client account* on instructions under rule 15;

(d)   money which, in accordance with a *trustee's* powers, is paid into or retained in an account of the *trustee* which is not a *client account* (for example, an account outside England and Wales), or properly retained in cash in the performance of the *trustee's* duties;

(e)   unpaid *professional disbursements* included in a payment of *costs* dealt with under rule 17.1(b);

(f)   In respect of payments from the Legal Aid Agency:

(i)   advance payments from the Legal Aid Agency withheld from *client account* (see rule 19.1(a)); and

(ii)   unpaid *professional disbursements* included in a payment of *costs* from the Legal Aid Agency (see rule 19.1(b)); and

(g)   money withheld from a *client account* on the written authorisation of the SRA. The SRA may impose a condition that the money is paid to a charity which gives an indemnity against any legitimate claim subsequently made for the sum received.

Guidance notes

(i)   If money is withheld from a client account under rule 16.1(a) or (b), rule 29 requires records to be kept of the receipt of the money and the payment out.

(ii)   If money is withheld from a client account under rule 16.1(d), rule 29 requires a record to be kept of the receipt of the money, and requires the inclusion of the money in the monthly reconciliations. (Money held by a trustee jointly with another party is subject only to the limited requirements of rule 9.)

(iii) It makes no difference, for the purpose of the rules, whether an endorsement is effected by signature in the normal way or by some other arrangement with the bank.

(iv) The circumstances in which authorisation would be given under rule 16.1(g) must be extremely rare. Applications for authorisation should be made to the Professional Ethics Guidance Team.

Rule 17 – Receipt and transfer of costs

17.1 When *you* receive money paid in full or part settlement of *your* bill (or other notification of *costs*) *you* **must follow one of the following five options:**

    (a) **determine the composition of the payment without delay, and deal with the money accordingly:**

        (i) if the sum comprises *office money* and/or *out-of-scope money* only, it must be placed in an *office account*;

        (ii) if the sum comprises only *client money*, the entire sum must be placed in a *client account*;

        (iii) if the sum includes both *office money* and *client money*, or *client money* and *out-of-scope money*, or *client money*, *out-of-scope money* and *office money*, you must follow rule 18 (receipt of mixed payments); or

    (b) **ascertain that the payment comprises only *office money* and/or *out-of-scope money*, and/or *client money* in the form of *professional disbursements* incurred but not yet paid, and deal with the payment as follows:**

        (i) place the entire sum in an *office account* at a *bank* or *building society* branch (or head office) in England and Wales; and

        (ii) by the end of the second working day following receipt, either pay any unpaid *professional disbursement*, or transfer a sum for its settlement to a *client account*; or

    (c) **pay the entire sum into a *client account* (regardless of its composition), and transfer any *office money* and/or *out-of-scope money* out of the *client account* within 14 days of receipt; or**

    (d) **on receipt of *costs* from the Legal Aid Agency, follow the option in rule 19.1(b); or**

    (e) **in relation to a cheque paid into a *client account* under rule 14.2(e), transfer the costs element out of the *client account* within 14 days of receipt.**

17.2 If *you* properly require payment of *your fees* from money held for a *client* or *trust* in a *client account*, you must first give or send a bill of *costs*, or other written notification of the *costs* incurred, to the *client* or the paying party.

17.3 Once *you* have complied with rule 17.2 above, the money earmarked for *costs* becomes *office money* and must be transferred out of the *client account* within 14 days.

17.4 A payment on account of *costs* generally in respect of those activities for which the practice is regulated by the SRA is *client money*, and must be held in a *client account* until *you* have complied with rule 17.2 above. (For an exception in the case of legal aid payments, see rule 19.1(a). See also rule 18 on dealing with mixed payments of *client money* and/or *out-of-scope money* when part of a payment on account of *costs* relates to activities not regulated by the SRA.)

17.5 A payment for an *agreed fee* must be paid into an *office account*. An 'agreed fee' is one that is fixed – not a *fee* that can be varied upwards, nor a *fee* that is dependent on the transaction being completed. An *agreed fee* must be evidenced in writing.

17.6 *You* will not be in breach of rule 17 as a result of a misdirected electronic payment or other direct transfer from a *client* or paying third party, provided:

(a)   appropriate systems are in place to ensure compliance;

(b)   appropriate instructions were given to the *client* or paying third party;

(c)   the *client's* or paying third party's mistake is remedied promptly upon discovery; and

(d)   appropriate steps are taken to avoid future errors by the *client* or paying third party.

17.7   *Costs* transferred out of a *client account* in accordance with rule 17.2 and 17.3 must be specific sums relating to the bill or other written notification of *costs*, and covered by the amount held for the particular *client* or *trust*. Round sum withdrawals on account of *costs* are a breach of the rules.

17.8   In the case of a *trust* of which the only *trustee(s)* are within the firm, the paying party will be the *trustee(s)* themselves. You must keep the original bill or notification of *costs* on the file, in addition to complying with rule 29.15 (central record or file of copy bills, etc.).

17.9   Undrawn *costs* must not remain in a *client account* as a 'cushion' against any future errors which could result in a shortage on that account, and cannot be regarded as available to set off against any general shortage on *client account*.

Guidance notes

(i)   This note lists types of disbursement and how they are categorised:

(a)   Money received for paid disbursements is office money.

(b)   Money received for unpaid professional disbursements is client money.

(c)   Money received for other unpaid disbursements for which you have incurred a liability to the payee (for example, travel agents' charges, taxi fares, courier charges or Land Registry search fees, payable on credit) is office money.

(d)   Money received for disbursements anticipated but not yet incurred is a payment on account, and is therefore client money.

(ii)   The option in rule 17.1(a) allows you to place all payments in the correct account in the first instance. The option in rule 17.1(b) allows the prompt banking into an office account of an invoice payment when the only uncertainty is whether or not the payment includes some client money in the form of unpaid professional disbursements. The option in rule 17.1(c) allows the prompt banking into a client account of any invoice payment in advance of determining whether the payment is a mixture of office and client money (of whatever description), or client money and outof-scope money, or client money, out-of-scope money and office money, or is only office money and/or out-of-scope money.

(iii)   If you are not in a position to comply with the requirements of rule 17.1(b), you cannot take advantage of that option.

(iv)   The option in rule 17.1(b) cannot be used if the money received includes a payment on account – for example, a payment for a professional disbursement anticipated but not yet incurred.

(v)   In order to be able to use the option in rule 17.1(b) for electronic payments or other direct transfers from clients, you may choose to establish a system whereby clients are given an office account number for payment of costs. The system must be capable of ensuring that, when invoices are sent to the client, no request is made for any client money, with the sole exception of money for professional disbursements already incurred but not yet paid.

(vi)   Rule 17.1(c) allows clients to be given a single account number for making direct payments by electronic or other means – under this option, it has to be a client account.

(vii)   'Properly' in rule 17.2 implies that the work has actually been done, whether at the end of the matter or at an interim stage, and that you are entitled to appropriate the money for costs. For example, the costs set out in a completion statement in a conveyancing transaction will become due on completion and should be transferred out of the client account within 14 days of completion in accordance with rule 17.3. The requirement to transfer costs out of the client account within a set time is intended to prevent costs being left on client account to conceal a shortage.

(viii)   Money is 'earmarked' for costs under rule 17.2 and 17.3 when you decide to use funds already held in client account to settle your bill. If you wish to obtain the client's prior approval, you will need to agree the amount to be taken with your client before issuing the bill to avoid the possibility of failing to meet the 14 day time limit for making the transfer out of client account. If you wish to retain the funds, for example, as money on account of costs on another matter, you will need to ask the client to send the full amount in settlement of the bill. If, when submitting a bill, you fail to indicate whether you intend to take your costs from client account, or expect the client to make a payment, you will be regarded as having 'earmarked' your costs.

(ix)   An amendment to section 69 of the Solicitors Act 1974 by the Legal Services Act 2007 permits a solicitor or recognised body to sue on a bill which has been signed electronically and which the client has agreed can be delivered electronically.

(x)   The rules do not require a bill of costs for an agreed fee, although your VAT position may mean that in practice a bill is needed. If there is no bill, the written evidence of the agreement must be filed as a written notification of costs under rule 29.15(b).

(xi)   The bill of an MDP may be in respect of costs for work of the SRA-regulated part of the practice, and also for work that falls outside the scope of SRA regulation. Money received in respect of the non-SRA regulated work, including money for disbursements, is out-of-scope money and must be dealt with in accordance with rule 17.

(xii)   See Chapter 1, indicative behaviour 1.21 of the SRA Code of Conduct in relation to ensuring that disbursements included in a bill reflect the actual amount spent or to be spent.

Rule 18 – Receipt of mixed payments

18.1   A 'mixed payment' is one which includes *client money* as well as *office money* and/or *out-of-scope money*.

18.2   A *mixed payment* must either:
   (a)   be split between a *client account* and *office account* as appropriate; or
   (b)   be placed *without delay* in a *client account*.

18.3   If the entire payment is placed in a *client account*, all *office money* and/or *out-of-scope money* must be transferred out of the *client account* within 14 days of receipt.

Guidance notes

(i)   See rule 17.1(b) and (c) for additional ways of dealing with (among other things) mixed payments received in response to a bill or other notification of costs.

(ii)   See rule 19.1(b) for (among other things) mixed payments received from the Legal Aid Agency.

(iii)   Some out-of-scope money may be subject to the rules of other regulators which may require an earlier withdrawal from the client account operated under these rules.

Rule 20 – Withdrawals from a client account

20.1   *Client money* may only be withdrawn from a *client account* when it is:
   (a)   properly required for a payment to or on behalf of the *client* (or other person on whose behalf the money is being held);

(b)   properly required for a payment in the execution of a particular *trust*, including the purchase of an investment (other than money) in accordance with the *trustee's* powers;

(c)   properly required for payment of a *disbursement* on behalf of the *client* or trust;

(d)   properly required in full or partial reimbursement of money spent by *you* on behalf of the *client* or trust;

(e)   transferred to another *client account*;

(f)   withdrawn on the *client's* instructions, provided the instructions are for the *client's* convenience and are given in writing, or are given by other means and confirmed by *you* to the *client* in writing;

(g)   transferred to an account other than a *client account* (such as an account outside England and Wales), or retained in cash, by a *trustee* in the proper performance of his or her duties;

(h)   a refund to *you* of an advance no longer required to fund a payment on behalf of a *client* or trust (see rule 14.2(b));

(i)   money which has been paid into the account in breach of the rules (for example, money paid into the wrong *separate designated client account*) – see rule 20.5 below;

(j)   money not covered by (a) to (i) above, where *you* comply with the conditions set out in rule 20.2; or

(k)   money not covered by (a) to (i) above, withdrawn from the account on the written authorisation of the SRA. The SRA may impose a condition that you pay the money to a charity which gives an indemnity against any legitimate claim subsequently made for the sum received.

20.2   A withdrawal of *client money* under rule 20.1(j) above may be made only where the amount held does not exceed £500 in relation to any one individual *client* or trust matter and *you*:

(a)   establish the identity of the owner of the money, or make reasonable attempts to do so;

(b)   make adequate attempts to ascertain the proper destination of the money, and to return it to the rightful owner, unless the reasonable costs of doing so are likely to be excessive in relation to the amount held;

(c)   pay the funds to a charity;

(d)   record the steps taken in accordance with rule 20.2(a)–(c) above and retain those records, together with all relevant documentation (including receipts from the charity), in accordance with rule 29.16 and 29.17(a); and

(e)   keep a central register in accordance with rule 29.22.

20.3   *Office money* may only be withdrawn from a *client account* when it is:

(a)   money properly paid into the account to open or maintain it under rule 14.2(a);

(b)   properly required for payment of *your costs* under rule 17.2 and 17.3;

(c)   the whole or part of a payment into a *client account* under rule 17.1(c);

(d)   part of a *mixed payment* placed in a *client account* under rule 18.2(b); or

(e)   money which has been paid into a *client account* in breach of the rules (for example, *interest* wrongly credited to a *general client account*) – see rule 20.5 below.

20.4   *Out-of-scope money* must be withdrawn from a *client account* in accordance with rules 17.1(a), 17.1(c) and 18 as appropriate.

20.5   Money which has been paid into a *client account* in breach of the rules must be withdrawn from the *client account* promptly upon discovery.

20.6   Money withdrawn in relation to a particular *client* or trust from a *general client account* must not exceed the money held on behalf of that *client* or trust in all *your general client accounts* (except as provided in rule 20.7 below).

20.7   You may make a payment in respect of a particular *client* or *trust* out of a *general client account*, even if no money (or insufficient money) is held for that *client* or *trust* in your *general client account(s)*, provided:

(a)   sufficient money is held for that *client* or *trust* in a *separate designated client account*; and

(b)   the appropriate transfer from the *separate designated client account* to a *general client account* is made immediately.

20.8   Money held for a *client* or *trust* in a *separate designated client account* must not be used for payments for another *client* or *trust*.

20.9   A *client account* must not be overdrawn, except in the following circumstances:

(a)   A *separate designated client account* operated in *your* capacity as *trustee* can be overdrawn if *you* make payments on behalf of the *trust* (for example, inheritance tax) before realising sufficient assets to cover the payments.

(b)   If a *sole practitioner* dies and his or her *client accounts* are frozen, overdrawn *client accounts* can be operated in accordance with the rules to the extent of the money held in the frozen accounts.

Guidance notes

(i)   Withdrawals in favour of firm, and for payment of disbursements

(a)   Disbursements to be paid direct from a client account, or already paid out of your own money, can be withdrawn under rule 20.1(c) or (d) in advance of preparing a bill of costs. Money to be withdrawn from a client account for the payment of costs (fees and disbursements) under rule 17.2 and 17.3 becomes office money and is dealt with under rule 20.3(b).

(b)   Money is 'spent' under rule 20.1(d) at the time when you despatch a cheque, unless the cheque is to be held to your order. Money is also regarded as 'spent' by the use of a credit account, so that, for example, search fees, taxi fares and courier charges incurred in this way may be transferred to your office account.

(c)   See rule 21.4 for the way in which a withdrawal from a client account in your favour must be effected.

(ii)   Cheques payable to banks, building societies, etc.

(a)   In order to protect client money against misappropriation when cheques are made payable to banks, building societies or other large institutions, it is strongly recommended that you add the name and number of the account after the payee's name.

(iii)   Drawing against uncleared cheques

(a)   You should use discretion in drawing against a cheque received from or on behalf of a client before it has been cleared. If the cheque is not met, other clients' money will have been used to make the payment in breach of the rules (see rule 7 (duty to remedy breaches)). You may be able to avoid a breach of the rules by instructing the bank or building society to charge all unpaid credits to your office or personal account.

(iv)   Non-receipt of electronic payments

(a)   If you withdraw money from a general client account on the strength of information that an electronic payment is on its way, but the electronic payment does not arrive, you will have used other clients' money in breach of the rules. See also rule 7 (duty to remedy breaches).

(v)   Withdrawals on instructions

(a)   One of the reasons why a client might authorise a withdrawal under rule 20.1(f) might be to have the money transferred to a type of account other than a client account. If so, the requirements of rule 15 must be complied with.

(vi)   Withdrawals where the rightful owner cannot be traced, on the SRA's authorisation and without SRA authorisation

(a)   Applications for authorisation under rule 20.1(k) should be made to the Professional Ethics Guidance Team, who can advise on the criteria which must normally be met for authorisation to be given. You may under rule 20.1(j) pay to a charity sums of £500 or less per client or trust matter without the SRA's authorisation, provided the safeguards set out in rule 20.2 are followed.

(b)   You will need to apply to the SRA, whatever the amount involved, if the money to be withdrawn is not to be paid to a charity. This situation might arise, for example, if you have been unable to deliver a bill of costs because the client has become untraceable and so cannot make a transfer from client account to office account in accordance with rule 17.2–17.3.

(c)   After a practice has been wound up, surplus balances are sometimes discovered in an old client account. This money remains subject to rule 20 and rule 21. An application can be made to the SRA under rule 20.1(k).

Part 3 – Interest

Rule 22 – When interest must be paid

22.1   When *you* hold money in a *client account* for a *client*, or for a person funding all or part of *your fees*, or for a *trust*, *you* must account to the *client* or that person or *trust* for *interest* when it is fair and reasonable to do so in all the circumstances. (This also applies if money should have been held in a *client account* but was not. It also applies to money held in an account in accordance with rule 15.1(a) (or which should have been held in such an account), or rule 16.1(d).)

22.2   You are not required to pay *interest*:

(a)   on money held for the payment of a *professional disbursement*, once counsel etc. has requested a delay in settlement;

(b)   on money held for the Legal Aid Agency;

(c)   on an advance from *you* under rule 14.2(b) to fund a payment on behalf of the *client* or *trust* in excess of funds held for that *client* or *trust*; or

(d)   if there is an agreement to contract out of the provisions of this rule under rule 25.

22.3   You must have a written policy on the payment of *interest*, which seeks to provide a fair outcome. The terms of the policy must be drawn to the attention of the *client* at the outset of a retainer, unless it is inappropriate to do so in the circumstances.

Guidance notes

(i)   Requirement to pay interest

(a)   Money is normally held for a client as a necessary, but incidental, part of the retainer, to facilitate the carrying out of the client's instructions. The main purpose of the rules is to keep that money safe and available for the purpose for which it was provided. The rules also seek to provide for the payment of a fair sum of interest, when appropriate, which is unlikely to be as high as that obtainable by the client depositing those funds.

(b)   An outcomes-focused approach has been adopted in this area, allowing firms the flexibility to set their own interest policies in order to achieve a fair outcome for both the client and the firm.

(c)   In addition to your obligation under rule 22.3, it is good practice to explain your interest arrangements to clients. These will usually be based on client money being held in an instant access account to facilitate a transaction. Clients are unlikely to receive as much interest as might have been obtained had they held and invested the money themselves. A failure to explain the firm's policy on interest may lead to unrealistic expectations and, possibly, a complaint to the Legal Ombudsman.

(d) The Legal Services Act 2007 has abolished the distinction in the Solicitors Act 1974 between interest earned on client money held in a general client account or a separate designated client account, meaning that interest earned on the latter type of account is, in theory, to be accounted for like interest on any other client money on a 'fair and reasonable' basis. In practice, however, a firm which wishes to retain any part of the interest earned on client money will need to hold that money in a general client account and continue to have interest paid to the office account (see rule 12.7(b)). The tax regime still treats interest arising on money held in a separate designated client account as belonging to the client, and requires banks to deduct tax at source from that interest (subject to the tax status of the individual client) and credit the interest to the separate designated client account. This makes it impracticable for firms to retain any part of the interest earned on a separate designated client account.

(e) Some firms may wish to apply a de minimis by reference to the amount held and period for which it was held, for example, providing that no interest is payable if the amount calculated on the balance held is £20 or less. Any de minimis will need to be set at a reasonable level and regularly reviewed in the light of current interest rates.

(f) It is likely to be appropriate for firms to account for all interest earned in some circumstances, for example, where substantial sums of money are held for lengthy periods of time.

(g) If sums of money are held in relation to separate matters for the same client, it is normally appropriate to treat the money relating to the different matters separately but there may be cases when the matters are so closely related that they ought to be considered together, for example, when you are acting for a client in connection with numerous debt collection matters. Similarly, it may be fair and reasonable in the circumstances to aggregate sums of money held intermittently during the course of acting for a client.

(h) There is no requirement to pay interest on money held on instructions under rule 15.1(a) in a manner which attracts no interest.

(i) Accounts opened in the client's name under rule 15.1(b) (whether operated by you or not) are not subject to rule 22, as the money is not held by you. All interest earned belongs to the client. The same applies to any account in the client's own name operated by you as signatory under rule 10.

(ii) Interest policy (rule 22.3)

(a) It is important that your clients should be aware of the terms of your interest policy. This should normally be covered at the outset of a retainer, although it may be unnecessary where you have acted for the client previously. It is open to you and your client to agree that interest will be dealt with in a different way (see rule 25).

(iii) Unpresented cheques

(a) A client may fail to present a cheque to his or her bank for payment. Whether or not it is reasonable to recalculate the amount due will depend on all the circumstances of the case. A reasonable charge may be made for any extra work carried out if you are legally entitled to make such a charge.

(iv) Liquidators, trustees in bankruptcy, Court of Protection deputies and trustees of occupational pension schemes

(a)   Under rule 8, Part 3 of the rules does not normally apply to liquidators, etc. You must comply with the appropriate statutory rules and regulations, and rules 8.3 and 8.4 as appropriate.

(v)   Joint accounts

(a)   Under rule 9, Part 3 of the rules does not apply to joint accounts. If you hold money jointly with a client, interest earned on the account will be for the benefit of the client unless otherwise agreed. If money is held jointly with another practice, the allocation of interest earned will depend on the agreement reached.

(vi)   Failure to pay interest

(a)   A client, including one of joint clients, or a person funding all or part of your fees, may complain to the Legal Ombudsman if he or she believes that interest was due and has not been paid, or that the amount paid was insufficient. It is advisable for the client (or other person) to try to resolve the matter with you before approaching the Legal Ombudsman.

Part 4 – Accounting systems and records

Rule 29 – Accounting records for client accounts, etc.

Accounting records which must be kept

29.1   You must at all times keep accounting records properly written up to show *your* dealings with:

(a)   *client money* received, held or paid by *you*; including *client money* held outside a *client account* under rule 15.1(a) or rule 16.1(d); and

(b)   any *office money* relating to any *client* or *trust* matter.

29.2   All dealings with *client money* must be appropriately recorded:

(a)   in a client cash account or in a record of sums transferred from one client ledger account to another; and

(b)   on the client side of a separate client ledger account for each *client* (or other person, or *trust*).

No other entries may be made in these records.

29.3   If *separate designated client accounts* are used:

(a)   a combined cash account must be kept in order to show the total amount held in *separate designated client accounts*; and

(b)   a record of the amount held for each *client* (or other person, or *trust*) must be made either in a deposit column of a client ledger account, or on the client side of a client ledger account kept specifically for a *separate designated client account*, for each *client* (or other person, or *trust*).

29.4   All dealings with *office money* relating to any *client* matter, or to any *trust* matter, must be appropriately recorded in an office cash account and on the office side of the appropriate client ledger account.

29.5   A cheque or draft received on behalf of a *client* and endorsed over, not passing through a *client account*, must be recorded in the books of account as a receipt and payment on behalf of the *client*. The same applies to cash received and not deposited in a *client account* but paid out to or on behalf of a *client*.

29.6   Money which has been paid into a *client account* under rule 17.1(c) (receipt of costs), or rule 18.2(b) (mixed money), and for the time being remains in a *client account*, is to be treated as *client money*; it must be appropriately identified and recorded on the client side of the client ledger account.

29.7   Money which has been paid into an *office account* under rule 17.1(b) (receipt of costs), rule 19.1(a) (advance payments from the Legal Aid Agency), or rule 19.1(b) (payment of costs from the Legal Aid Agency), and for the time being remains in an *office account* without breaching the rules, is to be treated as *office money*. Money paid into an *office account* under rule 19.2(b) (regular payments) is *office money*. All these payments must be appropriately identified and recorded on the office side of the client ledger account for the individual *client* or for the Legal Aid Agency.

29.8 *Client money* in a currency other than sterling must be held in a separate account for the appropriate currency, and *you* must keep separate books of account for that currency.

Current balance

29.9 The current balance on each client ledger account must always be shown, or be readily ascertainable, from the records kept in accordance with rule 29.2 and 29.3 above.

Acting for both lender and borrower

29.10 When acting for both lender and borrower on a mortgage advance, separate client ledger accounts for both *clients* need not be opened, provided that:

(a) the funds belonging to each *client* are clearly identifiable; and

(b) the lender is an institutional lender which provides mortgages on standard terms in the normal course of its activities.

Statements from banks, building societies and other financial institutions

29.11 *You* must, at least every 5 weeks:

(a) obtain hard copy statements (or duplicate statements permitted in lieu of the originals by rule 9.3 or 9.4 from *banks, building societies* or other financial institutions, or

(b) obtain and save in the *firm's* accounting records, in a format which cannot be altered, an electronic version of the *bank's, building society's* or other financial institution's on-line record,

in respect of:

(i) any *general client account* or *separate designated client account*;

(ii) any joint account held under rule 9;

(iii) any account which is not a *client account* but in which *you* hold *client money* under rule 15.1(a) or rule 16.1(d); and

(iv) any *office account* maintained in relation to the *firm*;

and each statement or electronic version must begin at the end of the previous statement.

This provision does not apply in respect of passbook-operated accounts, nor in respect of the *office accounts* of an *MDP* operated solely for activities not subject to SRA regulation.

Reconciliations

29.12 *You* must, at least once every five weeks:

(a) compare the balance on the client cash account(s) with the balances shown on the statements and passbooks (after allowing for all unpresented items) of all *general client accounts* and *separate designated client accounts*, and of any account which is not a *client account* but in which you hold *client money* under rule 15.1(a) or rule 16.1(d), and any *client money* held by *you* in cash; and

(b) as at the same date prepare a listing of all the balances shown by the client ledger accounts of the liabilities to *clients* (and other persons, and *trusts*) and compare the total of those balances with the balance on the client cash account; and also

(c)   prepare a reconciliation statement; this statement must show the cause of the difference, if any, shown by each of the above comparisons.

29.13 Reconciliations must be carried out as they fall due, or at the latest by the due date for the next reconciliation. In the case of a *separate designated client account* operated with a passbook, there is no need to ask the *bank*, *building society* or other financial institution for confirmation of the balance held. In the case of other *separate designated client accounts*, you must either obtain statements at least monthly or written confirmation of the balance direct from the *bank*, *building society* or other financial institution. There is no requirement to check that *interest* has been credited since the last statement, or the last entry in the passbook.

29.14 All shortages must be shown. In making the comparisons under rule 29.12(a) and (b), you must not, therefore, use credits of one *client* against debits of another when checking total client liabilities.

Bills and notifications of costs

29.15 *You* must keep readily accessible a central record or file of copies of:
  (a)   all bills given or sent by *you* (other than those relating entirely to activities not regulated by the SRA); and
  (b)   all other written notifications of *costs* given or sent by *you* (other than those relating entirely to activities not regulated by the SRA).

Withdrawals under rule 20.1(j)

29.16 If *you* withdraw *client money* under rule 20.1(j) *you* must keep a record of the steps taken in accordance with rule 20.2(a)–(c), together with all relevant documentation (including receipts from the charity).

Retention of records

29.17 *You* must retain for at least six years from the date of the last entry:
  (a)   all documents or other records required by rule 29.1 to 29.10, 29.12, and 29.15 to 29.16 above;
  (b)   all statements required by rule 29.11(a) above and passbooks, as printed and issued by the *bank*, *building society* or other financial institution; and/or all on-line records obtained and saved in electronic form under rule 29.11(b) above,
    for:
    (i)   any *general client* account or *separate designated client account*;
    (ii)   any joint account held under rule 9;
    (iii) any account which is not a *client account* but in which *you* hold *client money* under rule 15.1(a) or rule 16.1(d); and
    (iv)   any *office account* maintained in relation to the practice, but not the *office accounts* of an *MDP* operated solely for activities not subject to SRA regulation;
  (c)   any records kept under rule 8 (liquidators, trustees in bankruptcy, Court of Protection deputies and trustees of occupational pension schemes) including, as printed or otherwise issued, any statements, passbooks and other accounting records originating outside *your* office;
  (d)   any written instructions to withhold *client money* from a *client account* (or a copy of your confirmation of oral instructions) in accordance with rule 15;
  (e)   any central registers kept under rule 29.19 to 29.22 below; and
  (f)   copy letters kept centrally under rule 28.2 (dividend cheques endorsed over by nominee company).

29.18 You must retain for at least two years:

(a)   originals or copies of all authorities, other than cheques, for the withdrawal of money from a *client account*; and

(b)   all original paid cheques (or digital images of the front and back of all original paid cheques), unless there is a written arrangement with the *bank, building society* or other financial institution that:

(i)   it will retain the original cheques on *your* behalf for that period; or

(ii)   in the event of destruction of any original cheques, it will retain digital images of the front and back of those cheques on *your* behalf for that period and will, on demand by *you, your* reporting accountant or the SRA, produce copies of the digital images accompanied, when requested, by a certificate of verification signed by an authorised officer.

(c)   The requirement to keep paid cheques under rule 29.18(b) above extends to all cheques drawn on a *client account*, or on an account in which *client money* is held outside a *client account* under rule 15.1(a) or rule 16.1(d).

(d)   Microfilmed copies of paid cheques are not acceptable for the purposes of rule 29.18(b) above. If a *bank, building society* or other financial institution is able to provide microfilmed copies only, *you* must obtain the original paid cheques from the *bank* etc. and retain them for at least two years.

Centrally kept records for certain accounts, etc.

29.19 Statements and passbooks for *client money* held outside a *client account* under rule 15.1(a) or rule 16.1(d) must be kept together centrally, or *you* must maintain a central register of these accounts.

29.20 Any records kept under rule 8 (liquidators, trustees in bankruptcy, Court of Protection deputies and trustees of occupational pension schemes) must be kept together centrally, or *you* must maintain a central register of the appointments.

29.21 The statements, passbooks, duplicate statements and copies of passbook entries relating to any joint account held under rule 9 must be kept together centrally, or *you* must maintain a central register of all joint accounts.

29.22 A central register of all withdrawals made under rule 20.1(j) must be kept, detailing the name of the *client*, other person or *trust* on whose behalf the money is held (if known), the amount, the name of the recipient charity and the date of the payment.

29.23 If a nominee company follows the option in rule 28.2 (keeping instruction letters for dividend payments), a central book must be kept of all instruction letters to the share-owner's *bank* or *building society*, etc.

Computerisation

29.24 Records required by this rule may be kept on a computerised system, apart from the following documents, which must be retained as printed or otherwise issued:

(a)   original statements and passbooks retained under rule 29.17(b) above;

(b)   original statements, passbooks and other accounting records retained under rule 29.17(c) above; and

(c)   original cheques and copy authorities retained under rule 29.18 above.

There is no obligation to keep a hard copy of computerised records. However, if no hard copy is kept, the information recorded must be capable of being reproduced reasonably quickly in printed form for at least six years, or for at least two years in the case of digital images of paid cheques retained under rule 29.18 above.

Suspense ledger accounts

29.25 Suspense client ledger accounts may be used only when *you* can justify their use; for instance, for temporary use on receipt of an unidentified payment, if time is needed to establish the nature of the payment or the identity of the *client*.

Guidance notes

(i)   It is strongly recommended that accounting records are written up at least weekly, even in the smallest practice, and daily in the case of larger firms.

(ii)   Rule 29.1 to 29.10 (general record-keeping requirements) and rule 29.12 (reconciliations) do not apply to:

    (a)   liquidators, trustees in bankruptcy, Court of Protection deputies and trustees of occupational pension schemes operating in accordance with statutory rules or regulations under rule 8.1(i);

    (b)   joint accounts operated under rule 9;

    (c)   a client's own account operated under rule 10; the record-keeping requirements for this type of account are set out in rule 30;

    (d)   you in your capacity as a trustee when you instruct an outside administrator to run, or continue to run, on a day-to-day basis, the business or property portfolio of an estate or trust, provided the administrator keeps and retains appropriate accounting records, which are available for inspection by the SRA in accordance with rule 31. (See also note (v) to rule 21.)

(iii)   A cheque made payable to a client, which is forwarded to the client by you, is not client money and falls outside the rules, although it is advisable to record the action taken. See rule 14.2(e) for the treatment of a damages cheque, made payable to the client, which you pay into a client account under the Law Society's Conditional Fee Agreement.

(iv)   Some accounting systems do not retain a record of past daily balances. This does not put you in breach of rule 29.9.

(v)   'Clearly identifiable' in rule 29.10 means that by looking at the ledger account the nature and owner of the mortgage advance are unambiguously stated. For example, if a mortgage advance of £100,000 is received from the ABC Building Society, the entry should be recorded as '£100,000, mortgage advance, ABC Building Society'. It is not enough to state that the money was received from the ABC Building Society without specifying the nature of the payment, or vice versa.

(vi)   Although you do not open a separate ledger account for the lender, the mortgage advance credited to that account belongs to the lender, not to the borrower, until completion takes place. Improper removal of these mortgage funds from a client account would be a breach of rule 20.

(vii)   Section 67 of the Solicitors Act 1974 permits a solicitor or recognised body to include on a bill of costs any disbursements which have been properly incurred but not paid before delivery of the bill, subject to those disbursements being described on the bill as unpaid.

(viii) Rule 29.17(d) – retention of client's instructions to withhold money from a client account – does not require records to be kept centrally; however this may be prudent, to avoid losing the instructions if the file is passed to the client.

(ix)   You may enter into an arrangement whereby the bank keeps digital images of paid cheques in place of the originals. The bank should take an electronic image of the front and back of each cheque in black and white and agree to hold such images, and to make printed copies available on request, for at least two years. Alternatively, you may take and keep your own digital images of paid cheques.

(x)   Certificates of verification in relation to digital images of cheques may on occasion be required by the SRA when exercising its investigative and enforcement powers. The reporting accountant will not need to ask for a certificate of verification but will be able to rely on the printed copy of the digital image as if it were the original.

(xi)   These rules require an MDP to keep accounting records only in respect of those activities for which it is regulated by the SRA. Where an MDP acts for a client in a matter which includes activities regulated by the SRA, and activities outside the SRA's regulatory reach, the accounting records should record the MDP's dealings in respect of the SRA-regulated part of the client's matter. It may also be necessary to include in those records dealings with out-of-scope money where that money has been handled in connection with, or relates to, the SRA-regulated part of the transaction. An MDP is not required to maintain records in respect of client matters which relate entirely to activities not regulated by the SRA.

SRA Handbook Glossary [selected]

agreed fee

has the meaning given in Rule 17.5 of the SRA Accounts Rules.

bank

has the meaning given in section 87(1) of the SA.

building society

means a building society within the meaning of the Building Societies Act 1986.

client

means:

(i)   the *person* for whom you act and, where the context permits, includes prospective and former clients;

(ii)   in Parts 1-6 of the SRA Accounts Rules, the person for whom *you* act; and

(iii) in the SRA *Financial Services (Scope) Rules*, in relation to any *regulated activities* carried on by a *firm* for a trust or the estate of a deceased person (including a controlled trust), the trustees or personal representatives in their capacity as such and not any *person* who is a beneficiary under the trust or interested in the estate.

client account

has the meaning given in Rule 13.2 of the SRA Accounts Rules.

client money

has the meaning given in Rule 12 of the SRA Accounts Rules.

costs

means *your fees* and *disbursements*.

Court of Protection deputy

(i)   for the purposes of the SRA Accounts Rules includes a deputy who was appointed by the Court of Protection as a receiver under the Mental Health Act 1983 before the commencement date of the Mental Capacity Act 2005; and

(ii)   for the purposes of the SRA Authorisation Rules also includes equivalents in other *Establishment Directive* states.

director

means a director of a company; and in relation to a *societas Europaea* includes:

(i)   in a two-tier system, a member of the management organ and a member of the supervisory organ; and

(ii)   in a one-tier system, a member of the administrative organ.

disbursement

means, in respect of those activities for which the practice is regulated by the SRA, any sum spent or to be spent on behalf of the *client* or trust (including any VAT element).

fees

means *your* own charges or profit costs (including any VAT element).

firm

means:

(i)   save as provided in paragraphs (ii) and (iii) below, an *authorised body* or a body or *person* which should be authorised by the SRA as a *recognised body* or whose practice should be authorised as a recognised sole practice (but which could not be authorised by another *approved regulator*); and for the purposes of the SRA *Code of Conduct* and the SRA *Accounts Rules* can also include in-house practice;

(ii)   in the SRA *Indemnity Insurance Rules*:

(A)   any *recognised body* (as constituted from time to time); or

(B)   any *solicitor* or REL who is a *sole practitioner*, unless that *sole practitioner* is a *non-SRA firm*; or

(C)   any *partnership* (as constituted from time to time) which is eligible to become a *recognised body* and which meets the requirements applicable to *recognised bodies* set out in the SRA *Practice Framework Rules* and the SRA *Authorisation Rules*, unless that *partnership* is a *non-SRA firm* or an *Exempt European Practice*; or

(D)   any *licensed body* in respect of its *regulated activities*;

whether before or during any relevant *indemnity period*;

(iii) in the SRA *European Cross-border Practice Rules*, means any business through which a *solicitor* or REL carries on *practice* other than *in-house practice*.

general client account

has the meaning given in Rule 13.5 (b) of the SRA *Accounts Rules*.

interest

includes a sum in lieu of interest.

LLP

means a limited liability partnership incorporated under the Limited Liability Partnerships Act 2000.

MDP

means a *licensed body* which is a multi-disciplinary practice providing a range of different services, only some of which are regulated by the SRA.

mixed payment

has the meaning given in Rule 18.1 of the SRA *Accounts Rules*.

office account

means an account of the *firm* for holding *office money* and/or *out-of-scope money*, or other means of holding *office money* or *out-of-scope money* (for example, the office cash box or an account holding money regulated by a regulator other than the SRA).

office money

has the meaning given in Rule 12 of the SRA *Accounts Rules*.

out-of-scope money

means money held or received by an *MDP* in relation to activities that are not *regulated activities*.

partner

means a *person* who is or is held out as a partner in a *partnership*.

person

includes a body of persons (corporate or unincorporated).

principal

(i)   subject to paragraphs (ii) to (iv) means:

(A)   a *sole practitioner*;

(B)   a *partner* in a *partnership*;

(C)   in the case of a *recognised body* which is an *LLP* or *company*, the *recognised body* itself;

(D)   in the case of a *licensed body* which is an *LLP* or *company*, the *licensed body* itself;

(E)   the principal *solicitor* or *REL* (or any one of them) employed by a *non-solicitor employer* (for example, in a law centre or in commerce and industry); or

(F)   in relation to any other body, a member of its governing body;

(ii)   in the SRA Authorisation Rules, SRA Practice Framework Rules and SRA Practising Regulations, means a *sole practitioner* or a *partner* in a *partnership*;

(iii)   in the SRA Indemnity Insurance Rules means:

(A)   where the *firm* is or was:

(I)   a *sole practitioner* - that practitioner;

(II)   a *partnership* - each *partner*;

(III)   a *company* with a share capital - each *director* of that *company* and any *person* who:

(01)   is held out as a *director*; or

(02)   beneficially owns the whole or any part of a share in the *company*; or

(03)   is the ultimate beneficial owner of the whole or any part of a share in the *company*;

(IV)   a *company* without a share capital - each *director* of that *company* and any *person* who:

(01)   is held out as a *director*; or

(02)   is a *member* of the *company*; or

(03)   is the ultimate owner of the whole or any part of a *body corporate* or other legal person which is a *member* of the *company*;

(V)   an *LLP* - each *member* of that *LLP*, and any *person* who is the ultimate owner of the whole or any part of a *body corporate* or other legal person which is a *member* of the *LLP*;

(B)   where a *body corporate* or other legal person is a *partner* in the *firm*, any *person* who is within paragraph (A)(III) of this definition (including sub-paragraphs (01) and (03) thereof), paragraph (A)(IV) of this definition (including sub-paragraphs (01) and (03) thereof), or paragraph (A)(V) of this definition;

(iv)   in the SRA Indemnity Rules, means:

(A)   a *solicitor* who is a *partner* or a sole *solicitor* within the meaning of section 87 of the SA, or an *REL* who is a *partner*, or who is a *sole practitioner*, or an *RFL* or *non-registered European lawyer* who is a *partner*, and includes any *solicitor*, *REL*, *RFL* or *non-registered European lawyer* held out as a *principal*; and

(B)   additionally in relation to a *practice* carried on by a *recognised body* or a *licensed body* alone, or a *practice* in which a *recognised body* or a *licensed body* is or is held out to be a *partner*:

(I)   a *solicitor*, *REL*, *RFL* or *non-registered European lawyer* (and in the case of a *licensed body* any other person) who:

(01)   beneficially owns the whole or any part of a share in such *recognised body* or *licensed body* (in each case, where it is a *company* with a share capital); or

          (02)   is a member of such *recognised body* or *licensed body* (in each case, where it is a *company* without a share capital or an *LLP* or a *partnership* with legal personality); or

    (II)   a *solicitor*, *REL*, *RFL* or *non-registered European lawyer* (and in the case of a *licensed body* any other person) who is:

          (01)   the ultimate beneficial owner of the whole or any part of a share in such *recognised body* or *licensed body* (in each case, where the *recognised body* or *licensed body* is a *company* with a share capital); or

          (02)   the ultimate owner of a member or any part of a member of such *recognised body* or *licensed body* (in each case, where the *recognised body* or *licensed body* is a *company* without a share capital or an *LLP* or a *partnership* with legal personality).

professional disbursement

means, in respect of those activities for which the practice is regulated by the SRA, the fees of counsel or other *lawyer*, or of a professional or other agent or expert instructed by *you*, including the fees of interpreters, translators, process servers, surveyors and estate agents but not travel agents' charges.

recognised body

means a body recognised by the SRA under section 9 of the AJA.

regular payment

has the meaning given in Rule 19 of the *SRA Accounts Rules*.

separate designated client account

has the meaning given in Rule 13.5(a) of the *SRA Accounts Rules*.

SRA

means the Solicitors Regulation Authority, and reference to the SRA as an *approved regulator* or *licensing authority* means the SRA carrying out regulatory functions assigned to the *Society* as an *approved regulator* or *licensing authority*.

SRA Code of Conduct

means the SRA Code of Conduct 2011.

trustee

includes a personal representative, and 'trust' includes the duties of a personal representative.

without delay

means, in normal circumstances, either on the day of receipt or on the next working day.

you

means:

(i)   for the purposes of the *SRA Training Regulations* any person intending to be a *solicitor*, other than those seeking admission under the QLTSR;

(ii)   for the purposes of the *SRA Training Regulations* Part 3 a *solicitor* or an *REL*;

(iii) for the purposes of the *SRA Admission Regulations* any person intending to be a *solicitor*;

(iv) for the purpose of the *QLTSR* a person seeking admission as a *solicitor* via transfer in accordance with those regulations;

(v)   for the purpose of the *SRA Suitability Test* any individual intending to be a *solicitor*, and any person seeking authorisation as an *authorised role holder* under the *SRA Authorisation Rules*;

(vi) for the purposes of the *SRA Accounts Rules* (save for Part 7 (Overseas practice)):

    (A)   a *solicitor*; or

    (B)   an *REL*;

    in either case who is:

        (I)   a *sole practitioner*;

    (II)   a *partner* in a *partnership* which is a *recognised body*, *licensed body* or *authorised non-SRA firm*, or in a *partnership* which should be a *recognised body* but has not been recognised by the SRA;

    (III) an assistant, associate, professional support lawyer, consultant, locum or person otherwise employed in the practice of a *recognised body*, *licensed body*, *recognised sole practitioner* or *authorised non-SRA firm*; or of a *partnership* which should be a *recognised body* but has not been recognised by the SRA, or of a *sole practitioner* whose *practice* should be a *recognised sole practice* but has not been authorised by the SRA; and 'employed' in this context shall be interpreted in accordance with the definition of 'employee' for the purposes of the SRA *Code of Conduct*;

    (IV) employed as an in-house lawyer by a *non-solicitor employer* (for example, in a law centre or in commerce and industry);

    (V)   a director of a *company* which is a *recognised body*, *licensed body* or *authorised non-SRA firm*, or of a *company* which is a *manager* of a *recognised body*, *licensed body* or *authorised non-SRA firm*;

    (VI) a member of an LLP which is a *recognised body*, *licensed body* or *authorised non-SRA firm*, or of an LLP which is a *manager* of a *recognised body*, *licensed body* or *authorised non-SRA firm*; or

    (VII) a *partner* in a *partnership* with separate legal personality which is a *manager* of a *recognised body*, *licensed body* or *authorised non-SRA firm*;

(C)   an RFL practising:

    (I)   as a *partner* in a *partnership* which is a *recognised body*, *licensed body* or *authorised non-SRA firm*, or in a *partnership* which should be a *recognised body* but has not been recognised by the SRA;

    (II) as the *director* of a *company* which is a *recognised body*, *licensed body* or *authorised non-SRA firm*, or as the *director* of a *company* which is a *manager* of a *recognised body*, *licensed body* or *authorised non-SRA firm*;

    (III) as a member of an LLP which is a *recognised body*, *licensed body* or *authorised non-SRA firm*, or as a member of an LLP which is a *manager* of a *recognised body*, *licensed body* or *authorised non-SRA firm*;

    (IV) as a *partner* in a *partnership* with separate legal personality which is a *manager* of a *recognised body*, *licensed body* or *authorised non-SRA firm*;

    (V)   as an employee of a *recognised body*, *licensed body* or *recognised sole practitioner*; or

    (VI) as an employee of a *partnership* which should be a *recognised body* but has not been authorised by the SRA, or of a *sole practitioner* whose *practice* should be a *recognised sole practice* but has not been authorised by the SRA;

(D)   a *recognised body*;

(E)   a *licensed body*;

(F)   a *manager* or employee of a *recognised body* or *licensed body*, or of a *partnership* which should be a *recognised body* but has not been authorised by the SRA; or

(G)   an employee of a *recognised sole practitioner*, or of a *sole practitioner* whose *practice* should be a *recognised sole practice* but has not been authorised by the SRA;

(vii) for the purposes of the SRA *Higher Rights of Audience Regulations* means a *solicitor* or an *REL*;

(viii) for the purposes of the SRA *Insolvency Practice Rules* means a *solicitor* or an *REL*;

(ix) for the purposes of the SRA *Quality Assurance Scheme for Advocates (Crime) Notification Regulations* means a *solicitor* or an *REL*; and

(x)   for the purposes of the SRA *QASA Regulations* means a *solicitor* or an *REL*;

and references to 'your' and 'yourself' should be construed accordingly.

PROPOSALS FOR CHANGE

The SRA has formed the view that the Accounts Rules need simplifying and has consulted on possible amendments. In its Response to the Consultation published on June 2017, it said at para 5:

> The current Accounts Rules set out in minute detail how firms should run their accounting systems. This creates logistical problems for some firms to be compliant and makes it difficult for many firms to comply at all. Such complexity often ends up resulting in technical breaches. It drives confusion, cost and non-compliance rather than good practice.
>
> For example, a sole practitioner in a rural area has to drive to the bank several times a week to make sure cheques from clients are deposited within 48 hours of receipt as required by our rules. While sometimes this may be necessary, there is little flexibility for the solicitor to decide what is best in the circumstances and best for their clients overall.

And at para 7:

> It is our view that we need to put more trust in solicitors' professional judgement. We do not need pages and pages of prescriptive rules for a solicitor or firms to do the right thing and maintain professional standards.
>
> For instance, all good solicitors know that they should not steal money belonging to their clients. We do not think they need - or benefit - from more than 40 pages of detailed Accounts Rules setting out how to avoid stealing.

The SRA Accounts Rules 2018 were still in draft form when this book went to print. There may therefore be some changes before final implementation.

The Rules will apply to firms regulated by the SRA, their managers and employees. In relation to multi-disciplinary practices, the rules apply only in respect of regulated activities and not to 'out of scope money'.

1 Client money

The SRA had proposed changing the definition of client money to allow sums received in advance in respect of fees and disbursements to be treated as the firm's money. Respondents to the Consultation felt that this change would not be beneficial for firms or their clients. The general view was that this change would have a far-reaching impact on systems and processes and would result in additional costs for firms, and was therefore strongly opposed.

The SRA accepted this point and amended the definition of client money to include these sums, until the point at which they are billed to the client.

Rule 2.1 defines client money as money held or received:

(a)   relating to regulated services delivered to a client;

(b)   on behalf of a third party in relation to regulated services delivered (such as money held as agent, stakeholder or held to the sender's order);

(c)   as a trustee or as the holder of a specified office or appointment, such as donee of a power of attorney, Court of Protection deputy or trustee of an occupational pension scheme;

(d)   in respect of fees and any unpaid disbursements, if held or received prior to delivery of a bill for the same.

Rule 2.3 requires client money to be paid promptly into a client account unless:

(a)   in relation to money falling within 2.1(c), to do so would conflict with obligations under rules or regulations relating to the office or appointment;

(b)   the client money represents payments received from the Legal Aid Agency for costs; or

(c)   the firm agrees an alternative arrangement in writing with the client, or the third party, for whom the money is held.

Note: changes to legal aid payments

The bulk of the specific rules relating to payments from the Legal Aid Authority (LAA) are removed.

Rule 2.3(b), according to the SRA, mirrors the current position on LAA payments. Firms will be able to continue to take these payments into their business account. The only change from the current Accounts Rules is the removal of the rule that advanced payments for disbursements must be put back into client account if the party providing the professional services is not paid within the specified time.

The LAA has confirmed that they have no issue with the removal of this provision and they are content that the rules are workable from their perspective.

Removing the provision for disbursements to be held in a client account if they are not paid within a certain number of days does not mean that firms will be able to hold payments from the LAA in their business account indefinitely. If, for example, a firm does not pay an expert's fee (because the firm retains the money in their account to avoid increasing their overdraft) and thereby delays a client's matter, this would constitute a breach of the rule requiring payments to be made promptly. It is also likely that this would be a breach of the SRA Code of Conduct.

Client money must be available on demand unless an alternative arrangement in writing with the client, or the third party for whom the money is held, has been agreed (Rule 2.4). It must be returned promptly to the client, or the third party, as soon as there is no longer any proper reason to hold the funds (Rule 2.5)

Rule 2.2 provides that in circumstances where the only client money received falls within Rule 2.1(d), and:

(a)   money held for disbursements relates to costs or expenses incurred on behalf of the client and for which the firm is liable; and

(b)   the firm does not maintain a client account for any other reason,

the firm is not required to hold the money in a client account, *provided* it has informed the client in advance of where and how the money will be held. Rules 2.4 and 2.5 do not apply to such money.

The effect of Rule 2.2 is to provide an exemption so that where the only client money that a firm receives is advance payments for fees and unpaid disbursements for which the firm is liable, that money does not have to be held in client account, and firms that only handle these types of client money do not need to operate a client account. This is a significant benefit. These firms may benefit from potential cost savings in areas such as professional indemnity insurance and compliance, as no accountant's report will be required.

2   Client bank account

Rule 3 replicates the current requirements in relation to client bank accounts. So client bank accounts can only be maintained at a branch (or the head office) of a bank or a building society located in England and Wales.

The name of any client account must include the name of the firm and the word 'client' to distinguish it from any other type of account held or operated by the firm.

Rule 3.3 repeats the prohibition on using a client bank account to provide banking facilities to clients or third parties. Payments into, and transfers or withdrawals from, a client account must be in respect of the delivery of regulated services.

3   Keeping client money separate

Rule 4.1 requires firms to keep client money separate from their own money, and Rule 4.2 to allocate promptly any funds from mixed payments received to the correct client account or business account. Under the current Rules, where a mixed payment is paid into the client account, office money must be transferred out within 14 days. Many of those who responded to the SRA Consultation were unhappy with the use of the word 'promptly', describing the change as 'unnecessary'. Opponents of the change suggested that client money would be at greater risk of manipulation by firms. However, the SRA declined to amend the draft rule, content that the application of other rules such as acting with honesty and integrity will achieve compliance. The majority of respondents did see the change as a positive one, but requested the SRA issue guidance on the definition of 'prompt'.

Rule 4(3) provides:

> Where you are holding client money and some or all of that money will be used to pay your costs:
>
> (a)   you must give a bill of costs, or other written notification, to the client or the paying party;
>
> (b)   this must be done before you transfer any client money from a client account to make the payment; and
>
> (c)   any such payment must be for the specific sum identified in the bill of costs or other written notification, and covered by the amount held for the particular client or third party.

Significantly, the phrase that features in the equivalent provision in the current SRA Accounts Rules (Rule 20.3) – 'properly require' – is no longer in use. It is the presence of the words 'properly require' that prevents a firm from transferring funds from client to office bank account where a bill has been sent to the client but the work covered by the bill has not yet been completed. This important point is not covered under the draft SRA Accounts Rules 2018 which, at face value, seem to permit monies to be transferred from client to office bank account if a bill has been given to the client for work to be undertaken.

Another significant change is that the obligation to send or give a bill to the client prior to transferring funds from client to office account now applies to the firm's 'costs' rather than the firm's 'fees'. Critically, the definition of 'costs' comprises the firm's profit costs and disbursements, whereas the definition of 'fees', which is used in the equivalent provision within the current SRA Accounts Rules, is purely the profit cost element of the bill.

Therefore, it would appear that under the draft SRA Accounts Rules 2018, a firm will not be able to transfer funds held in client bank account, to cover disbursements paid out of office monies on behalf of the client, prior to giving a bill to the client.

4   Withdrawals from client account

Rule 5.1 provides that withdrawals of client money can only be made from a client account:

(a)   for the purpose for which it is being held; or

(b)   following receipt of instructions from the client, or the third party for whom the money is held; or

(c)   on the SRA's prior written authorisation or in prescribed circumstances.

The withdrawals must be 'appropriately' authorised and supervised (Rule 5.2).

As is the case under the current Rules, withdrawals of client money from the client bank account may only be made if sufficient funds are held on behalf of that specific client or third party (Rule 5.3).

6   Mistakes

Any breaches of the rules must be corrected promptly upon discovery. Any money improperly withheld or withdrawn from a client bank account must be immediately paid into the account or replaced as appropriate (Rule 6).

7   Payment of interest

Rule 7 imposes an obligation to account to clients or third parties for a fair sum of interest on any client money held on their behalf.

Rule 7.2 permits firms to come to a different arrangement in writing with the client or third party as to the payment of interest provided they have been given sufficient information to enable them to give informed consent.

8   Systems and controls

Rule 8 requires firms to keep and maintain accurate, contemporaneous and chronological records to:

(a)   record in client ledgers, identified by the client's name and an appropriate description of the matter to which they relate:

(i)   all receipts and payments which are client money on the client side of the client ledger account;

(ii)   all receipts and payments which are not client money and bills of costs, including transactions through the authorised body's accounts on the business side of the client ledger account;

(b)   maintain a list of all the balances shown by the client ledger accounts of the liabilities to clients (and third parties), with a running total of the balances;

(c)   provide a cash book showing a running total of all transactions through client accounts held or operated by the firm.

9   Operation of client's own account or a joint account with a client or third party

The Rules do not apply to these accounts rules save for:

(a)   Rule 8.2 – statements from banks, building societies and other financial institutions;

(b)   Rule 8.4 – bills and notifications of costs.

If operating the client's own account, Rule 8.3 (reconciliations) must be complied with.

10   Third party managed accounts

This is a new development. Rule 11 allows firms to enter into arrangements with a client to use a third party managed account (TPMA) for the purpose of receiving payments from or on behalf of, or making payments to or on behalf of, the client in respect of regulated services delivered by the firm in the following circumstances:

(a)   use of the account must not result in the firm receiving or holding the client's money; and

(b)   the firm takes reasonable steps to ensure, before accepting instructions, that the client is informed of and understands:

(i)   the terms of the contractual arrangements relating to the use of the TPMA, and in particular how any fees for use of the TPMA will be paid and who will bear them; and

(ii)   the client's right to terminate the agreement and dispute payment requests made by the firm.

The firm must obtain regular statements from the provider of the TPMA and ensure that these accurately reflect all transactions on the account.

These accounts will offer an alternative to operating a client bank account which will be attractive to some firms, particularly smaller firms that do not handle large amounts of client money. However, many firms will not find them a viable option due to uncertainty surrounding timings of payment and discomfort with control over client funds resting with a third party.

Money held in a TPMA is not held by the solicitor or firm, but by the TPMA provider.

It does not meet the definition of client money as set out in Rule 2.1. This means that the provisions in the Accounts Rules relating to holding client money do not apply to monies in a TPMA.

Regulation will be by the FCA and not by the SRA. The solicitor will not be responsible for the monies in the TPMA, as these are held by the TPMA provider and are not under the solicitor's direct control. However, firms using TPMAs will have to ensure that they comply with the standards in the Code of Conduct, including the duty to act in clients' best interests and safeguard money and assets belonging to clients. The SRA says that it would expect this would include an assessment of the suitability of the product in the particular circumstances and for the particular client.

11   Obtaining and delivery of accountants' reports

Rule 12 requires firms which have at any time during an accounting period held or received client money, or operated a joint account or a client's own account as signatory, to:

(a)   obtain an accountant's report for that accounting period within six months of the end of the period; and

(b)   deliver it to the SRA within six months of the end of the accounting period if the accountant's report is qualified to show a failure to comply with these rules, such that money belonging to clients or third parties is, or has been, or is likely to be, placed at risk.

Reports must be prepared and signed by an accountant who is a member of one of the chartered accountancy bodies and who is, or works for, a registered auditor

Firms are not required to obtain an accountant's report if:

(a)   all of the client money held or received during an accounting period is money received from the Legal Aid Agency; or

(b)   in the accounting period, the statement or passbook balance of client money held or received does not exceed:

(i)   an average of £10,000; and

(ii)   a maximum of £250,000,

or the equivalent in foreign currency.

However, under Rule 12.4, the SRA has the right to require a report where a firm ceases to operate as an authorised body and to hold or operate a client account, or it considers that it is otherwise in the public interest to do so. This will clearly relieve firms of an additional burden, although it will be interesting to see how often the SRA requires such a report, or what information it uses to judge whether one should be required.

Index